Chartered Financial Analyst® Program

Level I
Practice Examinations

2014

	Questions	Answers
Practice Examination 1		
Morning Session	1	33
Afternoon Session	57	89
Practice Examination 2		
Morning Session	111	143
Afternoon Session	165	197
Practice Examination 3		
Morning Session	221	251
Afternoon Session	275	307

BPP
LEARNING MEDIA

Published March 2014

ISBN 978 1 4727 0418 4
eISBN 978 1 4727 0442 9

British Library Cataloguing-in-Publication Data
A catalogue record for this book
is available from the British Library

Published by

BPP Learning Media Ltd
BPP House, Aldine Place
London W12 8AA

www.bpp.com/learningmedia

Printed in the United Kingdom by Ricoh UK Limited
Unit 2
Wells Place
Merstham
RH1 3LG

Your learning materials, published by BPP Learning Media Ltd, are printed on paper obtained from traceable sustainable sources.

A note about copyright

Dear Customer

What does the little © mean and why does it matter? Your market-leading BPP books, course materials and e-learning materials do not write and update themselves. People write them: on their own behalf or as employees of an organisation that invests in this activity. Copyright law protects their livelihoods. It does so by creating rights over the use of the content.

Breach of copyright is a form of theft – as well as being a criminal offence in some jurisdictions, it is potentially a serious breach of professional ethics.

With current technology, things might seem a bit hazy but, basically, without the express permission of BPP Learning Media:

- Photocopying our materials is a breach of copyright
- Scanning, ripcasting or conversion of our digital materials into different file formats, uploading them to facebook or e-mailing them to your friends is a breach of copyright

You can, of course, sell your books, in the form in which you have bought them – once you have finished with them. (Is this fair to your fellow students? We update for a reason.)

And what about outside the UK? BPP Learning Media strives to make our materials available at prices students can afford by local printing arrangements, pricing policies and partnerships which are clearly listed on our website. A tiny minority ignore this and indulge in criminal activity by illegally photocopying our material or supporting organisations that do. If they act illegally and unethically in one area, can you really trust them?

BPP
LEARNING MEDIA

The Chartered Financial Analyst® Program

Practice Examination 1
Morning Session

2014

The Morning Session of Practice Examination 1 consists of 120 multiple choice questions which must be completed in three hours. The topic areas covered are:

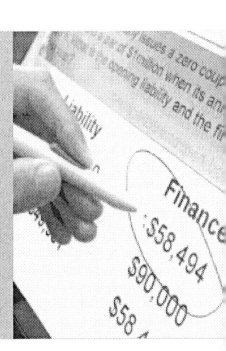

BPP
LEARNING MEDIA

Questions 1 through 18 relate to Ethical and Professional Standards

1. According to the CFA Institute Code of Ethics and Standards of Professional Conduct, all CFA candidates:

    A. must abide by the Code and Standards and must notify their employer of this responsibility.

    B. are encouraged to abide by the Code and Standards and notify their employer of this responsibility.

    C. must abide by the Code and Standards and are encouraged to notify their employer of this responsibility.

2. If the Designated Officer proposes a disciplinary sanction after an inquiry as a result of questionable conduct by a CFA Institute member and the sanction is rejected by the member, it is most likely that the:

    A. inquiry will be concluded with no disciplinary sanction.

    B. Designated Officer will propose a lesser disciplinary sanction.

    C. matter will be referred to a hearing by a panel of CFA Institute members.

3. Ted Larkin CFA is an analyst at an investment firm. He has been asked by his firm to meet with a prospective corporate finance client. During the meeting with the prospective client, Larkin states that his firm will guarantee comprehensive coverage of the client company by its analysts. After the meeting, Larkin has dinner with the prospective client, for which the prospective client pays. With respect to the Standard of Professional Conduct concerning Independence and Objectivity, it is *most likely* that Larkin has:

    A. not breached the standard.

    B. breached the standard by allowing for the prospective client to pay for his dinner.

    C. breached the standard by guaranteeing that his firm's analysts will provide comprehensive coverage of the company.

4. Walt Twain CFA is an analyst who is being paid by a company to prepare research notes on the company so as to generate investor interest. Twain negotiates a flat fee plus a commission based on how many new investors buy stock in the company. He then prepares a website where he publishes research on the company. He does not disclose details of his arrangement with the company on the website. With respect to the Standards of Professional Conduct concerning Independence and Objectivity and Misrepresentation, is it *most likely* that Twain has :

    A. breached both the Standard concerning Independence and Objectivity and the Standard concerning Misrepresentation.

    B. breached the Standard concerning Independence and Objectivity but not the Standard concerning Misrepresentation.

    C. not breached the Standard concerning Independence and Objectivity but has breached the Standard concerning misrepresentation.

5. John Baker CFA is an investment manager who is also actively involved in political and social causes that he believes to be just. He has recently attended a protest against the use of child labor in the manufacture of branded products by multi-national companies. At the protest, he was arrested for trespass on the property of such a company. He has not reported his arrest to his employer. In respect of the Standard of Professional Conduct concerning Misconduct it is *most likely* that Baker has:

    A. not violated the Standard.

    B. violated the Standard by engaging in acts of civil disobedience.

    C. violated the Standard by not reporting his arrest to his employer.

6. Hiroyuki Okada CFA has attended an analysts' meeting with a company specializing in clothes retail. At the meeting the company shows various new designs to the analysts, although these designs are not yet public knowledge. Subsequent to the meeting Okada discusses the designs with a number of fashion experts who express a view that the company's approach to designs is excessively conservative and unlikely to find favor with consumers. As a result, Okada makes a recommendation that the company's stock is a sell. He sells his own shares in the company and then distributes this recommendation before the company releases the details of the new designs in public. As a result of poor public perception of the new designs, the company's stock price falls. With respect to the Standard of Professional Conduct concerning Material Nonpublic Information, it is *most likely* that Okada has:

    A. not violated the Standard.

    B. violated the Standard by selling his own shares before the information was made public.

    C. violated the Standard by selling his own shares and releasing a sell recommendation before the information was made public.

7. Sunil Perera CFA is an investment manager whose firm owns a substantial shareholding in a very illiquid stock. He has decided that the stock is overvalued and wishes to dispose of the shareholding. He sells the stock in several large tranches and as a result of his sales, the stock falls significantly in value. Perera then decides that the value of the stock has fallen to below its intrinsic value and as a result decides to repurchase the stock. After his repurchases, the stock price recovers to a level that Perera considers to be around its fair value. With respect to the Standard of Professional Conducts concerning Market Manipulation and Material Nonpublic Information, it is *most likely* that Perera has:

    A. violated the Standard concerning Market Manipulation and violated the Standard concerning Material Nonpublic Information.

    B. violated the Standard concerning Market Manipulation but not violated the Standard concerning Material Nonpublic Information.

    C. not violated the Standard concerning Market Manipulation and not violated the Standard concerning Material Nonpublic Information.

8.	Russell King CFA is an analyst noted for his expertise in his industry areas. As a result, companies which he covers are always happy to meet him and give him explanations and guidance as to their future prospects. When he publishes his research notes, it is invariably the case that the stock price of the company concerned responds in the way suggested by his recommendation. When distributing a research note, King initially contacts his major institutional clients who pay the highest fees by e mail to give them a summary of the recommendation prior to the note being published. The note is then distributed to all of his clients. After the note is distributed, King contacts his major institutional clients by telephone to discuss the contents of the research note. In respect of the Standard of Professional Conduct concerning Fair Dealing, is it *most likely* that King has:

	A. violated the Standard by contacting his major institutional clients by email before distributing the note and by telephoning them afterwards.

	B. violated the Standard by contacting his major institutional clients by email before distributing the note but not by telephoning them afterwards.

	C. not violated the Standard by contacting his major institutional clients by email before distributing the note or by telephoning them afterwards.

9.	When a CFA Institute member who is simply executing specific investment instructions for a retail client rather than being in an advisory relationship receives an unsolicited trade request from the client that he or she knows to be unsuitable for the client in question, the member's *least appropriate* action according to the Standard of Professional Conduct concerning Suitability is to:

	A. refrain from making the trade.

	B. make the trade without question.

	C. seek an affirmative statement from the client that suitability is not a consideration.

10.	Robert Irving CFA has a client who is also a CFA Institute member. Both Irving and his client live in a country which requires that where a financial adviser has a reasonable suspicion that money laundering is taking place, the adviser must report this to the police, but otherwise forbids disclosure of confidential information about clients by their advisers to anyone except the country's tax authority when dealing with tax evasion. Irving has received a request from the CFA Institute Professional Conduct Program (PCP) to furnish them with confidential information concerning his client as a result of a written complaint received about his client's conduct. The course of action that Irving should follow to *most likely* be consistent with the requirements of the Standards of Professional Conduct is:

	A. to supply the information to the PCP.

	B. to supply the information to the country's tax authority.

	C. not to supply the information to the PCP or to the country's tax authority.

11. Oprah Flockhart CFA has recently resigned from her previous firm and is now at work for her new firm. When applying for the job at her new firm, she assured them that it was likely that clients from her previous firm would follow her with their business. She is now contacting these clients having obtained their contact details from a public directory with the intention of winning their business. Floyd Winters CFA has copied some confidential documents from his employer's records with the objective of disclosing these as evidence that his employer is engaging in market manipulation. Which of the following *most* accurately describes who has or has not violated the Standard of Professional Conduct concerning Loyalty?

   A. Both Flockhart and Winters have violated the Standard.

   B. Flockhart has violated the Standard but Winters has not violated the Standard.

   C. Neither Flockhart or Winters have violated the Standard.

12. Diane Conway CFA has supervisory responsibility over a number of members of staff, none of whom are CFA Institute members or candidates. Conway discovers that James Smith, one of the employees that she supervises who is neither a CFA Institute member nor a candidate in the CFA Program, has been frontrunning investment recommendations by buying shares for his own account before positive investment recommendations have been distributed and selling shares for his own account before negative recommendations have been distributed. Conway reprimands Smith and he assures her that he will not repeat the practice. Conway immediately investigates the problem to establish its scope and the compliance system to establish how it can be improved to avoid such a problem again. Having improved the compliance system, she takes no further action as Smith is otherwise a model employee. With respect to the Standard of Professional Conduct concerning Responsibilities of Supervisors, it is *most likely* that Conway has:

   A. violated the Standard.

   B. not violated the Standard because Smith is neither a CFA Institute member nor a candidate.

   C. not violated the Standard because she has made improvements to the compliance system to avoid a repetition of the problem.

13. Harry Milligan CFA is the chief investment officer of an investment firm specializing in the selection of small cap US stocks. As a result of the firm's diligent and thorough analysis and expertise, it has achieved high returns for its investors over a number of years. Harry Milligan has decided to increase the range of investments covered to include mid cap US stocks, and to apply the same investment approach for these stocks as for small cap stocks, regardless of the difference in size. Harry Milligan does not notify his firm's clients of this as he views it as not being a significant change. Which of the following *most* accurately describes whether Milligan has or has not violated the Standards of Professional Conduct concerning Diligence and Reasonable Basis and Communications with Clients and Prospective Clients?

   A. Milligan has violated both the Standard concerning Diligence and Reasonable Basis and the Standard concerning Communications with Clients and Prospective Clients.

   B. Milligan has violated the Standard concerning Diligence and Reasonable Basis but has not violated the Standard concerning Communications with Clients and Prospective Clients.

   C. Milligan has not violated the Standard concerning Diligence and Reasonable Basis but has violated the Standard concerning Communications with Clients and Prospective Clients.

14. In the absence of regulatory guidance, CFA Institute recommends in its Standard of Professional Conduct concerning record retention that records are retained for at least:

A. three years.

B. five years.

C. seven years.

15. Maggie Smith CFA works as an analyst for an investment firm. She has become aware that her firm is intending to sell a number of shares in a company in which her husband also owns shares. As the number of shares to be sold is substantial and is likely to affect the market price adversely, she telephones her husband and, without telling him the reason why, tells him to sell his stock immediately. Which of the following statements *most* accurately describes whether Smith has or has not breached the Standards of Professional Conduct concerning Material Nonpublic information and Priority of Transactions?

A. Smith has breached both the Standard concerning Material Nonpublic Information and the Standard concerning Priority of Transactions.

B. Smith has breached the Standard concerning Material Nonpublic Information but has not breached the Standard concerning Priority of Transactions.

C. Smith has not breached the Standard concerning Material Nonpublic Information but has breached the Standard concerning Priority of Transactions.

16. Shan Ru CFA works as portfolio manager for an investment firm. She is entitled to receive a bonus when she persuades clients and prospective clients to invest assets with the firm. She does not disclose this fact to her clients and prospective clients. Which of the following statements *most* accurately describes whether Ru has or has not breached the Standards of Professional Conduct concerning Disclosure of Conflicts and Referral Fees?

A. Ru has breached both the Standard concerning Disclosure of Conflicts and the Standard concerning Referral Fees.

B. Ru has breached the Standard concerning Disclosure of Conflicts but has not breached the Standard concerning Referral Fees.

C. Ru has not breached the Standard concerning Disclosure of Conflicts and has not breached the Standard concerning Referral Fees.

17. Ernest Barker CFA has disseminated a personal resume for himself in which he makes the following two statements:

Statement 1: I am one of an elite body who have passed all three exams in the CFA Program at the first attempt.

Statement 2: Completion of the CFA Program has enhanced my portfolio management skills.

Is it *most likely* that these statements violate the Standard of Professional Conduct concerning Reference to CFA Institute, the CFA Designation, and the CFA Program?

	STATEMENT 1	STATEMENT 2
A.	Yes	Yes
B.	No	Yes
C.	Yes	No

18. Which of the following industries do not have provisions specific to their industry within the GIPS Standards?
    A. Real estate
    B. Hedge funds
    C. Private equity

Questions 19 through 32 relate to Quantitative Methods

19. The present value of a regular cash flow of $1,000 each six months, starting in six months time and continuing to infinity when the effective interest rate is 6% is *closest to*:
    A. $16,181.
    B. $31,865.
    C. $33,826.

20. If the quoted interest rate is 7.78% with quarterly compounding, the number of months that it will take for a sum of money to double in value is *closest to*:
    A. 106 months.
    B. 108 months.
    C. 111 months.

21. A 100 day US Treasury bill has a bank discount yield of 6%. Its CD equivalent yield is *closest to*:
    A. 6.101%.
    B. 6.186%.
    C. 6.383%.

22. When a distribution has observations with different values, the geometric mean of the distribution will be:
    A. less than the harmonic mean and less than the arithmetic mean.
    B. greater than the harmonic mean and less than the arithmetic mean.
    C. greater than the harmonic mean and greater than the arithmetic mean.

23. Using Chebyshev's inequality, which of the following is *closest* to the minimum proportion of observations within 1.5 standard deviations of the arithmetic mean?
    A. 5%.
    B. 36%.
    C. 56%.

24. Details of two portfolios are as follows.

Portfolio	Skewness	Kurtosis
X	-1.4	4.9
Y	1.1	3.2

A researcher has made the following statements:

Statement 1: Portfolio X has a long tail to the left.

Statement 2: Portfolio Y is more peaked than a normal distribution.

It is *most likely* that the researcher's statements are:

A. correct for portfolio X and correct for portfolio Y.

B. correct for portfolio X and incorrect for portfolio Y.

C. incorrect for portfolio X and correct for portfolio Y.

25. The probability that a company's earnings per share will increase is 0.7 given that it increased in the previous period. The probability that a company's earnings per share will increase is 0.4 given that it decreased in the previous period. A company's earnings per share increased in 2012. The probability that it will decrease in 2012 is *closest to*:

A. 0.21.

B. 0.30.

C. 0.39.

26. An analyst has devised a screen to identify stocks that will outperform. 50% of stocks to which the screen is applied outperform. 40% of stocks fail the screen. The probability that a stock which outperforms passes the screen is 90%. The probability that a company will outperform given that it passes the test is *closest to*:

A. 0.60.

B. 0.75.

C. 0.90.

27. A company's interest expense is expected to be $5 million next year. The earnings before interest and tax is expected to lie in the range $2 million to $20 million, with all outcomes equally likely. What is the probability that the company's interest cover will be less than 2x?

A. 0.40.

B. 0.44.

C. 0.50.

28. Which of the following is *least likely* to be an assumption underlying the binomial distribution?

    A. Trials are independent from each other.

    B. The probability of success is constant for all trials.

    C. The distribution is described by the probability of success and the number of trials.

29. The standard error of the distribution of sample means is expressed as:

    A. $\dfrac{\sigma}{\sqrt{n}}$

    B. $\dfrac{\sigma}{n}$

    C. $\dfrac{\sigma}{\sqrt{n-1}}$

30. When calculating a range estimate of a normally distributed population's mean from a sample where the population variance is known, an increased sample size and an increased confidence level will:

    A. increase the range estimate.

    B. decrease the range estimate.

    C. increase or decrease the range estimate.

31. An analyst believes that the UK stock market is riskier than the US stock market. He has taken a sample of 48 months of observations for each stock market and found that the standard deviation of the UK stock market is 10% and the standard deviation of the US market is 7.9%. The alternative hypothesis for the appropriate significance test is of the:

    A. less than type and the test statistic is 1.3.

    B. greater than type and the test statistic is 1.3.

    C. greater than type and the test statistic is 1.6.

32. Which of the following is *most likely* to be an assumption underlying technical analysis? Prices of securities:

    A. move in trends that do not persist.

    B. are not affected by rational factors.

    C. are determined solely by the interaction of supply and demand.

Questions 33 through 44 relate to Economics

33. Cross-price elasticity of demand is:

    A. positive.

    B. negative.

    C. positive or negative.

---

34. If an economy faces an increase in labor productivity due to technological improvements, which of the following most accurately describes the impact on the short run aggregate supply curve (SRAS) and the long run aggregate supply curve (LRAS)?

    A. SRAS shifts leftward and there is no impact on the LRAS.

    B. SRAS shifts rightward and there is no impact on the LRAS.

    C. SRAS shifts rightward and LRAS shifts rightward.

---

35. The monthly demand function for a family buying DVDs is:

    $Q_{DVD} = 5 - 0.7P_{DVD} + 0.0003I - 0.23P_B$, where Q_{DVD} equals the number of monthly DVD purchases, P_{DVD} equals the average price of a DVD, I equals the household monthly income, and P_B equals the average price of a book.

    Given that the average price of a DVD is $10.82, household income is $2,500 and the average price of a book is $7.32, which of the following is closest to the own-price elasticity of demand?

    A. -2.63.

    B. -3.51.

    C. -7.48.

---

36. Almost every production process is *most likely* to exhibit:

    A. diminishing marginal returns.

    B. increasing then diminishing marginal returns.

    C. diminishing then increasing marginal returns.

---

37. Which of the following *best* describes a person who has a job but who has the qualifications to work a significantly higher-paying job?

    A. Discouraged worker.

    B. Underemployed.

    C. Voluntarily underemployed.

38. An economist has made the following two statements.

    Statement 1: In the long run, firms in monopolistic competition face a downward sloping demand curve.

    Statement 2: In the long run, firms in monopolistic competition will produce where average total cost is minimized.

    Is it *most likely* that the economist is correct with respect to statement 1 and statement 2?

	STATEMENT 1	STATEMENT 2
A.	Correct	Correct
B.	Correct	Incorrect
C.	Incorrect	Correct

39. When the growth rate of the money supply, measured by M2, is higher than the current inflation rate, this indicator most likely forecasts future economic:

    A. growth.

    B. decline.

    C. stability.

40. Which of the following would *least likely* be viewed as a lagging economic indicator?

    A. Inventory-sales ratio.

    B. Average bank prime lending rate.

    C. S&P 500 Stock Index.

41. An economist has the following views:

    (i) It is better to let aggregate demand and supply find their own equilibrium than have Governments intervening all the time

    (ii) The money supply needs to grow at a moderate rate; and

    (iii) Fiscal and monetary policy should be clear and consistent over time.

    The economist can *best* be describes as following which school of thought?

    A. Monetarist.

    B. Keynesian.

    C. New classical.

42. Assuming wages and prices are rigid, which of the following is *least* likely to be evident in an economy when easy fiscal policy is combined with tight monetary policy?

    A. There will be a rise in aggregate demand.

    B. Interest rates will rise.

    C. Private sector demand will increase.

43. All else being equal, when Government spending is financed by an increase in taxes, which of the following is the most likely impact on aggregate output?

A. Will rise.

B. Will fall.

C. No change.

44. All of the following are automatic stabilizers except:

A. induced taxes.

B. changes in tax rates.

C. needs tested spending.

Questions 45 through 69 relate to Financial Reporting and Analysis

45. When the auditors of a company believe that the company's financial statements materially depart from financial reporting standards, the auditors will *most likely* issue:

   A. a qualified opinion.

   B. an adverse opinion.

   C. a disclaimer of opinion.

46. A company paid a dividend of $1,000 during its financial year. Extracts from the company's financial statements for the year are as follows:

	$
Beginning retained earnings	3,000
Liabilities at the year end	1,700
Revenue for the year	10,000
Expenses for the year	8,500
Contributed capital at the year end	4,500

   Total assets at the end of the year for the company are *closest to*:

   A. $6,300.

   B. $9,700.

   C. $10,700.

47. All of the following are enhancing qualitative characteristics of financial information in the International Financial Reporting Standards Framework except:

   A. neutrality.

   B. comparability.

   C. understandability.

48. A US company, PartyMad, supplies party accessories to end users. PartyMad purchases the goods from a third party supplier and arranges for the goods to be shipped direct to the end user. PartyMad never holds the inventory. Under US GAAP revenue recognition rules, how should PartyMad disclose its sales?

   A. Gross, showing total sales value of all goods sold to the end user.

   B. Net, showing only the net difference between the sales value and the cost of the goods purchased from the third party.

   C. Gross, showing total sales value of all goods sold to the end user plus full disclosure in a note of net sales.

49. Which of the following is *most* likely to lead to a retrospective adjustment to the financial statements of a company?

   A. A company disposes of its overseas operations and will cease to make any further revenue from this part of the business.

   B. A change in the estimated useful life of all plant and machinery.

   C. A change in the method of accounting for stock options that results in a charge to the profit and loss account.

50. A company had 80,000,000 common shares in issue and $20,000,000 of convertible preferred stock in issue paying a dividend of 6% as at December 31 2011. The preferred stock is convertible into 105 ordinary shares per $100 of face value. The net income for the year was $190,000,000 and the tax rate is 30%. On 30 June 2011, there was a share repurchase of 20,000,000 shares. Which of the following is *closest to* the diluted earnings per share for the year ended December 31 2011?

   A. $1.71.

   B. $1.72.

   C. $1.88.

51. A company has inventories with a cost of $100,000. The inventories could be sold for $90,000, after future manufacturing costs of $5,000 have been incurred. The amount at which the inventories will be shown in the balance sheet is *closest to*:

   A. $85,000.

   B. $90,000.

   C. $95,000.

52. Under International Financial Reporting Standards, minority interest should be included in:

   A. equity.

   B. liabilities.

   C. its own section separate from equity and liabilities.

53. A company's long lived assets had a carrying value of $12,000 at the beginning of the year and $14,000 at the end of the year. During the year, the company purchased assets costing $4,200 and sold assets giving a loss on disposal of $600. The depreciation expense for the year was $800. Which of the following is *closest to* the company's cash flows from investing activities for the year?

   A. $3,400.

   B. $3,600.

   C. $5,000.

54. Under International Financial Reporting Standards, a decrease in a bank overdraft must be classified as:

    A. a cash outflow from financing activities.

    B. an increase in cash and cash equivalents.

    C. a cash outflow from financing activities or an increase in cash and cash equivalents.

55. A company had no inventories at December 31 2010. During the year ended December 31 2011, it purchased 15,000 units of inventory at a cost of $20 per unit, selling 10,000 of these units for $35 each. In the year ended December 31 2012, it purchased an additional 7,000 units of inventory at a cost of $22 per unit and sold 8,000 units at a price of $45 each. Assuming that the company uses the FIFO method of allocating inventory costs, the inventory value in the balance sheet at December 31 2012 is *closest to*:

    A. $80,000.

    B. $81,000.

    C. $88,000.

56. ABC Ltd has purchased inventory and subsequently written it down. Currently, the net realizable value is higher than the write-down value. ABC's inventory balance will *most likely* be:

    A. the same whether they use US GAAP or IFRS.

    B. lower if it complies with IFRS.

    C. lower if it complies with US GAAP.

57. Two companies, ABC Inc and XYZ Inc, have each purchased a piece of plant and machinery for $500,000 at the beginning of the year. Both companies assume the same useful life and residual value but ABC Inc uses the straight-line depreciation method and XYZ Inc uses double-declining balance method. All else being equal, at the end of the year XYZ Inc's return on asset ratio is *most likely* to be:

    A. lower than ABC Inc's return on asset ratio.

    B. higher than ABC Inc's return on asset ratio.

    C. lower or higher than ABC Inc's return on asset ratio, depending on the level of profits.

58. When a company uses straight line depreciation for a long lived asset, it is *most likely* that the company's return on equity will:

    A. increase over an asset's life.

    B. decrease over an asset's life.

    C. stay constant over an asset's life.

59. A long lived asset is currently being recognized in a company's balance sheet at a carrying amount of $24,000. The expected cash flows from the asset are $5,000 per year for the next five years, starting in one year's time. The discount rate to be applied to these flows is 6%. Using US GAAP, the amount at which the asset should be recognized in the balance sheet is *closest to*:

    A. $21,000.

    B. $24,000.

    C. $25,000.

60. Which of the following is *most likely* to give rise to a deferred tax asset?

    A. Balance sheet asset carrying value > tax base.

    B. Balance sheet liability carrying value < tax base

    C. Balance sheet liability carrying value > tax base.

61. An increase in a valuation allowance for deferred tax will *most likely*:

    A. increase assets and increase net income.

    B. decrease assets and decrease net income.

    C. increase liabilities and decrease net income.

62. A company has issued debt with an annual coupon of 5%, a bullet maturity of five years and a face value of $1,000,000. The issue proceeds were $918,000. Assuming that the company is following International Financial Reporting Standards, the balance sheet liability at the end of the first year is *closest to*:

    A. $932,300.

    B. $934,400.

    C. $945,100.

63. A company depreciates its assets on a straight line basis. It takes out a four year finance lease on January 1 2011. The lease involves four annual payments of $6,000 in arrears, payable on December 31. At the end of the lease, the asset will be worthless. The interest rate implicit in the lease is 6%. Which of the following is *closest to* the cash outflow for financing activities in the cash flow statement in the first year?

    A. $4,450.

    B. $4,752.

    C. $6,000.

64. If a lessor company structures a lease as a finance lease as compared to an operating lease, it is *most likely* that in the earlier years of the lease the company will have a:

    A. lower operating margin and a higher operating cash flow.

    B. higher operating margin and a higher operating cash flow.

    C. lower operating margin and a lower operating cash flow.

65. If a company's effective tax rate, interest coverage and EBIT margin all decrease, the company's net margin will *most likely*:

    A. increase.

    B. decrease.

    C. increase or decrease depending on the quantity of each of the above changes.

66. When prices are rising and inventory quantities are constant, use of the LIFO method of allocating costs to inventory compared to the FIFO method is *most likely* to:

    A. increase cost of sales.

    B. increase gross profit margin.

    C. increase inventory value.

67. Which of the following is least likely to be one of the five basic elements of financial statements in the International Financial Reporting Standards Framework?

    A. Cash.

    B. Assets.

    C. Income.

68. Extracts from a company's financial statements are as follows.

Year ended Dec 31	$ 2011	$ 2010
Inventories	12,000	10,560
Receivables	16,800	14,400
Cash	1,200	1,680
Current debt	7,200	2,400
Payables	11,520	11,040
Sales	72,000	69,600
Cost of goods sold	33,600	36,000

Which of the following is *closest to* the company's payables turnover for 2011?

    A. 2.98×.

    B. 3.04×.

    C. 3.11×.

69. Details of three companies are as follows:

	Net margin %	Asset turnover	Financial leverage
Company A	5	4.0	2.0
Company B	6	6.0	1.1
Company C	9	3.0	1.5

The company that is generating its return on equity through a high return on assets is:

A. company A.

B. company B.

C. company C.

Questions 70 through 78 relate to Corporate Finance

70. A company is assessing a new project. It will involve the purchase of some machinery at a cost of $50,000 and the use of some raw materials that originally cost $7,000 and would otherwise be disposed of at a cost of $10,000. The project would require office space and as a result would be allocated $15,000 of fixed overheads in the first year. The office space would otherwise have been rented out, bringing in rental income of $20,000 in the first year. The total cash flow to be used in assessing the project in its first year is *closest to*:

A. $60,000.

B. $80,000.

C. $82000.

71. A project's NPV profile has a positive intercept on the y axis and internal rates of return of 5%, 12% and 15%: The project should be accepted for investment between discount rates of:

A. 5% to 12%.

B. 12% to 15%.

C. 15% to 19%.

72. An analyst is trying to identify the weighted average cost of capital for company M. The analyst believes that company M has a target capital structure equal to average industry capital structure. The analyst has obtained the following data for peer companies that make up the industry:

Company	I	II	III
Debt to equity ratio	0.5	0.55	0.51

Company M has a beta of 1.2. The risk free rate of return is 4% and the return on the market is 7%. Debt costs 4.6% on a pre-tax basis and the tax rate is 30%. Company M's weighted average cost of capital is *closest to*:

A. 5.22%.

B. 6.10%.

C. 6.57%.

73. Use of the arithmetic mean when estimating the historical equity risk premium will *most likely* make the cost of equity:

A. lower than when using a geometric mean.

B. higher than when using a geometric mean.

C. lower or higher than when using a geometric mean, depending on the time period studied.

74. A company wishes to expand its short-term working capital portfolio. It wishes to invest in an instrument that can be up to a year in maturity, has an active secondary market and carries virtually no liquidity risk. The best suited short-term investment for the company is:

A. US Treasury bill.

B. Commercial paper.

C. Bank certificates of deposit.

75. A company is assessing the different short-term funding options available to it. It requires a facility that is reliable. Given that the company is relatively small and is considered by the banks to have a relatively poor financial strength, which of the following is the *most* likely short-term financing facility to be offered to the company by a bank?

    A. Uncommitted line.

    B. Commercial paper.

    C. Collateralised loan.

76. A company is able to pay its supplier on the terms 1/10 net 30. If the company always pays its account on the 30th day, which of the following is closest to effective cost of not taking up the opportunity of the trade discount?

    A. 18.85%.

    B. 20.13%.

    C. 23.40%.

77. Best practice for corporate governance would indicate that a company's Board should have:

    A. 50% independent Board members.

    B. a majority of independent Board members.

    C. more than one independent Board member.

78. Best practice for corporate governance would indicate that which of the following is *least likely* to be a satisfactory corporate policy with respect to shareholder voting rights?

    A. Anonymous voting is permitted.

    B. Voting is on a noncumulative basis.

    C. Shareholders are permitted to vote by proxy.

Questions 79 through 84 relate to Portfolio Management

79. An analyst is reviewing a stock, ABC Inc. Its required return using CAPM is 10%. The actual return of the stock based on its current trading price is 9%. Which of the following would the analyst *most* likely include in his stock report?

    A. ABC Inc is undervalued and recommends a buy action.

    B. ABC Inc is overvalued and recommends a sell action.

    C. ABC Inc is fairly valued and recommends a hold action.

80. An institutional investor is assessed as having the following investment needs:

    Time horizon : Long term

    Risk tolerance : High

    Liquidity needs : Low

    The institutional investor is *most* likely:

    A. a bank.

    B. a pension fund.

    C. a casualty insurance company.

81. Which of the following is *least likely* to be an assumption underlying Markowitz portfolio theory?

    A. Investors maximize one-period expected utility.

    B. Investor utility curves demonstrate increasing marginal utility of wealth.

    C. Investors base decisions solely on expected return and expected risk.

82. Details of the returns on two different asset classes are as follows:

Asset Class	Return %	Standard deviation of returns %
X	10%	12%
Y	7%	5%

    The correlation coefficient of returns for the asset classes is -0.3. The variance of a portfolio consisting of equal allocations to asset class X and asset class Y is *closest to*:

    A. 33.

    B. 51.

    C. 85.

83. Which of the following is *least likely* to be an assumption underlying the capital asset pricing model?

    A. Investments are infinitely divisible.

    B. All transaction costs are anticipated.

    C. Investors can borrow at the risk free rate of interest.

84. Details of the correlation with the market and standard deviation for a security are as follows:

Correlation with the market	Standard deviation
+0.2	40%

The standard deviation of the market is 65% The beta for the security is *closest to*:

A. 0.123.

B. 0.234.

C. 0.345.

Questions 85 through 96 relate to Equity

85. The annual dividend of a stock are expected to be $2.50 at the end of Year 1 and $2.62 at the end of Year 2. The stock is expected to have a value of £15.50 at the end of Year 3. Which of the following is closest to the current value of the stock, given an equity required return of 8%?

    A. $16.86.

    B. $18.32.

    C. $29.16.

86. Which of the following is *least* likely to be a feature of an Alternative Trading System (ATS)?

    A. Trading systems and subscribers are not regulated.

    B. Large orders are not displayed to other market participants.

    C. Trading systems are indistinguishable from the trading systems operated by exchanges.

87. Which of the following uses a price weighted method to calculate the index?

    A. TOPIX Index.

    B. Dow Jones Industrial Average Index.

    C. MSCI All Country World Index.

88. An unweighted arithmetic index *most likely* will:

    A. outperform a value weighted index when large stocks outperform.

    B. outperform a price weighted index when high growth stocks do stock splits.

    C. underperform an unweighted geometric index when the index components are highly volatile.

89. The weak form of the efficient market hypothesis can be tested by the use of:

    A. event studies.

    B. simulations of specific trading rules.

    C. predictions of cross sectional returns.

90. Which of the following is most likely to be a multiplier valuation model?

    A. Dividends.

    B. Free cash flow to equity.

    C. Enterprise value to EBITDA.

91. Where an industry has mainly intangible assets, the financial ratio that is *least likely* to be useful to calculate for companies in the industry is:

    A. interest cover.

    B. debt to equity.

    C. net profit margin.

92. When a company is earning a return on equity equal to its required return, the company's earnings multiplier is *least likely* to increase if there is:

   A. a decrease in the company's risk.

   B. a decrease in the risk free rate of interest.

   C. an increase in the retention rate of earnings.

93. An investor is valuing a stock for investment purposes which is expected to pay a dividend of €10 in a year's time, thereafter growing at a rate of 4%. The risk premium for the company is estimated at 8% and the risk free rate is 4%. The intrinsic value of the company is *closest to*:

   A. €100.

   B. €125.

   C. €200.

94. A company wishes to raise capital with low servicing costs and the ability to buy back the funding at a specified price before a specified date, Which of the following would be *best* suited to company as a source of financing?

   A. Cumulative preference stock.

   B. Callable common stock.

   C. Convertible preference shares.

95. An analyst has stated that since the economy is expected to improve significantly in the near future, portfolio managers should tilt their portfolios towards cyclical companies. An example of industries that he recommends for this is grocery chains. Is the analyst is *most likely* to be correct in respect of his statement that it is appropriate to tilt towards cyclical companies and his example of a cyclical industry?

	TILT TO CYCLICAL INDUSTRIES	EXAMPLE OF CYCLICAL INDUSTRY
A.	Correct	Correct
B.	Incorrect	Incorrect
C.	Correct	Incorrect

96. Details of a company's dividends and earnings are as follow:

	$
EPS	4.90
DPS	1.45
Return on equity	15%
Required rate of return	12%

   Which of the following is *closest* to the company's justified P/E?

   A. 20.0.

   B. 10.2.

   C. 7.8.

Questions 97 through 110 relate to Fixed Income

97. Which of the following is *least likely* to be an affirmative covenant in a bond indenture?
    A. Deliver collateral where necessary.
    B. Only raise additional debt with the consent of the lender.
    C. Give the lender access to the books and records of the borrower.

98. Which of the following is an example of external credit enhancement?:
    A. Surety bond.
    B. Overcollaterization.
    C. Turboing.

99. Security A is a 5% annual coupon fixed rate bond with a bullet maturity of 10 years. Security B is a 5% fixed rate mortgage pass through security with a maturity of 10 years. Security C is a zero coupon bond with a maturity of 20 years.

    Which of the above securities is *most likely* to have the greatest reinvestment risk?
    A. Security A.
    B. Security B.
    C. Security C.

100. A secondary bond market that has sufficient liquidity allows an investor to buy a bond at:
    A. a price at least equal to the selling price.
    B. the desired price.
    C. a price which is close to the bond's fair market value.

101. A bond issuer wants the right to take action and reduce borrowing costs if interest rate decline subsequent to issuing a bond. Which of the following bond instruments would *best* facilitate this need?
    A. Zero coupon bond.
    B. Callable bond.
    C. Step-up note.

102. A downward sloping spot curve is also called:
    A. the hypothetical yield curve.
    B. an inverted yield curve.
    C. an expected yield curve.

103. The term structure of interest rates *most likely* refers to the yield curve based on:
    A. forward rates.
    B. Treasury notes and bonds.
    C. spot rates.

104. An analyst has made the following two statements about bond spreads and yields:

Statement 1: The longer the deferred call period, the smaller the option adjusted spread is for a callable bond.

Statement 2: The yield ratio for a AAA Municipal bond over a Treasury bond is likely to be below 1.

Is the analyst *most likely* to be correct with respect to statement 1 and statement 2?

	STATEMENT 1	STATEMENT 2
A.	Correct	Correct
B.	Correct	Incorrect
C.	Incorrect	Correct

105. A zero coupon bond has a year to maturity and is trading on a yield of 10% (annual pay basis). The price of $100 par value of the bond is *closest to*:

A. $90.70.

B. $90.91.

C. $91.11.

106. When a bond is priced at a premium to par, it is *most likely* that the bond's:

A. coupon rate > current yield > yield to maturity.

B. coupon rate > yield to maturity > current yield.

C. coupon rate < current yield < yield to maturity.

107. Investors who believe that interest rates will fall will *most likely* invest in:

A. inverse floaters.

B. a fully amortizing bond.

C. a callable bond.

108. Details of quoted forward rates are as follows.

Period	Forward rate
0 – 6 months	2%
6 – 12 months	5%
12 – 18 months	8%

A 4% semi-annual coupon bond maturing in 18 months time will have a price *closest to*:

A. 92.01.

B. 94.56.

C. 98.65.

109. Which of the following securities is *least likely* to exhibit negative convexity?

    A. Putable bonds.

    B. Callable bonds.

    C. Mortgage passthroughs.

110. If interest rates are high and increase further, and yield volatility increases substantially, which of the following bonds is likely to have the greatest fall in price?

    A. Putable bond.

    B. Callable bond.

    C. Option free bond.

Questions 111 through 116 relate to Derivatives

111. Which of the following instruments can be described as a standardized instrument that is guaranteed against default and trades on an exchange?

A. Forward.

B. Future.

C. Options.

112. An investor has a position in a forward contract to buy a corporate bond in three months time. In this contract:

A. only the long position has default risk.

B. only the short position has default risk.

C. both the long position and the short position have default risk.

113. An investor has sold a futures contract priced at $720. The initial margin is $192 and the maintenance margin is $120. The price of the futures contract moves over the next four days as follows:

Day	Price
1	$710
2	$696
3	$864
4	$730

Assuming that the investor does not withdraw any margin, the total margin payments that the investor must make are *closest to:*

A. $192.

B. $288.

C. $336.

114. When a European put option price is less than the option's intrinsic value, the option is most likely:

A. overpriced.

B. underpriced.

C. in the money.

115. An option pricing model has given a put option a price of $10.00 when the market price of the option is $11.00. Which of the following is *least likely* to be the reason that the model has given a different price than the market price?

A. The strike price used into the model is lower than the actual strike price of the option.

B. The interest rate used into the model is lower than the actual interest rate in the market.

C. The volatility estimate used in the model is lower than the actual volatility of the stock.

116. An investor is seeking downside protection on an investment declining in value but wants to retain upside potential if the investment increases in value. He is willing to pay up front for the protection. Which of the following option strategies would best suit his requirement?

    A. Covered call.

    B. Protective put.

    C. Holder of a put option.

Questions 117 through 120 relate to Alternative Investments

117. Details of three different classes of share in a hedge fund are as follows:

	Fund A	Fund B	Fund C
Redemption fee %	1%	1%	0%
Incentive fee %	20%	10%	20%
Management fee %	1%	2%	2%

An investor is planning to hold shares in the hedge fund for three years. All three classes are expected to generate the same return each year. The investor is *most likely* to obtain the greatest value over three years through investing in:

A. class A shares.

B. class B shares.

C. class C shares.

118. A venture capital investment requires an initial investment of $1 million The investment is to be structured as convertible preferred shares with management retaining voting control of the company. This is an example of which of the following types of financing?

A. Mezzanine-stage financing.

B. Later-stage financing.

C. Formative-stage financing.

119. A merger has been announced between two companies, X and Y. The terms of the merger are that X will acquire Y by issuing one share in A for every two shares in Y. Shares in Y were previously trading at around $40 per share and are currently trading at $50. Shares in X are currently trading at $102. The merger is awaiting shareholder approval prior to being implemented. A merger risk arbitrage hedge fund would most likely go:

A. long in Y shares and short in X shares in the ratio 2:1.

B. short in Y shares and long in X shares in the ratio 2:1.

C. long in Y shares and short in X shares in the ratio 1:2.

120. A commodity futures market is said to exhibit backwardation when commodity spot prices are:

A. below the futures price.

B. above the futures price.

C. the same as the futures price.

Practice Examination 1
Morning Session Solutions

2014

ANSWERS

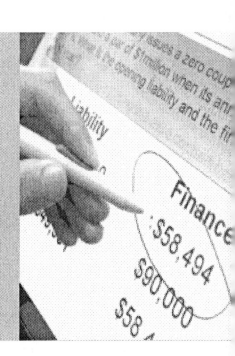

BPP
LEARNING MEDIA

Ethical and Professional Standards

1. **C**   The preamble states that CFA Institute members and candidates must abide by the Code and Standards and are encouraged to notify their employer of this responsibility.

        LOS 2a

2. **C**   The member may accept or reject the sanction proposed by the Designated Officer. If it is rejected, the matter is referred to a hearing by a panel of CFA Institute members.

        LOS 2a

3. **A**   Standard IB – Independence and Objectivity. It is not a problem to guarantee comprehensive coverage, so long as the coverage is independent and objective. A gift from a prospective client does not represent a potential breach of independence and objectivity.

        LOS 2a

4. **A**   The arrangement to receive a commission based on the number of new investors is a violation of rules concerning independence and objectivity (Standard IB Independence and Objectivity). Walt Twain should accept only a flat fee not based on his giving positive recommendations etc. The failure to disclose his relationship with the company on the website is misleading to investors and is a misrepresentation as a result (Standard IC Misrepresentation).

        LOS 2a

5. **A**   Standard ID Misconduct is not generally intended to cover acts of civil disobedience in support of personal beliefs.

        LOS 2a

6. **A**   Standard IIA Material Nonpublic Information. The information about the designs is nonpublic information but is not material since its impact on stock price is uncertain. Hiroyuki Okada has combined this information with the views of fashion experts to come to his conclusion i.e. the mosaic theory applies.

        LOS 2a

7. **C**   Sunil Perera has not used material nonpublic information so he has not violated Standard IIA Material Nonpublic Information. His actions in selling the stock and repurchasing the stock were based on investment opinions and were not intended to mislead the market by driving the price down before a subsequent repurchase. Therefore he has not violated Standard IIB Market Manipulation.

        LOS 2a

8. **B**   Standard IIIB Fair Dealing. It is unfair to other clients that he gives the information concerning his recommendations to major clients before releasing the information to other clients. However, it is not a problem that he gives a better service to his clients who pay higher fees etc. by discussing the note with them in detail afterwards.

        LOS 2a

9. **B** Standard IIIC Suitability. The member should refrain from making the trade or seek an affirmative statement that suitability is not a consideration.

LOS 2a

10. **C** Standard IIIE Preservation of Confidentiality states that the member must comply with the applicable law, which does not allow disclosure of such confidential information to anyone unless it relates to money laundering or tax evasion.

LOS 2a

11. **C** Standard IVA Loyalty. The standard does not prevent members from contacting clients of their previous employer, so long as the employer's records are not used and no anti competition clause is breached. Whistleblowing is permitted so long as it is for a purpose such as protecting market integrity and not for personal gain.

LOS 2a

12. **A** Standard IVC Responsibilities of Supervisors. After discovering a wrongdoing, the supervisor should respond promptly, investigate the activities to establish the scope of the problem and increase supervision of the wrongdoer pending the outcome of the investigation. Diane Conway did not increase supervision over James Smith pending the outcome of the investigation.

LOS 2a

13. **C** Standard VB Communications with Clients and Prospective Clients states that members should promptly disclose any changes to the investment process used. An increase in the investment universe represents a change that investors should be aware of, as they may have invested in the firm purely to obtain a small cap exposure and have a mid cap exposure elsewhere. There is no evidence that the firm is not being diligent and thorough in its investment approach, so there is no violation of Standard VA Diligence and Reasonable Basis.

LOS 2a

14. **C** Standard VC Record Retention recommends a minimum period of seven years.

LOS 2a

15. **A** Knowledge of pending transactions that will significantly affect the price is material nonpublic information according to Standard IIA Material Nonpublic Information. Hence she should not have caused her husband to deal on this information. Standard VIB Priority of Transactions states that firm and client transactions must take priority over personal transactions.

LOS 2a

16. **C** Clients should be aware that it is financially beneficial to Shan Ru He if she manages to obtain more assets under management, so there is no need to disclose bonuses received from the firm under Standard VIC Referral Fees. The same logic applies to Standard VIA Disclosure of Conflicts.

LOS 2a

17. **C** Standard VIIB Reference to CFA Institute, the CFA Designation, and the CFA Program. References to the rigor of the CFA Program and the relative merits of the CFA Program are permitted. Claims that the holder of the CFA designation is part of an elite are not acceptable.

LOS 2a

18. **B** Only real estate, private equity and separately managed accounts (SMA) portfolios have separate provisions within the GIPS Standards.

LOS 4d

Quantitative Methods

19. **C** The six monthly rate of interest is $(1.06)^{1/2} - 1 = 2.96\%$

The present value of a series from time 1 to infinity = 1000/0.0296= \$33,826. The formula $\dfrac{1}{r}$ gives the value one time period before the first flow.

LOS 5e

20. **B** The effective annual rate is $\left(1+\dfrac{0.0778}{4}\right)^{4} -1 = 8.01\%$. Trying out each answer in turn, 108 months = 9 years. $1.0801^{9} = 2.00$. Alternatively, you could calculate an effective monthly rate: $\left(1+\dfrac{0.0778}{4}\right)^{\frac{1}{3}} -1 = 0.644\%$. $1.00644^{108} = 2.00$.

LOS 5c

21. **A** Using the formula in the assigned reading: $\dfrac{360 \times 0.06}{360 - 100 \times 0.06} = 0.06101$ or 6.101%. Using first principles, the price of the T bill is $100 - 6 \times \dfrac{100}{360} = 98.333$. The CD equivalent (money market) yield is $\dfrac{100 - 98.333}{98.333} \times \dfrac{360}{100} = 0.06101$.

LOS 6e

22. **B** Generally, arithmetic mean > geometric mean > harmonic mean, unless all the observations have equal values in which case all three are equal to each other.

LOS 7e

23. **C** Using Chebyshev's inequality,

$x = 1-1/k^{2}$ $= 1-1/1.5^{2}$

$= 56\%$

LOS 7h

24. **A** Portfolio X has a negative skew, indicating that it has a very low value low probability item. This will extend the left tail outwards. Portfolio Y has kurtosis > 3, indicating that it is leptokurtic. This means that it is more peaked and has fatter tails than a normal distribution.

LOS 7l

25. **C** P(Increase 2013) = P(Increase 2011 decrease 2012) + P(decrease 2011 decrease 2012) = $(0.7 \times 0.3) + (0.3 \times 0.6) = 0.39$.

LOS 8f

26. **B** This can be solved by drawing a probability tree.

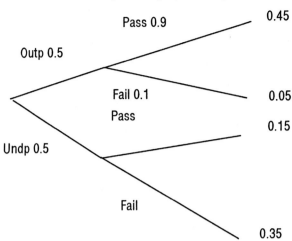

We know that 50% of stocks outperform and 50% underperform. We also know that given that a company outperforms, the probability that it will pas the screen is 0.9 (and therefore the probability that it will fail the screen is 0.1). This information enables us to complete the top half of the tree, as we can say that 0.45 of stocks will outperform and pass the screen and 0.05 of stocks will outperform and fail the screen. We also know that 40% of stocks fail the screen and therefore 60% pass the screen. This enables us to complete the bottom half of the tree, as 0.15 (0.6 − 0.45) of stocks which underperform must pass the screen and 0.35 (0.4 − 0.05) of stocks which underperform must fail the screen. The probability that a stock will outperform given that it passed the screen is: $\dfrac{0.45}{0.45+0.15} = 0.75$.

Alternatively, we can use Bayes theorem. The prior probability of outperforming is 0.5. We have been asked to calculate the posterior probability of outperforming given that the stock has passed the screen (passing the screen is the new information). The unconditional probability of the new information is 0.6 (60% of stocks pass the screen). The probability of the new information given the event (i.e. given that a stock outperforms, the probability that it will pass the screen) is 0.9. Using the Bayes Theorem formula: $\dfrac{0.9}{0.6} \times 0.5 = 0.75$.

LOS 8nand 8j

27. **B** This is a continuous uniform distribution. We want to know the probability of EBIT being between $10 million and $2 million: $\dfrac{10-2}{20-2} = 0.44$.

LOS 9i

28. **C** While this is a correct statement, it is not an assumption of the binomial distribution.

LOS 9f

29. **A** Deducting 1 from the sample size is only done when calculating the standard deviation of a sample. The variance of the distribution of sample means is calculated as $\dfrac{\sigma^2}{n}$.

LOS 10f

30.   C   A higher sample size will reduce the standard error ($\frac{\sigma}{\sqrt{n}}$). This will reduce the range estimate. A higher confidence level will increase the reliability factor and therefore increase the range estimate.

LOS 10j

31.   C   The null hypothesis is that the UK stock market has a variance equal to or less than the US stock market and the alternative hypothesis is that the UK stock market has a greater variance. The test statistic is $\frac{\sigma_a^2}{\sigma_b^2} = \frac{10^2}{7.9^2} = 1.60$

LOS 11a

32.   C   Trends are assumed to persist for appreciable periods of time and prices are affected by rational and irrational factors.

LOS 12a

Economics

33. **C**   Cross-price elasticity of demand is positive for a substitute and negative for a complement.

       LOS 13m

34. **C**   Improvements in productivity due to technological advances improves the efficiency of inputs. An increase in productivity decreases labor costs, improves profitability and results in higher output. Bothe the SRAS and the LRAS shift rightward.

       LOS 17h

35. **B**   Own price elasticity of demand = $-0.7 \times P_{DVD}/Q_{DVD}$.

       PED $= -0.7 \times (10.82/-3.51)$

       PED $= 2.15$

       Q_{DVD} $= 5 - 0.7P_{DVD} + 0.0003I - 0.23P_B$

                $= 5 - 0.7 \times \$10.82 + 0.0003 \times \$2,500 - 0.23 \times \$7.32$

                $= -3.51$

       LOS 13m

36. **B**   Increasing marginal returns arise due to specialization and division of labor. Diminishing marginal returns arise due to more workers using the same capital.

       LOS 15k

37. **B**   A discouraged worker is somebody who has stopped looking for a job. Voluntarily unemployed is somebody refusing an available job vacancy.

       LOS 18d

38. **B**   The downward sloping demand curve reflects the fact that each firm's products are different. In the long run, firms will produce where marginal revenue equals marginal cost and will make zero economic profit. At this point, average total cost will not be minimized, since price equals average total cost and the demand curve is downward sloping.

       LOS 16b

39. **A**   Growth in the money supply, measured by M2, indicates easing monetary conditions and a positive economic outlook, hence growth. It is a leading economic indicator.

       LOS 19c and 18j

40. **C**   The S&P 500 Stock Index is a leading economic indicator. Stock prices anticipate economic cycles.

       LOS 18i

41. **A**   All three points describe the beliefs of the monetarist school of thought.

       LOS 18c

42. **C** Easy fiscal policy means expansionary fiscal policy which will lead to a rise in aggregate output. Tight monetary policy will lead to a reduction in the supply of money and a rise in interest rates. High interest rates will lead to a *decrease* in private sector demand.

LOS 19l

43. **A** If Government raise spending by $Xk then aggregate output increases by $Xk. But if the tax rate is increased to finance this spending, and the marginal propensity to spend is less than 1, consumer spending will only reduce by MPC × $Xk. As a result, aggregate output will rise by (1-MPC) × $Xk. This is known as the balanced budget multiplier.

LOS 19n

44. **B** A change in tax rates is a discretionary fiscal policy.

LOS 19n

Financial Reporting and Analysis

45. **B** A qualified opinion is when there is some limitation or exception in the application of financial reporting standards. A disclaimer is when the auditor is unable to issue an opinion.

   LOS 22d

46. **B** Assets = Liabilities + Owners equity.

   Owners equity = Contributed capital + retained earnings.

   Retained earnings = Beginning retained earnings + net profit – dividends paid.

   Assets = 1,700 + 4,500 + 3,000 + (10,000 – 8,500) – 1,000 = 9,700

   LOS 23e

47. **A** There are two fundamental qualitative characteristics per the Conceptual Framework (2010): Relevance and Faithful Representation. In addition to this there are four characteristics that *enhance* the usefulness: Comparability, Verifiability, Timeliness and Understandability.

   LOS 24d

48. **B** If PartyMad bears no inventory risk, it is merely an agent for the supplier earning commission on sales (mark up on cost) and should show sales net.

   LOS 25b

49. **C** Discontinued operations are reported separately on the face of the income statement and are therefore not considered an adjustment but a disclosure requirement. Changes in accounting policy (such as changing the way of accounting for employee stock options) are adjusted for retrospectively, changes in accounting estimate (ie changes in useful life) are adjusted for prospectively.

   LOS 25e

50. **A** $$\frac{\text{Net income before preferred dividends}}{\text{Weighted average number of common shares} + \text{Shares issued on conversion}} \quad \frac{190m}{90m + 21m} = 1.71$$

   $$\text{Weighted average of ordinary shares} = \frac{100m \times 6 + 80m \times 6}{12} = 90m$$

   $$\text{Shares issued on conversion} = 20m \times \frac{105}{100} = 21m$$

   LOS 25g

51. **A** Show inventories at the lower of cost and market (net realizable value). NRV = estimated sales proceeds less future costs to complete and sell the inventories = 90,0000 – 5,000 = $85,000.

   LOS 26e

52. **A** IFRS require that minority interest is included in the shareholders' equity section.

   LOS 26a

53.   A

	$
Opening value	12,000
Capital expenditure	4,200
Depreciation expense	(800)
Value of assets sold	?
Closing value	14,000

Value of assets sold = $1,400

Sale proceeds = 1,400 – 600 = $800

Cash from investing activities = 4,200 – 800 = $3,400

LOS 27a

54.   B   Under US GAAP, an overdraft is treated as a bank loan i.e. a financing item, but under International Financial Reporting Standards, it is classified as cash and cash equivalents.

LOS 27a

55.   C   There are (15 – 10 + 7 – 8) 4,000 units in closing inventory. Under FIFO (first in first out), the last items purchased must be in closing inventories i.e. 4,000 × $22 = $88,000.

LOS 29c

56.   C   Inventory will be lower under US GAAP as it does not permit the reversal of write-down, whereas IFRS does if the value increases.

LOS 29f

57.   C   Double-declining balance method charges more depreciation in the year than straight-line depreciation. As a result, XYZ Inc's total assets will be lower but depreciation charge in the income statement will be higher. Therefore both the numerator and denominator in the ROA ratio will be lower, so no conclusion can be made unless the comparative value of profits to assets is known.

LOS 30c

58.   A   Since the depreciation expense is constant, other things being equal the profit will be constant. The book value of the asset is falling, meaning that return on equity will increase each year.

LOS 30c

59.   B   The undiscounted cash flows of $25,000 exceed the carrying value of the asset. Since the asset is recoverable, no write down is required. Had the total of the undiscounted cash flows been less than the carrying value of the asset, the asset should have been written down to the present value of the future cash flows.

LOS 30h

60.   C   Since the company has a net liability (compared to the tax carrying amount) in its balance sheet, the counterbalancing deferred tax effect will be the net liability × tax rate, giving a deferred tax asset.

LOS 31b

61.   **B**   An increase in a valuation allowance reduces deferred tax assets.

           LOS 31g

62.   **A**   We need to identify the IRR of the cash flows. The IRR is 7%:

Time	Flow	PV at 7%
0	(918,000)	(918,000)
1-4	50,000	169,361
5	1,050,000	748,639
		-

The balance at the end of the first year is:

	$
Opening balance	918,000
Finance cost at 7%	64,260
Coupon paid	(50,000)
Ending balance	932,260

           LOS 32a

63.   **B**   The value of the asset is the present value of four flows of $6,000 from time 1 to time 4, discounted at 6% i.e. $20,791. The interest expense in the first year is 6% × 20,791 = $1,247, meaning that the capital repayment is 6,000 – 1,247 = $4,752.

           LOS 32h

64.   **C**   Finance leases from the lessor's perspective will show interest revenue on the lease receivable (shown below operating profit). Operating leases from a lessor's perspective shows rent income and depreciation on the leased asset. It is therefore likely that under operating lease the operating profit will be higher than under a finance lease. Under a finance lease the interest portion of the lease payment only is shown in operating or investing cash flow, whereas under an operating lease the whole rental income is shown as an operating cash flow.

           LOS 32g

65.   **C**   EBIT margin falling causes net margin to fall. Interest coverage falling means that interest is a higher proportion of EBIT, so this will cause EBT margin to fall, causing net margin to fall. A fall in the effective tax rate will cause net margin to rise. The overall impact is uncertain.

           LOS 28c

66.   **A**   In times of rising prices, the last in first out means that cost of sales will be higher, gross profit margins will be lower. Inventory value on the balance sheet will be lower, as the 'cheaper' inventory will still be in stock.

           LOS 29d

67.   **A**   Cash is a type of asset.

           LOS 23a

68.   **C**   Purchases in 2010 = COGS + increase in inventories = 33,600 + (12,000 − 10,560) = 35,040.

$$\text{Payables turnover} = \frac{35,040}{\frac{1}{2}(11,520+11,040)} = 3.11$$

LOS 28b

69.   **B** $$\text{Return on assets} = \frac{\text{Net income}}{\text{Assets}} = \frac{\text{Net income}}{\text{Sales}} \times \frac{\text{Sales}}{\text{Assets}}$$

Company A: 5 × 4 = 20%

Company B: 6 × 6 = 36%

Company C: 9 × 3 = 27%

LOS 28d

Corporate Finance

70.　**A**

	$
Machinery	50,000
Lost rental income	20,000
Saved disposal cost	(10,000)
Net cash outflows	60,000

LOS 36b

71.　**B**　The NPV profile is as follows. Positive NPVs occur between 12% and 15%.

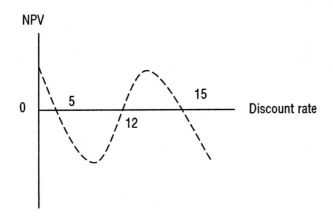

LOS 36d

72.　**B**　Average Debt to equity ratio of the industry = $\dfrac{0.5 + 0.55 + 0.51}{3} = 0.52$

Cost of equity = 4 + 1.2(7 − 4) = 7.6%

Pre tax cost of debt = 4.6%

$\text{WACC} = \dfrac{7.6\% \times 100 + 4.6\%(1 - 0.3) \times 52}{152} = 6.10\%$

Since the debt to equity ratio is 0.52, equity is 100 and debt is 52 of total finance.

LOS 37a

73.　**B**　Unless all values are equal, use of the arithmetic mean will give a value for the risk premium higher than the geometric mean, making the cost of equity estimate higher.

LOS 37h

74.　**A**　Both commercial paper and CDs have credit and liquidity risk.

LOS 40g

75.   **C**   Uncommitted lines of credit are not reliable as the bank can withdraw the facility at any time. Commercial paper is a non-bank source of short-term finance suited only to large corporations. A collateralized loan is reliable and suited to small companies with poor financial strength and hence requiring assets as security.

LOS 40g

76.   **B**   The cost of trade finance is given by:

Cost of trade finance: $\left(1+\dfrac{0.01}{0.99}\right)^{\frac{365}{20}} - 1 = 20.13\%$

LOS 40f

77.   **B**   There should be at least a majority of independent members.

LOS 41c

78.   **B**   Cumulative voting is preferred as it increases the likelihood that minority shareholders' will be represented on the Board. Proxy and anonymous (confidential) voting are desirable.

LOS 41g

Portfolio Management

79. **B** With an inflated market price the return would be lower than required with CAPM (return/price) and therefore return is only 9% when risk of the stock suggests that it should be 10%.

LOS 44h

80. **B** A bank tends to have a short time horizon and low risk tolerance. A casualty insurance company tends to have a high liquidity need to meet claims.

LOS 42b

81. **B** Investor utility curves demonstrate declining marginal utility of wealth.

LOS 43h

82. **A** $s^2 = 0.5^2 12^2 + 0.5^2 5^2 - 2 \times 0.5 \times 0.5 \times 12 \times 5 \times 0.3 = 33.25$

The correlation coefficient is negative so the last term is deducted.

LOS 43c

83. **B** There are no transaction costs.

LOS 44f

84. **A** The beta of the security is given by:

[Coefficient of correlation (i,m) × standard deviation (i)]/ standard deviation (m)

= [0.2 × 0.4]/0.65

= 0.123

LOS 44e

Equity

85.   **A** $V_0 = 2.50/(1.08) + 2.62/(1.08)^2 + 15.50/(1.08)^3$

   $= 2.31 + 2.25 + 12.30$

   $= 16.86$

   LOS 51e

86.   **A**   Alternative Trading Systems operate like exchanges but do not regulate subscribers. However, the trading and trading systems are fully regulated, as with an exchange.

   LOS 46b

87.   **B**   Both TOPIX and MSCI are market cap weighted indexes.

   LOS 47k

88.   **B**   A price weighted index will underperform when high growth stocks do stock splits as this will diminish their importance in a price weighted index.

   LOS 47d

89.   **B**   Simulations of specific trading rules see if it is possible to use market data to make supernormal profits.

   LOS 47d

90.   **C**   Although dividends or FCFE could be the basis for a multiplier based valuation, they are also used in present value based approaches. Enterprise value to EBITDA is explicitly a multiplier based approach.

   LOS 51b

91.   **B**   Since the company has few tangible assets, the balance sheet based debt to equity ratio is least likely to give useful information.

   LOS 50k

92.   **C**   Although an increase in the retention rate will increase the expected growth rate in earnings, it will reduce the dividend payout, meaning that the multiplier is less likely to increase.

   LOS 51e

93.   **B**   Required return = 4% + 8% = 12%

   $$\text{Value} = \frac{10}{0.12 - 0.04} = 125$$

   LOS 51e

94.   **B**   The ability to redeem the funding at a specified price means that there must be a callable option for the company. Common stock has no fixed servicing cost unlike preference shares and convertible preference shares.

   LOS 49b

95. **C** When the economy grows, cyclical companies should benefit most. However, a grocery chain supplies basic necessities and is more likely to be a defensive stock.

LOS 50c

96. **A** Justified P/E is given by:

$P/E = p/(r - g)$

Where p = dividend payout %

= 1.45/4.90 = 30%

P/E = 0.3/(0.12 − g)

where g, dividend growth rate = ROE × (1 − p)

= 0.15 × 0.7

= 10.5%

P/E = 0.3/(0.12 − 0.105) = 20

LOS 51h

Fixed Income

97. **B** Affirmative covenants are where the borrower agrees to do something. Negative covenants impose restrictions on the borrower, such as not borrowing additional money.

LOS 52b

98. **A** A surety bond is a form of external credit enhancement.

LOS 52b

99. **B** The amortizing feature of mortgage pass through securities means that the investor has to reinvest capital repayments as well as interest payments over the life of the bond. This increases reinvestment risk. Longer maturities also give greater reinvestment risk except for zero coupon bonds, which have no reinvestment risk.

LOS 53e

100. **C** Liquidity refers to the ability to buy and sell at fair market value.

LOS 53d

101. **B** Callable bond allows the company to repurchase the debt at a fixed price and then refinance at a lower interest rate. Zero coupon bonds give no option to refinance if interest rates decline. Step-up notes are designed to increase coupon payments over time.

LOS 52f

102. **B** A downward sloping yield curve is inverted as it shows short term yields as higher than long term yields, indicating that rates are expected to fall.

LOS 54g

103. **C** The term structure of interest rates is based on spot rates, which are the yields on zero coupon securities.

LOS 54g

104. **C** The OAS is unaffected by prepayment risk and therefore is not affected by the call feature. The nominal spread will be smaller for a longer deferred call. AAA rated municipal bonds have lower yields than Treasury bonds due to their tax advantage.

LOS 52f and 56j

105. **B** When using the equivalent annual yield, a year's time will be time 1.

$$\text{Price} = \frac{100}{1.1} = 90.91$$

LOS 54b

106. **A** Since the price is greater than 100, the coupon rate will exceed the current yield and since there will be a capital loss the current yield will exceed the yield to maturity.

LOS 54b

107. **A** The interest rate on an inverse floater will increase as rates decrease, which is of benefit to the holder. A fully amortizing bond will have a greater reinvestment risk when interest rates are falling, and a callable bond is more likely to be called, leaving the holder to reinvest at new lower yields.

LOS 52a

108. **C**

$$\frac{2}{1.01} + \frac{2}{1.01 \times 1.025} + \frac{102}{1.01 \times 1.025 \times 1.04} = 98.65$$

LOS 54h

109. **A** Both callable bonds and mortgage pass throughs give the borrower the right to repay early, so they exhibit negative convexity when interest rates are low.

LOS 55g

110. **B** At high interest rates that increase, the value of the option free bond will fall. The value of the call option will increase due to higher interest rate volatility, making the value of the callable bond fall even more (callable bond = option free bond – call option). The value of the put will increase, making the value of the putable bond fall less (putable bond = option free bond + put option). Therefore the callable bond suffers the greatest fall in price.

LOS 52f

Derivatives

111. **B** Forwards are customized instruments that are not guaranteed against default and traded off exchange. Options are not guaranteed against default and traded off exchange.

LOS 57a

112. **C** The long position has the risk that the short position will not deliver the bond. The short position has the risk that the long position will not pay for the bond.

LOS 58a

113. **C** Initial margin is $192. The price then rises to $864, giving (864 – 720) $144 of losses for the short position. The margin balance has therefore fallen to (192 – 144) $48, which is below the maintenance margin of $120. The variation margin payment is $144 (192 – 48), to restore his initial margin of $192. Total margin payments: 192 + 144 = $336.

LOS 59d

114. **C** Since the maximum value of a European put is the present value of the strike price (when the underlying price is zero), when a European put is deeply in the money it is possible for the option price to be less than the intrinsic value.

LOS 60k

115. **B** The model has given the put option a lower value than the market. A lower strike price would reduce the value and lower volatility would reduce the value. However, a lower interest rate would increase the value of a put, so use of a lower interest rate in the model would make the model based price higher than the actual market price.

LOS 60o and 60l

116. **B** A covered call generates cash up front but removes some of the upside potential. A put option without the underlying does not give the upside potential if the underlying goes up in value.

LOS 62b

Alternative Investments

117. **B**   Redemption fee is irrelevant as no exit planned for the next three years. Lowest incentive and management fee is fund B.

    LOS 63d

118. **C**   **LOS 63d**

119. **A**   Buy using $102 from shorting A to buy two shares in B for $100, the fund can make $2.00. If the merger is completed, the two shares in B will be exchanged for one share in A which can be used to close out the short position.

    LOS 63d

120. **B**   Backwardation is when future prices are below spot prices. Contango is when the future prices are above the forward price.

    LOS 63e

The Chartered Financial Analyst® Program

Practice Examination 1
Afternoon Session

2014

The Afternoon Session of Practice Examination 1 consists of 120 multiple choice questions which must be completed in three hours. The topic areas covered are:

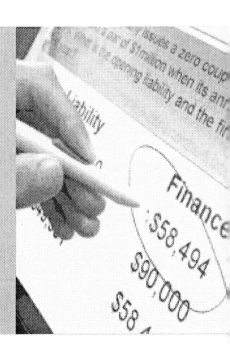

BPP
LEARNING MEDIA

Questions 1 through 18 relate to Ethical and Professional Standards

1. Which of the following is *least likely* to be required by the CFA Institute Code of Ethics? Members of CFA Institute and candidates for the CFA designation must:

   A. promote the integrity of capital markets.

   B. act with integrity when dealing with competing companies in the capital markets.

   C. place the interests of their employer above the interests of clients and their own personal interests.

2. James Joyce CFA lives in a country with minimal laws in respect of investment services and participation in equity initial public offerings (IPOs) by investment advisers. He provides investment services to clients living in a country where the laws prohibit participation in equity IPOs by investment advisers. The laws of the country where Joyce provides investment services to clients apply and state that the laws of the country where the investment adviser lives should apply to such investment services. In order to comply with the requirements and recommendations of the Standards of Professional Conduct, it is *most* likely that Joyce:

   A. is free to participate in any equity IPOs in the country where he provides investment services to clients.

   B. must not participate in any equity IPOs in the country where he provides investment services to clients.

   C. should obtain preclearance from his employer before participating in any equity IPOs in the country where he provides investment services to clients.

3. Which of the following is *least likely* to be a compliance procedure that will assist in avoiding violations of the Standard of Professional Conduct concerning Independence and Objectivity?

   A. Limit gifts.

   B. Create a restricted list.

   C. Permit special cost arrangements.

4. Emily Austen CFA has just prepared some promotional material for her firm which as a result of a typographical error overstates her firm's assets under management. The material is distributed to several clients before she realizes the mistake. Yukio Kawabata CFA has distributed material to clients of his firm for a number of years where it mistakenly states that he is a graduate of Tokyo University when in fact he left the university before completing his studies. Kawabata is not aware of the error in the material which was prepared by the marketing department. Which of the following *most* accurately describes who has or has not violated the Standard of Professional Conduct concerning Misrepresentation?

   A. Both Austen and Kawabata have violated the Standard concerning Misrepresentation.

   B. Austen has not violated the Standard concerning Misrepresentation but Kawabata has violated the Standard concerning Misrepresentation.

   C. Both Austen and Kawabata have not violated the Standard concerning Misrepresentation.

5. Jenny Buzan CFA recently attended an investment seminar on behalf of her employer. As a result of bad weather, she was forced to stay one night longer than anticipated and, to compensate for this additional time away from home, she overstated her expenses claim for the trip in lieu of receiving any other payment. Buzan also gives up some of her personal free time to assist in charity work unrelated to her employment. During this charity work, she has taken some goods donated to the charity for her own personal use to compensate for the time she gives up on behalf of the charity. When the charity discovered this, she was told that her donated time was no longer wanted. Which of the following statements most accurately describes whether Buzan has or has not violated the Standard of Professional Conduct concerning Misconduct?

   A. In respect of both her expense claim and her taking goods from the charity, Buzan has violated the Standard concerning Misconduct.

   B. In respect of her expense claim, Buzan has violated the Standard concerning Misconduct. In respect of her taking goods from the charity, Buzan has not violated the Standard concerning Misconduct.

   C. In respect of both her expense claim and her taking goods from the charity, Buzan has not violated the Standard concerning Misconduct.

6. Which of the following is *least likely* to be part of an effective set of compliance procedures designed to prevent violation of the Standard of Professional Conduct concerning Material Nonpublic Information?

   A. Control of interdepartmental communications through a clearance area.

   B. Use of a watch list to prevent trading in stocks on the list by employees.

   C. Documentation of the procedures designed to limit the flow of information between departments and any enforcement actions taken as a result of such procedures.

7. An investment firm has the following policy statements:

   Policy statement 1: The firm will vote all proxies unless a cost benefit analysis has decided that voting the proxy is not appropriate.

   Policy statement 2: The firm will always hold diversified portfolios for its clients in order to reduce the risk of loss, even if this is contrary to the client's investment objectives.

   Which of the two policy statements is *most likely* to be consistent with the Standard of Professional Conduct concerning Loyalty, Prudence and Care?

	STATEMENT 1	STATEMENT 2
A.	Consistent	Consistent
B.	Consistent	Inconsistent
C.	Inconsistent	Inconsistent

8. Which of the following is *least likely* to be a procedure for compliance that is consistent with the Standard of Professional Conduct concerning Fair Dealing?

   A. Maintain a list of clients and their holdings of securities and investments.

   B. Shorten the time frame between the decision to make an investment recommendation and its dissemination.

   C. Develop procedures to ensure that all clients are treated equally when disseminating investment recommendations.

9. Which of the following is *least likely* to mean that a CFA Institute member can meet his or her obligations under the Standard of Professional Conduct concerning Performance Presentation when making a performance presentation?

   A. Excluding terminated accounts from the performance history.

   B. Claiming compliance with Global Investment Performance Standards (GIPS).

   C. Presenting the performance of a weighted composite of similar portfolios rather than the performance of a representative portfolio.

10. Brigitte Birkin CFA is an investment adviser who has been approached by a client planning to make a substantial charitable donation which will reduce the client's tax liability. She asks Birkin if she knows of any charities which might be appropriate for a donation. Birkin suggests a local charity called Rabbits which offers support for disadvantaged children. Her client expresses an interest in contacting the charity and notes down its details. After the client has left, Birkin contacts the treasurer of Rabbits and suggests that they contact her client, giving the treasurer the client's contact details. With respect to the Standard of Professional Conduct concerning Preservation of Confidentiality, it is *most likely* that Birkin has:

    A. violated the Standard.

    B. not violated the Standard because the information released did not relate to the client's financial assets.

    C. not violated the Standard because the client asked Birkin for details of charities that might be appropriate and expressed an interest in the charity.

11. Philip Yeats CFA has received an offer from a client whereby if the client's portfolio achieves a return of more than 20% in a year, the client will provide Yeats with an expenses paid trip to Europe. Yeats achieves this return and takes advantage of the offer. With respect to the Standard of Professional Conduct concerning Additional Compensation Arrangements, it is *most likely* that Yeats:

    A. has not violated the Standard since this is a gift from a client.

    B. has violated the Standard because he did not disclose the offer to his employer and obtain the employer's consent.

    C. has violated the Standard because he did not disclose the offer to his employer and obtain his employer's and the client's written consent.

12. Louisa Ferguson CFA is a member of a team responsible for publishing research reports. Ferguson believes that it is likely that interest rates will remain stable for the foreseeable future and writes a report to the team to that effect. However, other team members adopt the view that interest rates are likely to increase for a number of reasons and the final fixed income report published by the team reflects this majority view that interest rates will increase. Ferguson recognizes that the other team members adopted sound procedures and have a reasonable basis in coming to their conclusions, but nevertheless holds the view that interest rates will remain stable. Ferguson's course of action that is *most likely* to be consistent with the Standard of Professional Conduct concerning Diligence and Reasonable Basis is to:

    A. demand that she be dissociated from the report.

    B. document her difference of opinion with the team.

    C. allow the report to be published without taking any additional action.

13. Peter Secombe CFA is an equity analyst who has just visited a mining company and been told by its managers that its reserves in its major mines are likely to be far higher than originally expected, although this is not yet public knowledge. The managers of the company expect this knowledge to have a significant impact on the stock price. On returning to the office Secombe writes and distributes a research note to his clients where he states that due to the likelihood that the company's reserves are far higher than expected, he recommends the company as a buy. It is *most likely* that Secombe has:

   A. not violated the Standards of Professional Conduct.

   B. violated only the Standard of Professional Conduct concerning Material Nonpublic Information.

   C. violated the Standards of Professional Conduct concerning Material Nonpublic Information and Communications with Clients and Prospective Clients.

14. Joe Roberts CFA has written a research report on ABC Inc. in which he recommended the stock as a purchase. Subsequent to writing and distributing the report, Roberts has received an inheritance of stock in ABC Inc. with a value of approximately $500,000. He has now been asked to write a second report on ABC Inc. by his firm. According to the Standard of Professional Conduct concerning Disclosure of Conflicts, best practice for Roberts would be to:

   A. dispose of his stockholding in ABC Inc.

   B. disclose his interest in ABC Inc. in the second report.

   C. ask his employer to assign another analyst to draft the second report.

15. Which of the following compliance procedures in respect of equity initial public offerings (IPOs) is *most likely* to be consistent with the Standard of Professional Conduct concerning Priority of Transactions?

   A. Employees may not invest in equity IPOs.

   B. Employees must preclear personal investment in equity IPOs.

   C. Employees must preclear personal investment in equity IPOs when there is a conflict of interest.

16. Mark Paxman CFA has written an article for publication in the Wall Street Journal in which he states that he believes that the CFA program is less rigorous than it was in previous years and that CFA Institute's policy with respect to continuing education needs significant improvement if it is to be relevant to investment practitioners. With respect to the Standard of Professional Conduct concerning Conduct as Members and Candidates in the CFA Program, it is *most likely* that Paxman has:

   A. not violated the Standard.

   B. violated the Standard by expressing opinions about CFA Institute without first obtaining preclearance.

   C. violated the Standard by expressing opinions about CFA Institute that are not based on factual evidence.

17. Which of the following usages in a resume when giving one's name or citing the CFA designation is *most likely* to be a violation of the Standard of Professional Conduct concerning Reference to CFA Institute, the CFA Designation, and the CFA Program?

   A. John Smith, C.F.A.

   B. CFA, 2005, CFA Institute.

   C. Level I candidate in the CFA program.

18. Which of the following is *most likely* to be a standard of competence which a CFA Institute member should reach in order to satisfy his or her ethical responsibilities under Standard 1A – Knowledge of the Law?

   A. Becoming an expert in compliance.

   B. Having detailed knowledge of all laws that could potentially govern the member's conduct.

   C. Having an understanding of applicable laws and regulations in all countries where the member provides investment services.

Questions 19 through 32 relate to Quantitative Methods

19. A bank deposit grows from $10,000 today to $11,900 in four years' time. What is the interest rate of the deposit if there is continuous compounding?

A. 4.56%.

B. 4.34%.

C. 4.24%.

20. A portfolio has an opening market value of $2,500. Six months later, the investor invests another $500 in the portfolio, at which time the market value is $2,800 before the $500 is invested. In a year's time, the portfolio value is $3,900 and the investor withdraws $1,000 of this. In two year's time, the portfolio value is $3,100, of which the investor withdraws $500. The annual money weighted rate of return for the portfolio is *closest to*:

A. 9.9%.

B. 19.0%.

C. 20.7%.

21. Which of the following calculations of yield for a T bill with a maturity of 180 days would *most likely* give the highest value?

A. Bank discount yield.

B. Money market yield.

C. Effective annual yield.

22. The following series of data relates to returns on a share over a number of months:

5% 7% 9% 12% 14%

The harmonic mean of the returns is *closest to*:

A. 8.2%.

B. 8.8%.

C. 9.4%.

23. An analyst has researched the returns on value and growth stocks, defining value stocks as those with low price to book ratios and growth stocks as those with high price to book ratios. He has analyzed stocks into three quartiles based on their price to book ratios and summarized his results as follows:

	Quartile 1	Quartile 2	Quartile 3
Median price to book ratio	1.2	1.9	2.4
Mean return	22%	18%	19%
Standard deviation of return	16%	13%	15%

The quartile with the highest relative dispersion is:

A. Quartile 1.

B. Quartile 2.

C. Quartile 3.

24. An investor needs $100,000 in five years' time and has found an investment vehicle that gives an annual interest rate of 6%. He is able to invest five equal lump sum payments starting from today and annually thereafter. How much should each lump sum payment be to ensure that he receives $100,000 after five years?

A. $14,543.

B. $15,675.

C. $16,736.

25. A technical analyst has plotted the price of a mining security over the last 6 months and has identified a head and shoulder pattern. The share price reached its highest at $110 and he estimates that the neckline is at $67. Which of the following is *closest to* the target price that the technician anticipates closing the investment position?

A. $110.

B. $67.

C. $24.

26. An analyst needs to construct an equally weighted portfolio of 4 different stocks from 10 stocks. The number of different portfolios that are possible is *closest to*:

A. 24.

B. 210.

C. 5,040.

27. When a project's internal rate of return is greater than the company's cost of capital, the company should:

A. always reject the project.

B. always accept the project.

C. sometimes reject and sometimes accept the project.

28. The probability density function for a continuous uniform distribution is described as:

A.

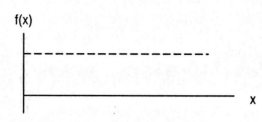

B.

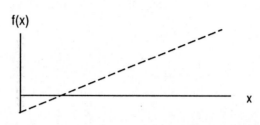

C.

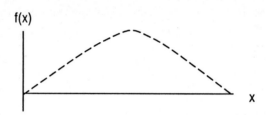

29. Which of the following statements is *least likely* to be correct? The arithmetic mean:

A. can be heavily influenced by extreme values.

B. cannot take one of the actual values of the data in the series.

C. can be explained through an analogy of the centre of gravity for a series of data.

30. When completing a hypothesis test on the mean of a population, a smaller sample size and a higher confidence level will:

A. increase the probability of a type I error.

B. decrease the probability of a type I error.

C. increase or decrease the probability of a type I error.

31. A researcher has made the following statements:

    Statement 1: A nonparametric test makes minimal assumptions about the population from which the sample comes and is used when data is given in ranks.

    Statement 2: When dealing with a large sample from any population where the population variance is unknown, the distribution of sample means will be approximately normally distributed.

    Is the researcher *most likely* to be correct in respect of statement 1 and statement 2?

	STATEMENT 1	STATEMENT 2
A.	Correct	Correct
B.	Correct	Incorrect
C.	Incorrect	Correct

32. Which of the following sentiment indicators is *most likely* to be a sign of positive sentiment in the market?

    A. The put/call ratio is at an extreme low.

    B. The level of margin debt is falling.

    C. The CBOE Volatility Index is rising.

Questions 33 through 44 relate to Economics

33. For an inferior good, the:
    A. income effect offsets part or all of the substitution effect.
    B. income and substitution effects reinforce one another.
    C. demand curve has a negative slope.

34. Which of the following is *least* likely to be an argument against being concerned about the size of a country's national debt compared to its GDP?
    A. The debt could be overstated because the debt is owed internally to the country's own citizens.
    B. The Government may print money which is likely to lead to a stimulus for the country's economy.
    C. A proportion of the borrowings could have been used for capital investment projects that could lead to higher future country output.

35. A country faces a large budget deficit. The government plans to cut spending and increase tax rates. Which of the following is least likely to be an impact of the Government's planned actions?
    A. The country's current account balance will improve.
    B. The country's imports are likely to reduce.
    C. The country's private sector savings are likely to increase.

36. An economist has made the following two statements.

    Statement 1: The marginal product curve cuts through the average product curve from above.

    Statement 2: Increases in the prices of factors of production will reduce marginal product.

    Is it *most likely* that the economist is correct with respect to Statement 1 and Statement 2?

	STATEMENT 1	STATEMENT 2
A.	Correct	Correct
B.	Correct	Incorrect
C.	Incorrect	Correct

37. A monopolist will set the price of its good at a point on the demand curve where demand is:
    A. elastic.
    B. inelastic.
    C. unit elastic.

38. In a duopoly which of the following is *least* likely to be a feature of the Nash model?
    A. The actions of the two firms are non co-operative.
    B. The firms will collude to maximize joint profits.
    C. Each company takes into account the other company's reaction when they select their strategy.

39. Which of the following is least likely to shift the aggregate demand curve to the right?

    A. Increases in stock prices.

    B. Increase in taxes.

    C. High expected future income levels.

40. Details of the Price Index are as follows.

Year	2008	2009	2010	2011
Price Index	100	105	110	115

    The inflation rate is:

    A. constant.

    B. increasing.

    C. decreasing.

41. All of the following are included in M1 in the United States except for:

    A. travelers checks.

    B. checking deposits.

    C. bank currency holdings.

42. Which of the following is *least* likely to be an impact of unanticipated inflation in an economy?

    A. Increased information content of market prices.

    B. Inequitable transfers of wealth between borrowers and sellers.

    C. Risk premia in borrowing rates.

43. An exchange rate regime whose currency is pegged to the US$ at a fixed rate and has fixed horizontal intervention bands of +/-2% is best known as:

    A. crawling peg.

    B. target zone.

    C. fixed parity.

44. The USD/EUR spot rate is 1.4230. The GBP/USD spot rate is 0.7824. Which of the following is closest to the GBP/EUR spot rate?

    A. 1.1134.

    B. 1.8188.

    C. 0.5498.

Questions 45 through 68 relate to Financial Reporting and Analysis

45. Under US GAAP in which of the following categories is interest paid *most likely* to be included?
    A. Investing activities.
    B. Operating activities.
    C. Financing activities.

46. Which of the following is most likely to be included in a company's year end liabilities?
    A. Unearned revenue.
    B. Prepayment.
    C. Unbilled revenue.

47. All of the following are underlying assumptions in the preparation of financial statements in the International Financial Reporting Standards Framework except:
    A. accrual accounting.
    B. consistency.
    C. going concern.

48. When the outcome of a long term contract cannot be measured reliably, revenue recognized each year over the life of a contract before its completion under International Financial Reporting Standards compared to revenue recognized each year under US GAAP will *most likely* be:
    A. lower.
    B. higher.
    C. the same.

49. A company had 100,000,000 common shares in issue as at December 31 2011. On July 1 2011, the company completed a 4 for 1 stock split. The net income for the year ended December 31 2011 was $90,000,000 and a preferred dividend of $20,000,000 was paid to 10,000,000 preferred shares and a dividend of $30,000,000 to the common shares. Which of the following is *closest to* the earnings per share for the year ended December 31 2011?
    A. $0.40.
    B. $0.70.
    C. $1.12.

50. In the year ended December 31 2011, a company had earnings per share of $1.50, based on a weighted average number of common shares of 400,000. The company paid a preferred dividend of $20,000 and an ordinary dividend of $10,000. At the year end, stockholders equity was $6,000,000 and at the year beginning stockholders equity was $4,500,000. There was a share issue during the year which raised $400,000. Which of the following is *closest to* the company's other comprehensive income for the year?

    A. $510,000.

    B. $530,000.

    C. $1,100,000.

51. Into which of the following elements of financial statements is the account for prepaid expenses *most likely* to be included?

    A. Costs.

    B. Assets.

    C. Liabilities.

52. A company's income statement shows sales of $40,000 for the year ended December 31 2013. Extracts from the company's balance sheets are as follows:

Balance sheet at	December 31 2012 $	31 December 2013 $
Receivables	3,000	2,000
Unearned income	5,000	1,000
Accrued expenses	1,400	400

    Cash flow from sales for the company for the year ended December 31 2013 is *closest to*:

    A. $37,000.

    B. $43,000.

    C. $45,000.

53. A company's net income for the year ended December 31 2013 is $1,500. Extracts from the company's financial statements are as follows.

Balance sheet at December 31	2013 $	2012 $
Inventories	900	700
Receivables	1,300	1,000
Cash	50	30
Long lived assets	1,800	1,100
Total assets	4,050	2,830
Payables	600	450
Debt	1,070	800
Stockholders' equity	2,380	1,580
	4,050	2,830

Long lived assets were purchased during the year costing $900. There were no disposals of long lived assets.

Which of the following is *closest to* the company's cash flow from operating activities for the year?

A. $1,150.

B. $1,350.

C. $2,050.

54. An accountant has made the following statements:

Statement 1: Under International Financial Reporting Standards, if a company receives dividends and interest from investments they are treated as operating cash flows, whereas under US GAAP they can be treated as operating or investing cash flows.

Statement 2: Under IFRS, dividends to stockholders can be classified as operating or financing cash flows, whereas under US GAAP they are classified as financing activities only.

Is the accountant *most likely* to be correct in respect of Statement 1 and Statement 2?

	STATEMENT 1	STATEMENT 2
A.	Correct	Correct
B.	Correct	Incorrect
C.	Incorrect	Correct

55. A company was started in 2012. During 2012, it purchased 40,000 units of inventory at a cost of $50 per unit, and sold 35,000 units at a price of $110 each. In 2013, it purchased an additional 50,000 units of inventory at a cost of $60 per unit and sold 45,000 units at a price of $100 each. Of the units sold in 2012, 4,000 units were actually purchased in 2012 and 41,000 units were purchased in 2013. Assuming that the company uses the LIFO method of allocating inventory costs, the inventory value in the balance sheet at December 31 2013 is *closest to*:

A. $500,000.

B. $550,000.

C. $590,000.

56. When inventory prices are rising and inventory quantities are constant, the gross profit and ending inventory value of a company using the FIFO method of allocating inventory costs compared to a company using the LIFO method are most likely to be:

	GROSS PROFIT	ENDING INVENTORY VALUE
A.	Lower	Same
B.	Higher	Lower
C.	Higher	Higher

57. Where a company is replacing its assets and prices of fixed assets are not changing, return on equity for a company using double declining balance depreciation compared to straight line depreciation will *most likely* be:

A. lower.

B. higher.

C. the same.

58. When a company wishes to increase its reported profits in future years, it will *most likely*:

A. write down the value of its fixed assets.

B. reduce the expected salvage value of its fixed assets.

C. reduce the expected useful economic life of its fixed assets.

59. Deferred tax assets are *most likely* to arise when:

A. an excess amount is paid for income taxes and the company expects to recover this excess.

B. a deficit amount is paid for income taxes and the company expects to eliminate this deficit.

C. it is more likely than not that a company will generate future taxable profits in excess of future taxable losses.

60. Which of the following *most accurately* describes the accounting equation relationship?

A. Assets = Liabilities + Owner's equity + Retained earnings.

B. Assets = Liabilities + Contributed capital + Owner's equity.

C. Assets – Liabilities + Expenses = Contributed capital + Opening retained earnings + Revenue.

61. Which of the following elements of financial statements is most closely related to the measurement of performance?

A. Assets.

B Equity.

C. Income.

62. A company has issued a bond at a discount to its face value. The company uses the effective interest rate method to account for the bond. Which of the following is most likely to be true?

   A. On issuance, the balance sheet will show a liability equal to the face value of the bonds.

   B The annual interest expense in the income statement is given by the carrying value of the bond multiplied by the coupon rate.

   C. The annual interest payment shown in the cash flow statement is given by the face value of the bond multiplied by the coupon rate.

63. When a lessee treats a lease as an operating lease, it is most likely that compared to a finance lease, the company will have a higher:

   A. debt to equity ratio.

   B. cash flow from financing activities.

   C. cash flow from operating activities.

64. A company has a return on equity of 56%, a net margin of 6% and its stockholders equity is equal to its total liabilities. Which of the following is closest to the company's asset turnover?

   A. 4.7.

   B. 7.3.

   C. 9.3.

65. Compared to the completed contract method, over the life of a long term contract the percentage of completion method will most likely give a:

   A. higher current ratio and lower financial leverage.

   B. lower current ratio and higher financial leverage.

   C. higher current ratio and higher financial leverage.

66. A company has debt of $7,000 and stockholders equity of $9,000 in its balance sheet. It has disclosed that it is committed to operating leases with a present value of $2,000. An analyst wishes to assess the solvency of the company and make suitable adjustments to treat the lease as an ongoing financial commitment. The company's debt to equity ratio calculated by the analyst would be closest to:

   A. 78%.

   B. 82%.

   C. 100%.

67. Details of three companies are as follows.

	Scale and diversification	Financial policies	Operational efficiency
Company A	Small scale and undiversified	Strong	Average
Company B	Small scale and undiversified	Average	Average
Company C	Large scale and diversified	Strong	High

Which company is *most likely* to have the lowest credit rating?

A. Company A.

B. Company B.

C. Company C.

68. All of the following represent an opportunity for a company's management to over-report the company's earnings except:

A. high turnover rates of staff.

B. significant related party transactions.

C. excessive pressure to meet financial targets.

Questions 69 through 78 relate to Corporate Finance

69. If a conventional project has a discounted payback period of three years it *most likely*:

A. may not have a positive internal rate of return.

B. will have a payback period of more than three years.

C. will not be rejected when using the net present value methodology.

70. Project X and project Y are mutually exclusive projects with the same level of risk, the same amount of initial investment required and conventional cash flows. Project X has a shorter discounted payback period than project Y. The discount rate at which both projects have the same net present value is 7% and the internal rate of return for project Y is 12%. At a cost of capital of 10%, the correct investment decision is *most likely* to be to accept:

A. project X.

B. project Y.

C. both project X and project Y.

71. A company has some debt in issue with a five year maturity and semi annual paying a coupon of 6%. The original issue price of the debt was 95 and it is currently priced at 96. The tax rate is 30%. The company's post tax cost of debt is *closest to*:

A. 4.87%.

B. 4.88%.

C. 4.96%.

72. Details of a company's cost of capital schedule are as follows.

Amount of new debt $m	After tax cost of debt %	Amount of new equity finance $m	Cost of equity %
0 - 2	3.0	0 – 6	9
2 – 5	3.4	6 – 12	10
>5	4.0	>12	11

The company raises finance so as to maintain a debt to total capital ratio of 40%. Which of the following is closest to the second breakpoint when raising capital for the company?

A. $5 million.

B. $10 million.

C. $13 million.

73. All of the following are pulls on liquidity for a company except:

A. reducing credit limits.

B. making payments early.

C. uncollected receivables.

74. Two mutually exclusive projects are being reviewed by a company looking to expand. Project A has an IRR of 20% and Project B has an IRR of 24%. At the company's discount rate of 12%, Project A has an NPV of $560,000 and Project B has an NPV of $450,000. Given this information, which of the following is the best investment decision for the company?

    A. Project A.

    B. Project B.

    C. Projects A and B.

75. Company X produces power boats and has fixed operating costs of $12 million per annum. It has debt that attracts annual interest of $20 million. The selling price of each power boat is $35,000 and the variable cost per power boat is $22,000. Which of the following is closest to the company's operating breakeven point?

    A. $920.

    B. $1,450.

    C. $2,460.

76. A 91 day $100,000 US T-bill is issued at a discount of 6.4%. Which of the following is closest to the money market yield?

    A. 6.2%.

    B. 6.5%.

    C 8.1%.

77. Best practice for corporate governance would indicate that a benefit of having a classified Board is *most likely*:

    A. protection against takeovers.

    B. continuity of Board expertise.

    C. greater flexibility to appoint new members.

78. Best practice for corporate governance would *least likely* indicate that a remuneration committee should:

    A. consist of independent and non independent Board members.

    B. link executive compensation to long term profitability for the company.

    C. have access to external advisers without needing approval from the Board.

Questions 79 through 84 relate to Portfolio Management

79. An investor is in the accumulation phase of his lifecycle. He suffers a high rate of tax on any income received and a low rate of tax on realized capital gains. The investment strategy that is *most likely* to be suitable for the investor is:

    A. total return.

    B. capital preservation.

    C. capital appreciation.

80. Using CAPM, calculate the required return of an equity stock whose beta is estimated at 1.1. The return of the market is 10%, the risk free rate is 4% and the correlation coefficient of the equity stock with the market is 0.45.

    A. 8.5%.

    B. 8.8%.

    C. 10.6%.

81. Which of the following statements is *most likely* to be correct with respect to the covariance of returns?

    A. Covariance can take on any value.

    B. The magnitude of covariance is determined exclusively by the variances of the two variables concerned.

    C. Covariance is a measure of the relative degree to which two variables move together relative to their individual mean values over time.

82. An investor who is highly tolerant of risk is *most likely* to select an investment on the efficient frontier where the slope of the frontier is:

    A. steep.

    B. unitary.

    C. shallow.

83. Which of the following statements is *least likely* to be correct with respect to the capital market line? The capital market line:

    A. dominates the efficient frontier.

    B. only consists of portfolios that have only systematic risk.

    C. identifies the expected return on a security for its level of risk.

84. When a portfolio of risky assets is combined with a risk free asset, the relationship between return and standard deviation of the portfolio is:

    A. linear.

    B. convex.

    C. concave.

Questions 85 through 97 relate to Equity

85. A market where dealers provide liquidity by buying and selling shares is referred to as a:
     A. order driven market.
     B. pure auction market.
     C. quote driven market.

86. An investor who owns shares currently priced at $10 wishes to sell them if the market price falls to $8. The investor should place a:
     A. limit order.
     B. market order.
     C. stop loss order.

87. When small cap stocks are outperforming relative to large cap stocks, an index that will *most likely* underperform is a:
     A. price weighted index.
     B. equal weighted index.
     C. value weighted index.

88. Which of the following is *least likely* to be a characteristic of a well-functioning financial system?
     A. Security prices adjust rapidly to reflect new information.
     B. Announcements of new information regarding securities is independent and timely.
     C. Security prices respond to demands for liquidity made by traders.

89. The disposition effect is where:
     A. investors are rational and risk averse when analyzing prospective returns for a stock.
     B. investors tend to avoid realizing losses but seek to realize gains.
     C. investors determine future stock prices through a mixture of rational and irrational motives which determine supply and demand.

90. When an analyst identifies pricing anomalies by analyzing the performance of current mutual funds over a period of time, he is *most likely* introducing into his sample:
     A. selection bias.
     B. survivorship bias.
     C. data mining bias.

91. A company is expected to start paying dividends in three years' time. The first dividend is expected to be $24.00 and it is expected to subsequently grow at 5% per year. If common stock investors require a return of 12% the intrinsic value of the stock is *closest to*:

A. $244.

B. $273.

C. $300.

92. The crucial relationship that determines the value of a stock is *most likely* to be the difference between the:

A. retention rate and the dividend payout ratio.

B. marginal return on equity and the average return on equity.

C. required rate of return and the expected growth rate in dividends.

93. Three companies have the same earnings multiplier. Additional details about the three companies are as follows.

Company	Cost of equity	Expected growth rate in dividends
A	15%	9%
B	12%	5%
C	9%	4%

Which company is *most likely* to be overvalued?

A. Company A.

B. Company B.

C. Company C.

94. A strategic group is *most likely*:

A. the same as an industry group.

B. a group of industries with similar characteristics.

C. a group of companies sharing a distinct business model.

95. Which of the following statements relating to the secondary bond market is least accurate?

A. Newly issued corporate bonds are issued in the secondary market.

B. Secondary bond markets are where bonds are traded between investors.

C. The major participants in secondary bond markets globally are institutional investors.

96. An analyst has stated that empirical evidence indicates that long run returns on stocks are related to price to book ratios but not to price to sales ratios. Is the analyst *most likely* to be correct with respect to price to book ratios and price to sales ratios?

	PRICE TO BOOK	PRICE TO SALES
A.	Correct	Correct
B.	Correct	Incorrect
C.	Incorrect	Correct

97. When interest rates increase, which of the following embedded options is *most likely* to be exercised?

A. Put feature.

B. Conversion option.

C. Accelerated sinking fund provision.

Questions 98 through 110 relate to Fixed Income

98. Modified duration measures the risk of a change in a bond's price due to:

    A. parallel shifts of the yield curve.

    B. non parallel shifts of the yield curve.

    C. parallel and non parallel shifts of the yield curve.

99. Which of the following securities is *most likely* to have the largest fall in price if interest rates are initially low but rise by a small amount and interest rate volatility falls substantially?

    A. Putable bond.

    B. Callable bond.

    C. Fixed rate bond.

100. Which of the following is *most likely* to be a government sponsored enterprise (GSE)?

    A. Farmers Housing Administration.

    B. Federal National Mortgage Association.

    C. Government National Mortgage Association.

101. A minimum debt service coverage ratio for municipal bonds will measure available revenue to cover:

    A. capital interest payments after operating expenses.

    B. capital and interest payments before operating expenses.

    C. interest payments only after expenses.

102. Which of the following *best* describes the components of credit risk?

    A. Default probability and loss severity.

    B. Default probability and spread risk.

    C. Loss severity and recovery rate.

103. A bond investor who expects the economy to go into recession would *most likely* go:

    A. short Treasury bonds and long corporate bonds.

    B. long Treasury bonds and short corporate bonds.

    C. short Treasury bonds and short corporate bonds.

104. A bond paying an annual coupon of 5% has four years to maturity and is trading on a yield of 7%. A year later the bond is trading on a yield of 6%. The change in value of a holding of $1,000 par value due to the passage of time is *closest to*:

    A. $15.25.

    B. $25.76.

    C. $41.01.

105. A 5% semi annual coupon Treasury bond has two years to maturity and is trading on a yield of 5.0%. The term structure of interest rates for Treasury securities is as follows.

Time	Spot rate
6 months	3%
12 months	4%
18 months	5%
24 months	6%

Which of the following is *closest to* the arbitrage free value of $1,000 par value of the bond?

A. $982.57.

B. $1,000.00.

C. $1,010.11.

106. When the level of interest rates increases during a bond's life, it is *most likely* that the achieved yield to maturity of the bond will:

A. equal the promised yield to maturity.

B. be lower than the promised yield to maturity.

C. be higher than the promised yield to maturity.

107. When valuing a noncallable corporate bond, it is most likely appropriate to use:

A. nominal spread.

B. zero volatility spread.

C. option adjusted spread.

108. A corporate bond has a nominal spread of 5%, a z-spread of 4% and an option adjusted spread of 1%. The option cost is *closest to*:

A. 3%.

B. 4%.

C. 5%.

109. A bond has a price of 97.42, an effective duration of 5.1 and a convexity of 40. If interest rates increase by 2%, the price of bond is *closest to*:

A. 85.92.

B. 89.04.

C. 108.92.

110. An analyst has made the following two statements:

Statement 1: When calculating duration for an option free bond, modified duration is an appropriate measure.

Statement 2: Modified convexity may be negative for a callable bond.

Is the analyst *most likely* to be correct with respect to Statement 1 and Statement 2?

	STATEMENT 1	STATEMENT 2
A.	Correct	Correct
B.	Correct	Incorrect
C.	Incorrect	Correct

Questions 111 through 110 relate to Derivatives

111. Which of the following strategies for the holder of an equity stock exposes the investor to limited downside risk if the stock declines in value and unlimited upside potential if the stock rises in price?

    A. Protective put.

    B. Covered call.

    C. Sell an equity forward contract.

112. An investor has bought a 1 x 3 forward rate agreement at a rate of 5% with a principal amount of $1,000,000. Details of the rates for LIBOR in the subsequent months are as follows:

Time	60 day LIBOR	90 day LIBOR
One month's time	6%	7%
Two months' time	8%	9%
Three months' time	10%	11%

    The amount which the investor will pay or receive on the forward rate agreement is *closest to*:

    A. receive $1,650.

    B. pay $1,667.

    C. receive $1,667.

113. Delivery options on Treasury bond futures are exercised by the:

    A. buyer.

    B. seller.

    C. clearinghouse.

114. Using put-call parity, which of the following strategy is equivalent to a long bond?

    A. Long put + long underlying + short call.

    B. Long call + long underlying + short put.

    C. Short put + short underlying + long put.

115. An investor has a $20 million portfolio invested equally in equities and bonds. The investor wishes to increase her allocation to bonds as part of a review of investment objectives but has a view that in the short term interest rates are going to increase. The investor is considering two swaps.

    Swap 1: exchanging the return on the S & P 500 with fixed rate flows.

    Swap 2: exchanging fixed rate flows for floating rate flows.

    In order to satisfy her revised investment objectives and her tactical view on interest rates, the investor should *most likely*:

    A. pay the equity return on swap 1 and pay the fixed return on swap 2.

    B. pay the equity return on swap 1 and receive the fixed return on swap 2.

    C. receive the equity return on swap 1 and pay the fixed return on swap 2.

116. Which of the following most accurately describes a protective put position?

A. Synthetic long call.

B. Long stock and short put.

C. Long stock and short call.

Questions 117 through 120 relate to Alternative Investments

117. An analyst has made the following statements:

    Statement 1: Hedge funds employ long and short positions, are often highly leveraged and aim to perform well even if the broad market is in decline.

    Statement 2: A benefit of hedge funds is that they are one of the more liquid alternative investments and exiting from a hedge fund investment is simple and cost free. Is the analyst *most likely* to be correct in respect of Statement 1 and Statement 2?

	STATEMENT 1	STATEMENT 2
A.	Correct	Correct
B.	Correct	Incorrect
C.	Incorrect	Correct

118. A hedge fund that takes short positions in securities identified as overvalued is described as following which of the following strategies?

    A. Equity hedge.

    B. Macro.

    C. Relative-value.

119. Which of the following private equity exit strategy is most likely to provide the highest price?

    A. Recapitalisation.

    B. IPO.

    C. Trade sale.

120. Which of the following would not be an adjustment made in a comparable sales approach to valuing real estate?

    A. Location.

    B. Depreciation.

    C. Age of property.

Practice Examination 1
Afternoon Session Solutions

2014

ANSWERS

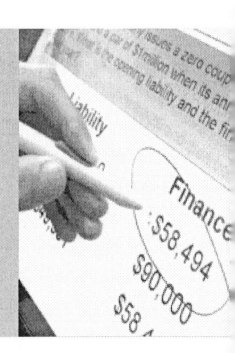

BPP
LEARNING MEDIA

Ethical and Professional Standards

1. **C** The Code of Ethics requires members and candidates to place the interests of clients above their own personal interests.

    LOS 2a

2. **C** Since the laws of the country where James Joyce lives apply to the situation, he should follow the Standards of Professional Conduct which are stricter than the laws of the country, according to Standard IA – Knowledge of the Law. Standard IVB – Priority of Transactions states in its recommended procedures that members should preclear participation in equity IPOs.

    LOS 2a

3. **C** Special cost arrangements should be restricted under Standard IB Independence and Objectivity.

    LOS 2a

4. **B** Standard IC Misrepresentation. Emily Austen did not knowingly make the representation about the firm's assets since it arose through a typographical error. However, having noticed the error, she should now immediately rectify this. Yukio Kawabata has been using the material for a number of years and should have spotted the misrepresentation by now. Therefore he has breached the Standard.

    LOS 2a

5. **A** Standard ID Misconduct covers professional conduct involving dishonesty etc. and also any act that reflects adversely on integrity.

    LOS 2a

6. **B** Standard IIA Material Nonpublic Information. A watch list is known only to a few people such as compliance officers, and is used to monitor trading. It may be combined with a restricted list.

    LOS 2a

7. **B** Standard IIIA Loyalty, Prudence and Care. Proxies should be voted in the client's best interests, unless a cost benefit analysis has shown that voting would be beneficial to the client. Diversification is appropriate unless the diversification is inconsistent with plan guidelines or contrary to the account objectives.

    LOS 2a

8. **C** Standard IIIB Fair Dealing states that all clients should be treated fairly, i.e. not discriminating between clients, when disseminating investment recommendations, but does not specify equally since this would not be possible due to unique client needs etc.

    LOS 2a

9. **A** Standard IIID Performance Presentation. Including terminated accounts in the performance history avoids survivorship bias and therefore presents performance more fairly and completely.

    LOS 2a

10. **A** Standard IIIE Preservation of Confidentiality. Brigitte has released confidential information about her client received in the course of their business relationship without the client's permission.

   LOS 2a

11. **C** Standard IVB Additional Compensation Arrangements. The member should obtain written consent from the employer and client where the benefit could reasonably expected to create a conflict of interest with the employer's interest.

   LOS 2a

12. **B** Standard VA Diligence and Reasonable Basis. Members may request to have their name removed from the report but if they are satisfied that the report has a sound and reasonable basis (as is the case with Laura), they do not have to do this. Instead, they can just document their difference of opinion.

   LOS 2a

13. **B** Standard IIA Material Nonpublic Information prohibits a member causing others to trade in securities on the basis of material nonpublic information. The significantly higher reserves is a material fact and it is stated in the question that it is nonpublic information. Standard VB Communications with Clients and Prospective Clients has not been violated.

   LOS 2a

14. **C** Standard VIA Disclosure of Conflicts. In this circumstance, it is best practice to avoid such a significant conflict rather than just to disclose it.

   LOS 2a

15. **B** Standard VIB Priority of Transactions. Investment in equity IPOs should be restricted and employees should preclear participation in IPOs, even where there is no conflict of interest.

   LOS 2a

16. **A** Standard VIIA Conduct as Members and Candidates in the CFA Program is not intended to prevent opinions being expressed about the CFA Program or CFA Institute.

   LOS 2a

17. **A** Standard VIIB Reference to CFA Institute, the CFA Designation, and the CFA Program. Periods should not be used, so John Smith, CFA would be correct.

   LOS 2a

18. **C** Standard IA – Knowledge of the Law. Members are not expected to become experts in compliance or have a detailed knowledge of all laws that might potentially govern their conduct.

   LOS 2a

Quantitative Methods

19. **B** $FV_N = PVe^{rN}$ $11,900 = 10,000e^{r4}$

Ln(11,900/10,000) = r x 4

r = 0.0434

LOS 5e

20. **C**   The money weighted return is the IRR. Calculate the six monthly IRR first of all (using the CF function on your calculator), treating the initial market value and investments as outflows and the closing market value and withdrawals as inflows:

CF	
0	(2,500)
1	(500)
2	1,000
4	3,100

Six monthly IRR = 9.88%. Annual IRR = 1.0988^2 - 1 = 0.2074 or 20.7%

LOS 6a and 6d

21. **C**   The discount yield is based on par rather than market value, so this will give the lowest value. The money market yield is calculated as $r \times \dfrac{360}{n}$. Where r is the return for n days.

The effective annual yield is calculated as $(1+r)^{\frac{365}{n}}$. Since this uses 365 days rather than 360 days and compounds the return, it will give a higher value than the money market yield.

LOS 6e

22. **A** $\dfrac{5}{\dfrac{1}{5}+\dfrac{1}{7}+\dfrac{1}{9}+\dfrac{1}{12}+\dfrac{1}{14}} = 8.21$

LOS 7e

23. **C**   We need to calculate the coefficient of variation since we are measuring relative dispersion. Quartile 3 has the highest relative dispersion.

Quartile 1: $\dfrac{16}{22} = 0.727$

Quartile 2: $\dfrac{13}{18} = 0.722$

Quartile 3: $\dfrac{15}{19} = 0.789$

LOS 7f

24. **C** $FV5 = A(1+r)5 + A(1+r)4 + A(1+r)3 + A(1+r)2 + A(1+r)1$

$100,000 = A(1.06)^5 + A(1.06)^4 + A(1.06)^3 + A(1.06)^2 + A(1.06)^1$

$100,000 = A1.338 + A1.262 + A1.191 + A1.124 + A1.06$

$100,000 = 5.975A$

$A = 16,736$

LOS 5e

25. **C** To profit from a head and shoulders pattern, a technician will set a target price that he expects the share price to fall to – this is below the neckline, so C is the only sensible answer. The price target can be calculated as follows:

Target price = Neckline – (Head – Neckline)

$= 67 - (110 - 67)$

$= \$24$

If you were unsure of this detail, you should remember that a head and shoulders pattern is a reversal pattern, so the stock price is heading down from its previous high.

LOS 12d

26. **B** We are selecting 4 items out of 10 items where the order does not matter (since the portfolio is equally weighted). $\dfrac{10!}{6!4!} = 210$. Use the combination function on your calculator nc_r as a quicker way of working this out.

LOS 8o

27. **C** There are a number of circumstances when the IRR rule of accepting projects where the IRR exceeds the cost of capital is not appropriate, e.g. when comparing mutually exclusive projects.

LOS 6b

28. **A** All outcomes are equally likely so the line is horizontal. The cumulative density function would show the straight line with a positive slope. The bell shape is characteristic of the normal distribution rather than the uniform distribution.

LOS 9c

29. **B** It may take one of the values, but it need not do so.

LOS 7e

30. **B** The probability of a type I error is equal to the significance level of the test. A higher confidence level indicates a smaller rejection area and gives a lower probability of a type I error (the probability of incorrectly rejecting the null hypothesis). The sample size does not affect the probability of a type I error.

LOS 11c

31. **A** Nonparametric testing can also be used when data is not normally distributed, or the hypothesis does not address a parameter.

LOS 11j

32.   A   If the put/call ratio is at an extreme low, then market sentiment is extremely positive. Investors who buy call options are likely to be bearish and those that buy put options are likely to be bearish. So, the lower the ratio the more likely sentiment in the market is positive. If margin debt is falling this indicates a more negative market sentiment, as investors are not borrowing to invest. If the CBOE Volatility Index is rising, this implies the price of the put options are rising, indicating a more negative market sentiment.

LOS 12e

Economics

33.   **A**   For a normal good the demand curve is negatively sloped and the income and substitution effects reinforce one another.

LOS 14f

34.   **B**   Governments will print money to meet the fiscal deficit if citizens lose confidence in them. This is likely to lead to inflation rather than a boost to the economy.

LOS 19m

35.   **C**   Spending cuts and tax rises will improve the current account balance. The country's imports are likely to reduce because spending cuts will mean less demand from the government of overseas goods. The tax rises will mean less private household disposable income and therefore less private sector savings.

LOS 20g

36.   **B**   Marginal product increases then decreases, meaning that it will cut through average product from above. Increases in prices of factors of production will affect costs but not marginal product, which is the increase in total production through adding one more unit of a factor of production.

LOS 15j

37.   **A**   The monopolist will set the price and quantity where marginal revenue = marginal cost. This will be on the elastic part of the demand curve.

LOS 16b

38.   **B**   the Nash model assumes that the companies do not co-operate with each other; they work to maximise their own profit, not the joint profit. Each firm considers how the other firm will react before selecting a strategy. The Nash equilibrium means that the companies have no incentive to change strategy.

LOS 16d

39.   **B**   High expected future income will increase consumer confidence and shift AD to the right. An increase in stock prices is a positive economic signal, likely to increase consumer consumption and shift AD to the right. Increasing taxes will reduce household wealth and reduce consumption, shifting AD to the left.

LOS 17h

40.   **C**   Since the absolute increase in the Price Index is constant, the percentage increase (= inflation rate) is decreasing.

LOS 18f

41.   **C**   Currency held by banks is not viewed as part of M1.

LOS 19b

42. **A**   Unanticipated inflation will *reduce* the information content of prices. For example, increase in prices could be translated as increased demand or reduced supply rather than just purely inflationary increases.

LOS 19f

43. **B**   Fixed parity has narrower bands of up to +/- 1% either side of the pegged rate, rather than the wider band of the target zone. Crawling pegs are an adjustment that takes into account moving inflation rates.

LOS 19h

44. **A**   GBP/EUR = USD/EUR × GBP/USD

$$= 1.4230 \times 0.7824$$

$$= 1.1134$$

LOS 21e

Financial Reporting and Analysis

45. **B** Interest is part of net income. Net income is considered as an operating activity under US GAAP.

    LOS 27a

46. **A** Unearned revenue occurs when a company receives cash but has not yet fulfilled all its obligations of a sale, e.g. receipt of a twelve month magazine subscription. The initial entry is to increase cash and create a liability since the revenue can not yet be recognized on the profit and loss account. Prepayments are included as assets. Unbilled revenue is when a company earns revenue, has not yet received the cash, and has not yet recognised the sale. The entry to recognise the sale is to increase sales, and increase trade receivables. The trade receivables will be included as a current asset until the money is received.

    LOS 23d

47. **B** Both accruals accounting and going concern are assumptions that underlie IFRS financial statements. Consistency is not an underlying assumption but is a general feature of accounts as described by IAS 1.

    LOS 24d

48. **B** When the outcome cannot be reliably measured, International Standards use the cost recovery method, where revenue is recognized each year to the extent that costs have been incurred, with costs being written off in the year that they are incurred. US GAAP uses the completed contract method, which only recognizes revenue in the year the contract is completed.

    LOS 25b

49. **B** $$\frac{\text{Net income after preferred dividends}}{\text{Weighted average number of common shares}}$$

    $$\frac{90m - 20m}{100m} = 0.70$$

    Since the increase in shares was due to a stock split, there is no need to do a weighted average calculation.

    LOS 25g

50. **A**

	$
Beginning equity	4,500,000
Share issue	400,000
Net income after preferred dividends (1.50 × 400,000)	600,000
Ordinary dividend	(10,000)
Other comprehensive income	?
Ending equity	6,000,000

    Other comprehensive income = $510,000

    LOS 25l and 26f

51. B   When an expense is prepaid, it is not yet charged as a cost in the income statement, but carried forward as an asset in the balance sheet.

LOS 26a

52. A

	$
Sales	40,000
Decrease in receivables	1,000
Decrease in unearned income	(4,000)
Cash flow from sales	37,000

LOS 27f

53. B

	$
Net income	1,500
Increase in inventories	(200)
Increase in receivables	(300)
Increase in payables	150
Depreciation expense	200
Operating cash flow	1,350

Depreciation:

	$
Opening value of fixed assets	1,100
Capital expenditure	900
Depreciation expense	?
Closing value	1,800

Depreciation expense = $200

LOS 27f

54. C   The first statement should be swapped to read IFRS instead of US GAAP and US GAAP instead of IFRS, in order to be correct.

LOS 27c

55. B   At the end of 2012, there are (40 – 35) 5,000 items in inventory. At the end of 2013, there are an additional (50 – 45) 5,000 items in inventory. Using LIFO (last in first out), the last items bought are the first items sold, so the inventory value is $5,000 \times 50 + 5,000 \times 60 = \$550,000$.

LOS 29c

56. C   When inventory prices are rising, LIFO will allocate a higher amount to cost of goods sold, since it is allocating the latest costs to COGS while FIFO is allocating the earlier costs to COGS. Therefore FIFO will have the higher profits. FIFO means that the more recent, more expensive inventory will be left on the balance sheet, meaning ending inventory value is high compared to LIFO.

LOS 29e

57. **B** The profits will be the same under both methods, since assets are being replaced and prices are not changing. However, double declining balance depreciation writes off assets more quickly than straight line, meaning that the balance sheet value of assets will be lower for double declining balance, giving a higher return on equity.

    LOS 30c

58. **A** Writing down the value will give a charge against profits in the current year, but lower depreciation expense in future years, increasing profits. A lower salvage value and shorter useful life will increase the depreciation expense in future years.

    LOS 30c

59. **A** When a company has paid an excess amount of tax now and expects to recover this later, it has an asset from a tax viewpoint.

    LOS 31b

60. **C** In a more standard form, it is: Assets = Liabilities + Contributed capital + Opening retained earnings + Revenue − Expenses. Note that retained earnings and contributed capital are components of owners' equity.

    LOS 23b

61. **C** Income and expenses relate to performance. Assets, liabilities and equity relate to financial position.

    LOS 23a

62. **C** The initial bond liability will be the discounted value received on issuance, not the face value. The interest in the income statement will be given by the carrying value of the bond and the effective interest rate (not the coupon rate). The cash flow statement will show the actual cash payment made which is the face value multiplied by the coupon rate.

    LOS 32b

63. **B** An operating lease shows no asset or matching debt on the balance sheet so it has a lower debt to equity ratio. For an operating lease, the whole of the lease payment is treated as an operating cash flow whereas for a finance lease, part of the lease payment (the capital portion) is treated as a financing cash outflow, so a finance lease has lower cash flow from financing activities and an operating lease has lower cash flow from operating activities.

    LOS 32h

64. **A** ROE = AT × net margin × financial leverage

    56 = AT × 6 × 2

    AT = 4.7

    LOS 28d

65.   **A**   The percentage of completion method recognizes sales and profit over the life of the contract, meaning that current assets and stockholders equity will be higher than for the completed contract method. The current ratio will be higher. Assets and equity will both be higher by the same dollar amount, but because equity will have a lower value than assets (unless a company has no liabilities, which is extremely unlikely), the proportionate effect on equity is higher, meaning that financial leverage (assets divided by equity) will be lower.

LOS 25b

66.   **C**   The analytical adjustment is to increase fixed assets and increase debt. Revised debt balance = \$9,000. The stockholders equity is unaffected, making the debt to equity ratio $\frac{9,000}{9,000} = 100\%$.

LOS 35e

67.   **B**   Company B is small scale and undiversified, has only average financial policies and average operational efficiency, which means that it comes lowest in each category.

LOS 28e

68.   **C**   Excessive pressure to meet targets represents an incentive/pressure rather than an opportunity.

LOS 33a

Corporate Finance

69. **C**   If the discounted payback period is three years, the undiscounted cash flows must have a payback period of less than three years. Since the future cash flows are at least equal to the initial outflow on a discounted basis, the project will have a positive IRR and a NPV of zero or greater. If the NPV is not negative, the appraiser will be indifferent (if the NPV is zero) or will accept the project (if the NPV is positive).

LOS 36d

70. **A**   Since the projects have the same initial cash investment, have conventional cash flows and have a discount rate where the NPVs are equal, the fact that X has a shorter discounted payback period means that its NPV declines as a slower rate than Y's NPV (since cash flows closer to time 0 are less affected by higher discount rates than projects with more distant cash flows), so X's NPV at zero must be lower. The NPV profiles are as follows.

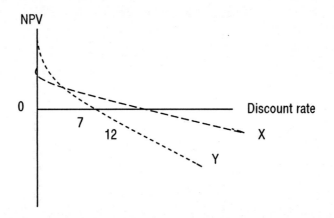

It can be seen that at a discount rate of 10%, X has a higher NPV than Y and therefore should be accepted. Both projects will not be accepted because they are mutually exclusive.

LOS 36d

71. **A**   First we need to calculate the IRR of the semi annual flows. This is 3.48%.

Time	Flow	PV at 3.48%
0	(96)	(96.00)
1-9	3	22.84
10	103	73.16
		-

The post tax cost of debt = $3.48\% \times 2 \times (1 - 0.7) = 4.872\%$.

The issue price of the debt is irrelevant, since we are calculating the company's cost of debt today.

LOS 37f

72. B The first breakpoint is when $2 million of debt is raised, when total finance raised = $\dfrac{2}{0.4}$ = $5m . The second breakpoint is when $6 million of equity is raised, when total finance raised = $\dfrac{6}{0.6}$ = $10m . The third breakpoint is when $5 million of debt is raised, when total finance raised = $\dfrac{5}{0.4}$ = $12.5m

LOS 37f

73. C A pull on liquidity is when disbursements are paid too quickly or credit availability is limited. A drag on liquidity is when receipts lag.

LOS 40a

74. B The highest NPV should be chosen over IRRs. Both projects would be viable, as they both have positive NPVs, if they were not mutually exclusive.

LOS 36e

75. A Operating breakeven point excludes interest payments and is calculated by dividing total fixed costs by contribution per unit:

= 12,000,000/(35,000 − 22,000)

= 923

LOS 38d

76. A Purchase price = $100,000 − [(0.0640)(91/360)($100,000)]

= $98,382.23

Money market yield = [1,617.77/98,382.23] × [360/91]

= 6.5%

LOS 40e

77. B A classified Board is where Board members are elected on a staggered basis for multiple year terms (contrast annual elections for all Board members). This gives continuity but makes it more difficult to change the Board composition significantly.

LOS 41b

78. A There should only be independent members on the remuneration committee.

LOS 41b

Portfolio Management

79. **C** The investor is in the accumulation phase, so capital preservation is unlikely to be suitable. The high rate of tax on income means that capital appreciation (returns based on capital gains) is more likely to be suitable than total return (returns based on capital gains and reinvested income).

LOS 45e

80. **C** Using CAPM:

$$E(Ri) = Rf + \beta [E(Rm) - Rf]$$
$$= 4\% + 1.1\times [10\% - 4\%]$$
$$= 10.6\%$$

LOS 44g

81. **A** Covariance is an absolute measure, not a relative measure and its magnitude is determined by the standard deviations of the two variables and their relationship with one another.

LOS 43c

82. **C** The slope of the efficient frontier is shallow at the top end. This indicates that a relatively large increase in risk is compensated for by a relatively small increase in return. This is appropriate for an investor who is highly tolerant of risk.

LOS 43g

83. **C** It is the security market line that gives the expected return on a security given its level of risk.

LOS 44b and 44f

84. **A** There is a straight line relationship between return and risk for a risky asset + risk free asset.

LOS 44a

Equity

85. **C** Dealers provide quotes.

LOS 46j

86. **C** A stop loss order specifies the price at which the shares should be sold to prevent further losses.

LOS 46h

87. **C** The value weighted index weights performance to large cap stocks, so it will underperform if small cap stocks outperform.

LOS 47c

88. **C** Prices reflect fundamental values so that prices vary primarily in response to changes in fundamental values and not to demands for liquidity made by uninformed traders.

LOS 46k

89. **B** The disposition effect is a behavioural bias where investors tend to avoid realizing losses but seek to realize gains.

LOS 48g

90. **B** By only looking at hedge funds currently in existence, the analyst is looking at survivors and ignoring hedge funds who disappeared over the period.

LOS 47j

91. **B** Intrinsic value = $\dfrac{24}{0.12-0.05} \times \dfrac{1}{1.12^2} = 273.32$

LOS 51e

92. **C** Since value $\dfrac{D}{k-g}$, changes in k − g give potentially large changes in value (assuming that the dividend remains constant).

LOS 51e

93. **B** Given that they all have the same multiplier, the company with the largest spread between its cost of equity and the growth rate is most likely to be overvalued, since this is the crucial relationship. A larger spread indicates a lower intrinsic value.

Company	k − g
A	15 − 9 = 6%
B	12 − 5 = 7%
C	9 − 4 = 5%

LOS 51e

94.   C   For example, a group of companies within an industry may all target the same customer segment.

        LOS 50e

95.   A   Newly issued bonds are traded in the primary market.

        LOS 53d

96.   B   Long run returns are related to both price to book and price to sales ratios.

        LOS 51h

97.   A   Investors will put the bond back to the issuer and reinvest the proceeds at the higher interest rates available in the market.

        LOS 52f

Fixed Income

98. **A** Duration only measures changes in price due to parallel shifts in yields.

   LOS 55b

99. **A** Since the value of a bond with an embedded option = option free bond +/- put/call option, the issue here is how the value of the options change as interest rates change and interest rate volatility changes. The option free bond is common to all three answers.

   Impact of fall in interest rate volatility: A fall in interest rate volatility will reduce the value of the put option and the call option. Since the value of a callable bond = option free bond – call option, this will cause the value of the callable bond to increase. Since the value of a putable bond = option free bond + put option, this will cause the value of the putable bond to decrease.

   Impact of slight increase in interest rates: The small increase in interest rates will cause the prices of all the bonds to fall. As the call option moves out of the money, the fall in its value will be relatively large (making the increase in the callable bond's value larger) whereas the put option will still be deeply out of the money so its value is unlikely to increase significantly (i.e. it will cause the bond value to increase only slightly).

   Overall, the putable bond is likely to have the greatest fall in price as the fall in put option value due to lower interest rate volatility will have a greater impact than the increase in option value due to the put option moving slightly less out of the money.

   LOS 52f

100. **B** Both FHA and GNMA are federally related institutions.

   LOS 53e

101. **A** The minimum debt service coverage ratio measures available revenue to cover capital and interest payments after operating expenses.

   LOS 56j

102. **A** The two components of credit risk are default probability (or default risk) and loss severity.

   LOS 56a

103. **B** The spreads between Treasury bonds and corporate bonds will widen in a recession. The investor who is long T bonds and short corporate bonds will obtain positive returns as a result.

   LOS 54i

104. **A** The change due to the passage of time is the difference between the present value for the four year maturity at 7% and the three year maturity at 7%.

   Four years: $\dfrac{50}{1.07} + \dfrac{50}{1.07^2} + \dfrac{50}{1.07^3} + \dfrac{50}{1.07^4} = 932.26$

   Three years: $\dfrac{50}{1.07} + \dfrac{50}{1.07^2} + \dfrac{1,050}{1.07^3} = 947.51$

   $947.51 - 953.26 = 15.25$

   LOS 54b

105. **A** The arbitrage free valuation is taken by valuing the bond using the spot rates (which are the quoted spot rates divided by 2):

$$\text{Price} = \frac{25}{1.015} + \frac{25}{1.02^2} + \frac{25}{1.025^3} + \frac{1,025}{1.03^4} = 982.57$$

LOS 54h

106. **C** Since coupons can be reinvested at higher rates of interest, the achieved yield will be higher than the promised yield.

LOS 54b

107. **B** OAS is only needed when valuing a callable bond. Nominal spread is based on YTM and therefore is flawed.

LOS 54i

108. **A** z-spread = OAS + Option cost

4 = 1 + Option cost

Option cost + 3

LOS 54i

109. **B** Percentage fall in price due to duration = 5.1% × 2 = 10.2%

Percentage increase in price due to convexity = 40 × 0.02² × 100 = 1.6%

Overall fall in price = 10.2% − 1.6% = 8.6%

New price = 97.42 − 8.6% × 97.42 = 89.04

LOS 55g

110. **B** Modified duration and modified convexity assume that the cash flows of the bond do not change if interest rates change. Since this is the case for option free bonds, modified duration will give an appropriate estimate of duration. However, it means that modified convexity will not be negative, even for callable bonds, meaning that effective convexity is a better measure to use for callable bonds, which exhibit negative convexity at lower interest rates.

LOS 55c and 55g

Derivatives

111. **A**   A protective put provides a limit on the downside and no limit on the upside. A covered call limits upside potential and has significant downside risk. An equity forward contract will provide income at the forward price and reduce losses but will not provide any limit, unlike an option contract.

           LOS 60h

112. **A**   In one month's time, 60 day LIBOR is 6%,, meaning that the investor has made a profit of 1%, since he bought the 1 × 3 (i.e. from 30 days time to 90 days time) FRA. The receipt is the present value of the 1% discounted back by 60 days at the prevailing LIBOR, since the cash flow takes place at the beginning of the period rather than the end of the period and interest is normally paid at the end of the period.

$$\text{Receipt} = \$1,000 \times \left(6\% - 5\%\right) \times \frac{60}{360} \times \frac{1}{1 + 0.06 \times \frac{60}{360}} = 1,650$$

           LOS 58g

113. **B**   The short future has the choice of which bond to deliver etc.

           LOS 59a

114. **A**   Using put-call parity,

            Long bond = $p_0 + S_0 - c_0$

           LOS 60m

115. **A**   In order to swap out of equities and into bonds, the investor should pay the equity return and receive the fixed return on the equity swap. In order to avoid losses on fixed rate returns from interest rates rising, the investor should pay the fixed rate and receive the floating rate swap.

           LOS 61b

116. **A**   A protected put gives a limited loss as the stock price falls and unlimited potential profits as the stock price rises, i.e. the same payoff as a long call.

           LOS 62b

Alternative Investments

117. **B**   Hedge funds often have redemption clauses and often charge redemption fees.

      LOS 63d

118. **A**   This strategy is known as short bias and is a type of equity hedge strategy.

      LOS 63d

119. **B**   Trade sale is likely to give a lower price than IPO. A recapitalization is not a full exit strategy and likely to yield a dividend only.

      LOS 63d

120. **B**   Depreciation would be a consideration in the income approach to property valuation when deriving net operating income.

      LOS 63d

BPP LEARNING MEDIA

The Chartered Financial Analyst® Program

Practice Examination 2
Morning Session

2014

The Morning Session of Practice Examination 2 consists of 120 multiple
choice questions which must be completed in three hours. The topic
areas covered are:

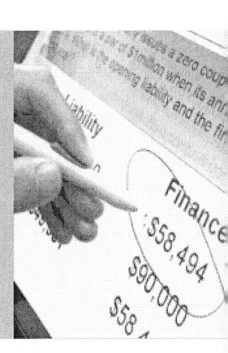

BPP
LEARNING MEDIA

Questions 1 through 18 relate to Ethical and Professional Standards

1. Valerian Clot CFA manages several funds which invest in equity securities in illiquid stock markets. He wishes to sell a security which is currently held by all of his funds but is concerned that the illiquidity of the stock market concerned will result in a disadvantageous price for his funds below the fair price of the security. As a result, he trades the security between his funds to give an impression of higher liquidity and demand for the security. Subsequently, he is able to liquidate the funds' holdings at a higher price than he would have otherwise achieved, to the benefit of the investors in the funds. It is *most likely* that the trading of securities between his funds by Clot has:

    A. violated Standard IIB – Market Manipulation.

    B. not violated Standard IIB – Market Manipulation because the trading is in an illiquid stock market.

    C. not violated Standard IIB – Market Manipulation because the trading is for the purpose of benefiting the investors in the funds concerned.

2. Edward Martins CFA is a portfolio manager managing individual accounts at an investment firm. His accounts comprise individuals with a wide range of investment objectives and constraints, some having a high growth mandate and others having a stable value income focus, for example. Martins goes to a restaurant one night and sees the chief executive officers of two companies that he follows deep in discussion over a meal together. Martins wonders if there might be the possibility of a merger between the two companies and the next morning analyzes both companies in detail. He decides that they are an excellent fit, noting that both companies pay low dividends and have high returns on investment. Accordingly he buys stock in both companies for all of his individual accounts. Soon afterwards, there is a merger announced between the two companies and the investments make substantial profits for all the individual portfolios.

    With respect to Standard IIA – Material Nonpublic Information and Standard IIIC – Suitability, it is *most likely* that Martins has violated:

    A. Standard IIA but not Standard IIIC.

    B. Standard IIIC but not Standard IIA.

    C. neither Standard IIIC nor Standard IIA.

3. Apex Investment Management operates in a country where local laws state that records should be kept for five years. In order to comply with the requirements and recommendations of CFA Institute's Code of Ethics and Standards of Professional Conduct, Apex should retain its records for a minimum of:

    A. 5 years.

    B. 7 years.

    C. 10 years.

4. John Wilson is a CFA charterholder. Wilson will *most likely* violate Standard of Professional Conduct IA – Knowledge of the Law if he does not:

   A. have a detailed knowledge of all the laws which could govern his professional activities.

   B. dissociate himself from activities by his employer that he has reasonable grounds to believe are unethical but not illegal.

   C. report to CFA Institute potential violations of CFA Institute's Code of Ethics and Standards of Professional Conduct by fellow members and candidates.

5. Elspeth Montez CFA has been recruited by XYZ investment management firm as its compliance officer. The firm issues an announcement of her appointment which states the following.

   "XYZ Investment Management is pleased to announce the appointment of Elspeth Montez CFA as its compliance officer. As a Chartered Financial Analyst, Montez has extremely detailed knowledge of ethical and compliance issues in the investment industry, meaning that our clients can have every confidence in the strength of our compliance procedures and the integrity of our ethical conduct."

   Elspeth Montez was shown the announcement prior to its publication and agreed that it is appropriately worded and can be published.

   It is *most likely* that Montez has:

   A. not violated CFA Institute Standards of Professional Conduct.

   B. violated CFA Institute Standards of Professional Conduct by her use of the CFA designation.

   C. violated CFA Institute Standards of Professional Conduct by exaggerating the meaning and implications of membership in CFA Institute.

6. The compliance procedure that is *most likely* recommended in Standard IB – Independence and Objectivity in order to ensure compliance with the standard is to:

   A. require disclosure by employees to their supervisors of all gifts above a specified value.

   B. prohibit employee participation in equity or equity-related initial public offerings (IPOs).

   C. restrict the use of special cost arrangements for employees provided by issuers when attending meetings with an issuer at its headquarters.

7. Clay Bell CFA works as an analyst for an investment firm. He regularly takes an early lunch at 11 am where he consumes a bottle of wine before returning to the office where he has a cognac and coffee prior to starting work in the afternoon. He is inebriated as a result of his lunchtime drinking and sometimes forgets to do work as a result. His colleagues at work are aware of this and ensure that they always double check that all his important work has been completed by the end of the day.

   Stringer Davis CFA works for an investment firm as a portfolio manager. Davis has a strong belief in the importance of socially responsible investing and is actively persuading his firm to adopt a stance on this matter. Outside of work, he regularly attends non violent demonstrations and has been arrested several times as a result of this.

   With regard to Standard ID – Misconduct, it is *most likely* that:

   A. neither Bell nor Davis have violated the standard.

   B. Bell has violated the standard but Davis has not violated the standard.

   C. Davis has violated the standard but Bell has not violated the standard.

8. Linda Els CFA was an employee of Intrepid Investment Management, a firm that provides investment services for high net worth individuals with assets of $10 million or more. Prior to resigning from Intrepid Investment Management with the intention of setting up her own investment boutique which will provide investment services to individuals with assets of $2 million or more, she registered her new business with the relevant investment regulator. After she handed in her resignation but before the resignation was effective, she contacted individuals with assets in the range of $2 million to $5 million to inform them of her new business. She had previously spoken to these individuals when they contacted Intrepid Investment Management to enquire about its services. With respect to Standard IVA – Loyalty, it is *most likely* that Els has:

   A. not violated the standard.

   B. violated the standard by contacting the potential clients before her resignation is effective.

   C. violated the standard by registering her new investment business before resigning from Intrepid Investment Management.

9. When a CFA Institute member is managing a portfolio for a defined benefit pension plan, the duty of loyalty to the client is achieved by having a duty of loyalty to the plan:

   A. sponsor and plan beneficiaries.

   B. sponsor but not to the plan beneficiaries.

   C. beneficiaries but not to the plan sponsor.

10. Patrick Sharpe CFA volunteered his time as a moderator for the CFA Level III examination. Having completed this task, he returned to his work place in Europe. Richard Harper is an employee of the same investment firm as Sharpe. Harper is sitting level III of the CFA examinations in the next year and he asks Sharpe for an indication of the type of questions that were examined in the previous year. Sharpe states that as a moderator with privileged access to the examination, he is not permitted to give details of the questions that were examined. However, he does give Harper an indication of the broad topical areas that were covered in the examination, since these details will be released by CFA Institute as part of its information program. It is *most likely* that:

    A. Sharpe and Harper have both violated CFA Institute Standards of Professional Conduct.

    B. Sharpe has violated CFA Institute Standards of Professional Conduct but Harper has not violated them.

    C. Harper has violated CFA Institute Standards of Professional Conduct but Sharpe has not violated them.

11. Sharon Bennett CFA is currently studying for a Masters in Business Administration (MBA) at a leading European school of business studies. In order to assist with her living costs, she has continued working on a part time basis for her previous employer, Jordan Investment Analysis. Her role is to provide reports on a number of companies in a sector that she follows, based on her previous knowledge as a full time employee and incorporating her knowledge from her current studies and ongoing research. It is not disclosed to clients of Jordan that Bennett is only working part time. At times, Bennett finds juggling the commitments of study and work somewhat demanding. Recently, she published a research article for Jordan's clients based on her general knowledge of the sector and some recent developments highlighted in newspapers she read where one company was singled out as likely to outperform. It is *most likely* that Bennett has violated:

A. Standard VIA – Disclosure of Conflicts.

B. Standard VA – Diligence and Reasonable Basis.

C. Standard VB – Communications with Clients and Prospective Clients.

12. An investment firm segregates its clients into first class and second class categories, based on the amount of assets under management. First class clients receive superior levels of service due to their higher level of assets under management. The availability of this service to all clients who meet the specified asset level is disclosed to all clients. The firm's statement of ethics and professional conduct contains the following statement.

"When making investment recommendations, all clients should be notified of the recommendation as soon as possible. After notifying all clients of the recommendation, employees should then contact their first class clients to explain the recommendations in more detail and how fits in with their mandated investment strategy."

With respect to Standard IIIB – Fair Dealing, the investment firm's statement of ethics and professional conduct *most likely*:

A. complies with the standard.

B. violates the standard, which states that all clients must receive equal treatment in the dissemination of investment recommendations.

C. violates the standard, which states that different levels of assets under management must not be used as the basis for differentiating between clients.

13. Maria Santos CFA is advising an individual client as to his tax affairs. Santos recommends that the client makes some substantial charitable donations before the end of the tax year. The client agrees with this and states that he is particularly favorably disposed to charities dedicated to the eradication of poverty. He will therefore make donations to such charities. After the meeting, Stantos telephones a contact at such a charity and suggests that he contacts the client. The client subsequently makes a large donation to the charity. Considering Standard IIIE – Preservation of Confidentiality, it is *most likely* that Santos has:

A. violated the standard by contacting the charity.

B. not violated the standard because the client has agreed to make donations to such charities.

C. not violated the standard because the client indicated their willingness to be contacted through subsequently making a donation.

14. Sanjiv Woods CFA works for a broker dealer firm. He has established links with Emma Goldsmith CFA, an investment adviser. He refers his clients to Goldsmith for investment advice services, receiving a referral fee from her. Woods discloses to his clients details of the referral fee that he receives. Goldsmith does not make such a disclosure to the clients concerned, on the basis that it is the responsibility of the individual receiving the fee to make such a disclosure. It is *most likely* that CFA Institute's Code of Ethics and Standards of Professional Conduct have been violated by:

   A. Woods and Goldsmith.

   B. Woods but not Goldsmith.

   C. Goldsmith but not Woods.

15. According to CFA Institute Standards of Professional Conduct, on discovery of a violation of applicable laws by someone subject to their authority, it is *least likely* to be appropriate for a supervisor to:

   A. respond promptly to the violation.

   B. conduct a thorough investigation into the violation.

   C. maintain supervision on the wrongdoer pending the outcome of any investigation.

16. James Mason CFA is an equity analyst who covers the automobile sector for his employer. Mason owns shares in MN Autos Inc. with a value of $10,000. In addition, his son owns one share in XY Autos Inc. with a value of $40. The share was given to his son as a birthday present by his grandmother to encourage the virtues of saving and investment. CFA Institute's Code of Ethics and Standards of Professional Conduct *most likely* indicate that Mason should disclose in his research reports:

   A. his shareholding in MN Autos Inc. and his son's shareholding in XY Autos Inc.

   B. his shareholding in MN Autos Inc. but not his son's shareholding in XY Autos Inc.

   C. neither his shareholding in XY Autos Inc. nor his son's shareholding in XY Autos Inc.

17. When a professional conduct inquiry on a member's conduct has been initiated and the Designated Officer either issues a cautionary letter or proposes a disciplinary sanction, the member in question can refuse to accept:

   A. a cautionary letter or a proposed disciplinary sanction.

   B. a cautionary letter but not a proposed disciplinary sanction.

   C. a proposed disciplinary sanction but not a cautionary letter.

18. A firm claims compliance with the Global Investment Performance Standards (GIPS®). When reporting the performance of a portfolio to an individual client, the manager tells the client that the performance of the portfolio is calculated in accordance with the Global Investment Performance Standards. The manager's statement *most likely*:

   A. does not violate the requirements of the GIPS standards.

   B. violates the requirements of the GIPS standards, which state that firms must comply with all the requirements of the GIPS standards.

   C. violates the requirements of the GIPS standards, which state that firms must not make any statements that may indicate partial compliance with the GIPS standards.

Questions 19 through 32 relate to Quantitative Methods

19. A perpetual preferred stock pays a dividend of $1,000 every six months. The required return on the investment is 13%, compounded annually. The amount that an investor would be willing to pay for the preferred stock is *closest to*:

   A. $14,410.

   B. $15,390.

   C. $15,870.

20. A couple wish to invest in an annuity payment of $3,000 a year for 10 years, starting in 3 years time. At the end of the fifteenth year, they wish to have the payments grow to a sum of $55,000 to give to their child. The annual rate of interest that the couple must earn over the whole period to achieve their desired final value is *closest to*:

   A. 4.8%.

   B. 7.9%.

   C. 8.1%.

21. When a rational wealth maximizing investor is selecting between mutually exclusive projects, she should *most likely* select the project with the highest:

   A. internal rate of return even if does not have the highest net present value.

   B. net present value even if does not have the highest internal rate of return.

   C. net present value or the highest internal rate of return, since both approaches are equivalent.

22. A 70 days Treasury bill is trading at a discount of 5.32%. The effective annual yield on the T bill is *closest to*:

   A. 5.45%.

   B. 5.51%.

   C. 5.57%.

23.   Three cumulative frequency distributions are as follows.

Distribution A

Distribution B

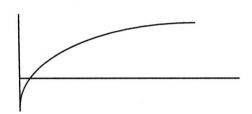

Distribution C

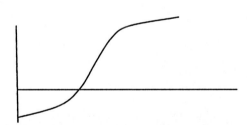

The distribution which is *most likely* fits a normal distribution is:

A.   distribution A.

B.   distribution B.

C.   distribution C.

24.   A population distribution that is symmetrical will *most likely* have a mean absolute deviation that is:

A.   equal to its standard deviation.

B.   less than its standard deviation.

C.   greater than its standard deviation.

25. An analyst estimates that there is a 0.7 probability of interest rates staying the same or falling. If interest rates fall, there is a probability of 0.7 that a company's earnings per share will stay the same or increase. If interest rates rise, there is a probability of 0.4 that earnings per share will stay the same or increase. It turns out that the company's earnings per share increased. The probability that interest rates increased is *closest to*:

    A. 0.20.

    B. 0.36.

    C. 0.55.

26. A portfolio consists of 10 corporate bonds, all of which are rated BB. The probability of a BB rated bond defaulting is considered to be 15%. Assuming that the probability of each bond defaulting is independent from all the other bonds in the portfolio, the probability of at least 8 bonds not defaulting is *closest to*:

    A. 0.27.

    B. 0.62.

    C. 0.82.

27. A pension fund is to pay its beneficiaries $500k per annum for twenty years, starting in eight years' time. What is the present value of the pension liability if the annual discount rate is 6%?

    A. $6,976k.

    B. $5,734k.

    C. $3,814k.

28. The z statistic is *least likely* to be appropriate to use when the distribution of sample means based on a sample size of 100 items has been constructed from a:

    A. normal distribution with a known variance.

    B. normal distribution with an unknown variance.

    C. nonnormal distribution with a known variance.

29. A pension fund wishes to identify whether a particular manager has the skill to be able to achieve an acceptable alpha. In order to test whether this is the case at the 5% error level, the pension fund examines 100 monthly returns for the manager compared to his benchmark and identifies that the manager's mean alpha is 2.1% with a standard deviation of 12%. The pension fund will *most likely*:

    A. reject the null hypothesis.

    B. accept the null hypothesis.

    C. fail to reject the null hypothesis.

30. An analyst is considering two situations. In the first situation, a company is considering whether to offer credit terms to its customers. It will conduct a statistical test designed to identify credit risks. It is more concerned with losing new customers unnecessarily through rejecting them as a bad credit risk than with suffering excessive credit losses. In the second situation, an investment management firm is seeking to identify stock market anomalies. The investment management firm is more concerned to avoid adopting an incorrect investment strategy than missing out on some potential profitable strategies. Which type of statistical error is more important to minimize in each situation?

	FIRST SITUATION	SECOND SITUATION
A.	Type I	Type I
B.	Type II	Type I
C.	Type I	Type II

31. Elliot wave theory is *most likely* used in technical analysis for:

A. short term trading analysis.

B. long term economic analysis.

C. short term trading analysis and long term economic analysis.

32. The left shoulder of a head and shoulders pattern has a high price of $58 before falling to a trough at a price of $50. The head has a high price of $67 before declining to a price of $50. The right shoulder shows a rally to a price of $58 before the price starts another decline. The price target for a technical analyst is *closest to*:

A. $33.

B. $41.

C. $42.

Questions 33 through 44 relate to Economics

33. When marginal product starts to decline as one more unit of labor is added, it is *most likely* that average product will:

    A. decline and total product will decline.

    B. decline and total product will increase.

    C. increase and total product will increase.

34. If the Fed uses monetary policy to fight inflation, it is *most likely* that there will be a:

    A. a decrease in the interest rate.

    B. a decrease in the supply of loanable funds.

    C. an increase in open market purchases by the Fed.

35. In a monopoly, it is *least likely* that:

    A. the social cost of the monopoly is equal to the deadweight loss.

    B. a marginal cost pricing rule will maximize the total surplus for a regulated monopoly industry.

    C. the monopolist could eliminate the whole of the consumer surplus through price discrimination between each unit of output.

36. An economy has suffered inflation which is caused by a rise in the price of wheat and other basic foodstuffs. This is best described as being:

    A. a supply shock.

    B. a demand shock.

    C. a deflationary gap.

37. When cross elasticity of demand is positive, the relationship between the goods is *most likely* described as their being:

    A. substitutes.

    B. complements.

    C. unrelated goods.

38. The potential sustainable growth rate of an economy may be best measured as:

    A. long term growth rate in labour productivity.

    B. aggregate hours worked multiplied by labour productivity.

    C. long term growth rate in labour productivity plus long term growth rate of the labour force.

39. Which of the below might *least* well be described as the actions of an automatic stabilizer?

    A. Government spending on unemployment benefits rising as the economy slows.

    B. Government spending on capital projects to stimulate an economy and reduce unemployment during a downturn.

    C. Progressive taxes rising as the economy booms.

40. In monopolistic competition, it is *most likely* in the long run that:

    A. a firm will produce where average total cost is at a minimum.

    B. the profit maximizing quantity is where price equals average total cost.

    C. a firm can earn a positive economic profit due to product differentiation.

41. When there is a maximum rent for housing below the equilibrium rent but the rent control is very loosely enforced, the black market rent is *most likely* close to the:

    A. unregulated rent.

    B. maximum rent ceiling.

    C. highest price that renters can afford to pay.

42. The GDP deflator in 2012 is 240, the GDP deflator in 2010 was 220. Which value is the closest to the annual growth rate of the overall price level?

    A. 4.45%.

    B. 6.67%.

    C. 9.10%.

43. An increase in the money wage rate will *most likely*:

    A. have no effect on short run aggregate supply and long run aggregate supply.

    B. cause short run aggregate supply and long run aggregate supply to decrease.

    C. cause short run aggregate supply to decrease and have no effect on long run aggregate supply.

44. A short run decision that needs to be made by a firm in perfect competition is *most likely* whether to:

    A. shut down.

    B. stay in the industry.

    C. change its plant size.

Questions 45 through 68 relate to Financial Reporting and Analysis

45. Common size statements are *most likely* a form of:

    A. time series analysis tool.

    B. cross sectional analysis tool.

    C. time series or cross sectional analysis tool.

---

46. Northern Rockport Design started business in 2013 and uses the FIFO method. During 2013 it purchased 20,000 units of inventory at $12 each and sold 12,000 units at $25 each. In 2014 it purchased another 50,000 units at $14 each and sols 35,000 for $22 each. Its 2014 ending inventory balance ($ thousand) is closest to:

    A. $422.

    B. $433.

    C. $462.

---

47. A company constructed a building for its own use over the period 2011 to 2012, capitalizing borrowing costs relating to the construction. The building was completed at the beginning of 2013 and is estimated to have a useful life of 50 years. Compared to if the borrowing costs had not been capitalized, the company's financial statements for the year ended December 31 2013 will have a net margin that is:

    A. lower and debt to equity ratio that is lower.

    B. lower and a debt to equity ratio that is higher.

    C. higher and a debt to equity ratio that is lower.

---

48. A company acquired a long lived asset on January 1 2012 at a cost of $60,000. The asset is expected to have a three year life and a zero residual value at the end of its life. It is to be depreciated using straight line depreciation for accounting purposes, but the whole of the cost is allowed as a tax recoverable expense in the first year, as the company is operating in a special investment zone. The corporate tax rate is 30% in 2012 but changes to 20% in 2013. The deferred tax liability in the balance sheet as at December 31 2013 is *closest to*:

    A. $4,000.

    B. $6.000.

    C. $8,000.

---

49. When charging the premium on the issue of a bond, the effective interest rate method is *most likely*:

    A. required under both US GAAP and International Financial Reporting Standards.

    B. required under US GAAP and preferred under International Financial Reporting Standards.

    C. preferred under both US GAAP and required under International Financial Reporting Standards.

50. A company is undertaking a long term contract for which it has reliable estimates of both costs and revenue over its life. The company is reasonably certain that the revenue will be realized. It is incurring a loss on the contract as it wishes to maintain good relations with the government which is sponsoring the contract. Under International Financial Reporting Standards, the loss should be recognized:

    A. immediately.

    B. at the end of the contract.

    C. over the life of the contract.

51. Extracts from a company's financial statements for the year ended December 31 2012 are as follows, prepared under US GAAP.

December 31	2012	2011
	$	$
Cash	100	25
Receivables	1,200	1,100
Inventories	890	920
Current assets	2,190	2,045
Long lived assets	4,225	3,810
Total assets	6,415	5,855
Payables	750	710
Short term notes	1,000	800
Current liabilities	1,750	1,510
Long term debt	2,000	1,500
Deferred tax liability	200	290
Stockholders equity	2,465	2,555
	6,415	5,855

    The company had a net income of $800 in the year and repurchased shares for a price of $890. No dividends were paid. Long lived assets costing $500 were purchased in the year. There were no disposals of long lived assets and the depreciation expense was $85.

    The cash flow from operating activities for the year ended December 31 2012 is *closest to*:

    A. $680.

    B. $765.

    C. $855.

52. When analyzing a company for risk factors relating to poor quality financial reporting, an analyst would *most likely* classify a risk factor as relating to pressures when:

    A. the company needs to raise additional debt.

    B. there is high turnover of senior management.

    C. management has frequent disputes with the auditors.

53. A company has revenue of $50,000 and cost of goods sold of $20,000. It accounts for inventories using the LIFO method The company pays corporate taxes at a rate of 30% and has a net margin of 10%. Assuming inventory prices have been consistently rising, using the FIFO method which of the following is *most likely* to be true:

   A. gross profit margin would be higher and closing inventory would be higher.

   B. gross profit margin would be lower and closing inventory would be higher.

   C. gross profit margin would be lower and closing inventory would be higher.

54. When a company's financial statements materially depart from accounting standards, it will *most likely* receive an audit report that is:

   A. adverse.

   B. qualified.

   C. a disclaimer.

55. An increase in inventory turnover *most likely* indicates:

   A. the risk of obsolescent inventories.

   B. window dressing by a company at its year end.

   C. a company taking advantage of prompt payment discounts on purchases of inventory.

56. A company using a periodic inventory system has beginning inventories of 50 units valued at $1,000. Purchases of inventories and sales through the year in chronological order are as follows.

	Units	$
Purchases	80	1,800
Sales	90	4,500
Purchases	20	500

   The difference between the company's gross profit using first in first out (FIFO) and last in first out (LIFO) inventory valuation methods is *closest to*:

   A. $50.

   B. $100.

   C. $175.

57. When a company is replacing its long lived assets and prices are stable, compared to an accelerated depreciation method, straight line depreciation will give a return on equity that is:

   A. lower.

   B. higher.

   C. the same.

58. At December 31 2011, a company has temporary timing differences relating to deferred tax liabilities of $100,000. A year later, the temporary differences relating to deferred tax liabilities are $120,000. The corporate tax rate was 30% in 2011, but increased to 40% in 2012. The deferred tax expense for the year ended December 31 2012 is *closest to*:

    A. $6,000.

    B. $8,000.

    C. $18,000.

59. Under IFRS which of the following components of the movement in the net pension asset/liability are recognized in the profit and loss account?

    A. Employees' service costs and net interest expense.

    B. Employees' service costs and actuarial gains and losses.

    C. Net interest expense and actual return on plan assets.

60. When preparing a cash flow statement, use of the direct method is:

    A. encouraged under International Financial Reporting Standards and US GAAP.

    B. encouraged under International Financial Reporting Standards but not under US GAAP.

    C. encouraged under US GAAP but not under International Financial Reporting Standards.

61. Details of three companies are as follows.

    Company A: has businesses in a range of diversified segments, is vertically integrated and has a low EBITDA margin.

    Company B: has wide geographical diversification and a high and stable EBITDA margin.

    Company C: has a tight focus on one business stream, low debt levels and a stable and moderate EBITDA margin.

    The company that is *most likely* to have the highest credit rating is:

    A. company A.

    B. company B.

    C. company C.

62. Extracts from a company's financial statements are as follows.

Year ended December 31

	2011	2010
	$m	$m
Inventories	430	430
Receivables	670	620
Cash and cash equivalents	100	5
Payables	520	480
Short term debt	1,000	300
Sales	5,090	4,800
Cost of goods sold	4,100	3,800

The net operating cycle for the year ended December 31 2011 is *closest to*:

A. 40 days.

B. 52 days.

C. 85 days.

63. A company following US GAAP that decides to change from using the FIFO method of accounting for inventories to the LIFO method must account for this on a:

A. cumulative basis.

B. retroactive basis.

C. prospective basis.

64. A company spends $750,000 on development costs in one financial year. The tax treatment of development costs is to expense over five years. The accounting treatment for development costs is to amortise over ten years. Which of the following is closest to the tax base and the temporary difference of the development costs in the financial year?

	TAX BASE	TEMPORARY DIFFERENCE
A.	$600,000	$75,000
B.	$675,000	$(75,000)
C.	$750,000	$0

65. When there are unrealized gains on investments that are held as available-for-sale, they are *most likely*:

A. not recognized until they become realized.

B. recognized as part of net income for the year.

C. recognized as part of other comprehensive income.

66. When analyzing return on assets as computed by most databases, it is *most likely* that the ratio:

    A. is based on pre-tax income.

    B. is potentially distorted by the use of financial leverage.

    C. measures the return to equity investors based on their investment in the company.

---

67. A company following International Financial Reporting Standards recognized the impairment of a long lived asset below its cost amount in the year ended December 31 2011. In the year ended December 31 2012, the company reverses the impairment out due to an increase in the recoverable amount of the asset. Compared to if the impairment had not been recognized and reversed, the financial statements for the year ended December 31 2012 will have:

    A. a lower return on assets.

    B. a higher return on assets.

    C. the same return on assets.

---

68. Bilko inc had net income of $20 million, the weighted average number of shares is 1 million. Three years ago the company issued $1 million nominal value 5% convertible bonds. The bonds were convertible into 250,000 common shares. Assuming a tax rate of 40%, what is the diluted EPS?

    A. $13.82.

    B. $14.68.

    C. $16.02.

Questions 69 through 78 relate to Corporate Finance

69. A company is making a decision as to which of two mutually exclusive projects to accept. Details of the projects are as follows.

	Project X	Project Y
NPV at 11%	$1,340	$1,100
Internal rate of return	14%	18%

The interest rate at which both projects have the same net present value is 12%. Project Y should be selected for any cost of capital:

A. above 12%.

B. between 12% and 18%.

C. between 14% and 18%.

70. A company's stock has a price of $172. It has just paid a dividend of $10 per share, which is expected to grow at a rate of 3% indefinitely. The company's debt investors have a required rate of return of 5%. The company has a debt to equity ratio of 50% in book value terms and 40% in market value terms. The company pays corporate taxes at an average rate of 35% and a marginal rate of 30%. The company's weighted average cost of capital is *closest to*:

A. 6.8%.

B. 7.3%.

C. 7.4%.

71. A company has net income of $5 million, after paying corporate taxes at a rate of 30%. It has 3 million shares in issue and plans to repurchase 500,000 shares using borrowed funds at an interest rate of 4%. The stock price is currently $20. The earnings per share after the repurchase is *closest to*:

A. $1.53.

B. $1.84.

C. $1.89.

72. A company is being offered credit terms of 2/10 net 60. The company's borrowing cost is 10% on an effective annual basis. The cost to the company of accepting the credit terms, if the account is paid on the 20th day, is *closest* to:

A. 109%.

B. 75%.

C. 45%.

BPP LEARNING MEDIA

73. Ratios extracted from a company's accounts are as follows.

Operating margin	10%
Effect of non operating items	1.1
Tax effect	0.65
Asset turnover	1.4
Financial leverage	1.8

The company's return on assets is *closest to*:

A. 9.1%.

B. 10.0%.

C. 18.0%.

74. A supervisory board in a two-tier board system should *most likely* consist of:

A. independent board members only.

B. independent and non executive board members.

C. independent, non executive and executive board members.

75. A company has days of inventory on hand of 25, days sales outstanding of 52, and days of payables of 20. The company's operating cycle is *closest to*:

A. 57.

B. 77.

C. 97.

76. A company has sales of $350,000 and net income of $49,000. Its degree of operating leverage is 1.5 and its degree of financial leverage is 2.0. The tax rate is 30%. If sales increase by 50%, the profit before fixed costs is *closest to*:

A. $310,000.

B. $315,000.

C. $318,000.

77. When examining the effectiveness of corporate governance policies for a company, an analyst would *most likely* favor:

A. noncumulative voting.

B. independent directors having access to specialized help.

C. non executive directors holding board positions for many different companies.

78. Which of the following describes the breakeven point for a manufacturer?

A. The number of units produced and sold at which revenues v equal fixed costs and fixed financial cost.

B. The number of units produced and sold at which the company's net income is zero.

C. The number of units produced and sold at which revenues are equal to fixed costs.

Questions 79 through 84 relate to Portfolio Management

79. Janet Perry, aged 30, is a professional executive with a good salary. She has a family with two children. She inherited a large house from her father and as a result her salary is more than adequate to cover family expenses. Her mother has now given her $200,000 to invest and she plans to use this to start a portfolio to finance her retirement years. She believes that successful investing in investments is largely down to luck and that risk analysis should therefore be based on downside loss analysis. It is *most likely* that Janet has:

    A. low ability to take risk and low willingness to take risk.

    B. high ability to take risk and low willingness to take risk.

    C. high ability to take risk and high willingness to take risk.

80. Which of the following *best* describes a difference between the capital allocation line (CAL) and the capital market line (CML)?

    A. The CAL is a kinked line whereas the CML is an upward sloping straight line.

    B. On a graph with the y axis being the expected portfolio return and the x axis being the portfolio standard deviation, the CAL goes through the y axis at zero whilst the CML cuts the y axis at the risk free rate.

    C. The CAL shows the risk and return profile of the risk free asset and a risky portfolio, the CML shows the risk and return of the risk free asset and the market portfolio.

81. The investor type that is *most likely* to have the longest time horizon for a portfolio is:

    A. a university endowment.

    B. an individual just starting work.

    C. a defined benefit pension plan where the average participant age is 45.

82. Details of the expected return and risk of two asset classes are as follows.

	Expected return %	Standard deviation of returns %
Stocks	8	10
Bonds	5	8

    The covariance of returns between stocks and bonds is 48.

    The standard deviation of a portfolio invested 70% in equities and 30% in bonds is *closest to*:

    A. 7.4%.

    B. 8.7%.

    C. 9.4%.

83. The security characteristic line *most likely*:

    A. has the risk free rate as its intercept.

    B. has a gradient equal to the beta of the security.

    C. gives the expected return premium over the risk free rate for a security given its beta.

---

84. A young individual in work without any savings has received an inheritance of $50,000, which he plans to invest for the long term with a high return and high risk objective. An investment vehicle that is *most likely* to be suitable for the individual is a:

    A. mutual fund.

    B. hedge fund.

    C. separately managed account.

Questions 85 through 96 relate to Equity

85. A comparables based approach to valuation using price to sales multiples *least likely*:

    A. relies on the law of one price.

    B. incorporates growth expectations.

    C. assumes companies have the same net margins.

86. In the shakeout phase of the industry life cycle, sales growth is *most likely* to be described as:

    A. low.

    B. slowing.

    C. negative.

87. An investor buys 1,000 shares at a price of $80 per share on margin. The initial margin requirement is 30% and the maintenance margin requirement is 25%. The stock price at which a margin call will be triggered is *closest to*:

    A. $20.

    B. $60.

    C. $75.

88. The broad based index which is *most likely* to outperform when small cap stocks are performing better than large cap stocks is *most likely*:

    A. price weighted.

    B. equal weighted.

    C. value weighted.

89. A PIPE transaction is *most likely* where a:

    A. public company makes a private placement of shares.

    B. public company invests in shares in a private enterprise.

    C. private equity house makes an investment in a public enterprise.

90. A fundamental analyst would *most likely* argue that the form of efficient market hypothesis that does not apply is the:

    A. strong form.

    B. weak form only.

    C. semi strong form only.

91. An overseas company wishes to develop and broaden its US investor base without issuing new shares to US investors. The most appropriate form of American Depositary Receipt for the company to sponsor would be:

    A. level II.

    B. level III.

    C. rule 144A.

92. Details from an open order book are as follows.

Quantity	Price	Price	Quantity
1,000	52	54	700
500	50	56	500
300	49	57	500
800	48	60	300

    The price of a marketable limit buy order put into the system is *most likely*:

    A. 51.

    B. 53.

    C. 55.

93. Hedge fund indices based on databases of hedge fund returns *most likely*:

    A. are market value weighted.

    B. are subject to survivor bias.

    C. have their constituents determined by the index provider.

94. An airline company requires the ability to run a large fleet of expensive airplanes, which can be leased with low upfront costs. The cost of running a flight is substantially fixed, due to the cost of fuel. *Based on these two factors only*, the airline industry is *most likely* to be:

    A. competitive.

    B. uncompetitive.

    C. competitive or uncompetitive, depending on the relative importance of the two factors.

95. A company has just paid a dividend of $5.00 a share. The dividend is expected to grow for three years at a rate of 8% per year. Thereafter, it is expected to grow at a rate of 2% a year indefinitely. The cost of capital for the company is 9%. The intrinsic value of the share is *closest to*:

    A. $79.26.

    B. $79.75.

    C. $85.60.

96. Data mining *most likely*:

    A. is an autocorrelation based test.

    B. describes how sample data is used to construct a hypothesis which can then be tested.

    C. provides supportive evidence for a stock market anomaly based on technical trading rules.

BPP
LEARNING MEDIA

Questions 97 through 110 relate to Fixed Income

97. Details of LIBOR over the next year are as follows.

	90 days	180 days	270 days	360 days
LIBOR	4%	4%	4%	4%

90 days LIBOR over the next year is *most likely* expected to:

A. increase.

B. decrease.

C. stay constant.

98. Which of the following is an example of an external credit enhancement structure for an asset-backed security?

A. A corporate guarantee.

B. Reserve fund.

C. Special purpose vehicle.

99. A bond can be redeemed by the borrower at a price that is the higher of the principal value of the bond or the present value of all the remaining scheduled payments on the note, discounted at the relevant Treasury bond yield plus 50 basis points. This type of call provision is *most likely* referred to as:

A. deferred provision.

B. refundable provision.

C. make whole provision.

100. The modified duration of a bond *most likely*:

A. measures yield curve risk.

B. is determined partly by the bond's yield to maturity.

C. will be higher for a corporate bond with credit risk than for a government bond.

101. Details of three bonds with the same yield to maturity and their price changes for a 1% change in yield are as follows.

Bond	Price change for a 1% increase in yields	Price change for a 1% decrease in yields
A	-5.22%	5.34%
B	-5.22%	5.01%
C	-5.15%	5.34%

The bond which is *most likely* to be a callable bond is:

A. bond A.

B. bond B.

C. bond C.

102. A five year bond paying an annual coupon of 4% has a yield to maturity of 6%. A year later, the yield to maturity has changed to 5%. The price change for $1,000 par value due to the change in discount rate is *closest to*:

    A. $33.84.

    B. $40.96.

    C. $48.79.

103. Three bonds have a yield to maturity of 8% and the same maturity. Bond A is priced at 95, bond B is priced at 98 at bond C is priced at 101. The bond with the highest level of reinvestment risk is *most likely*:

    A. bond A.

    B. bond B.

    C. bond C.

104. A bond covenant that is *least likely* to be an affirmative covenant is to:

    A. pay interest on a timely basis.

    B. maintain the borrower's properties in good repair.

    C. only raise new debt if the debt to equity is below a specified maximum.

105. The spread on a Ginnie Mae pass through security relative to a comparable Treasury security is *most likely* due to:

    A. credit risk only.

    B. prepayment risk only.

    C. credit risk and prepayment risk.

106. Where P is the original price of a bond, P_1 is the price of the bond predicted by modified duration when interest rates fall by 1% and P_2 is the price of the bond predicted by duration when interest rates rise by 1%, it is *most likely* the case that:

    A. $P_1 - P > P - P_2$

    B. $P_1 - P < P - P_2$

    C. $P_1 - P = P - P_2$

107. The type of bond issued by a multilateral agency, such as World Bank, is *best described* as a:

    A. supranational bond.

    B. sovereign bond.

    C. quasi-government bond.

108. A yield curve which has been constructed from various yields to maturity on zero coupon bonds covering a range of maturities is known as:

    A. par curve.

    B. strip curve.

    C. forward curve.

109. The impact of an increase in interest rate volatility assumed in a valuation model for a putable bond on the z spread of the bond is that the z spread will *most likely*:

    A. increase.

    B. decrease.

    C. stay the same.

110. Which of the following is a benefit to the issuer?

    A. Conversion option.

    B. Put option.

    C. Call option.

Questions 111 through 116 relate to Derivatives

111. A company has entered into a plain vanilla interest rate swap where it is receiving fixed and paying floating rate. The company believes that interest rates are going to rise in the future and wishes to have the ability to terminate the swap if this occurs. The *most appropriate* method of achieving the company's objectives is to:

    A. take out a pay fixed swaption.

    B. agree with the counterparty that the swap can be terminated on payment of the swap's market value at the termination date.

    C. take out a swap where the company pays fixed and receives floating rate and the swap commences on a specified date in the future.

112. Delivery options on the expiration of a futures contract are exercised by the:

    A. long investor.

    B. short investor.

    C. clearinghouse.

113. Details of three put options on a stock which all have a three months expiration are as follows.

Put option	X	Y	Z
Strike price	50	60	70

    An investor owns the stock at a price of 60 and wishes to create a protective put position at the lowest upfront cost possible. He notes that the lowest premium is 6 and the highest premium is 18.

    Given the investor's objectives, the highest loss that the overall position will suffer in three months time is *closest to*:

    A. 6.

    B. 16.

    C. 24.

114. Which of the following is a characteristic of an over-the-counter derivative?

    A. Subject to Government regulation.

    B. The parties set all their own terms.

    C. Guaranteed against from loss due to default.

115. In a forward contract for the physical delivery of tin, it is *most likely* that:

    A. only the long position has default risk.

    B. only the short position has default risk.

    C. both the long and short positions have default risk.

116. A European put option has a strike price of $50 and a year to expiration. The asset price is $42 and the risk free interest rate is 4%. The value below which the put option price should not fall is *closest to*:

    A. $0.

    B. $6.08.

    C. $7.70.

Questions 117 through 120 relate to Alternative Investments

117. An investment in a mortgage REIT has the risk and return profile most similar to which of the following?

A. Fixed income.

B. Equity.

C. Call option.

118. Which of the following characteristic of hedge fund investments is *least* likely to contribute to the valuation issues faced by investors?

A. The level of investor redemptions.

B. Poor liquidity of underlying investments results in the need for liquidity discounts.

C. Non traded investments have no reliable market value.

119. A commodity futures market will *most likely* enter backwardation when prices are:

A. low and volatile.

B. high and stable.

C. high and volatile.

120. A commodity index strategy is *most likely* generally to be considered as:

A. a passive strategy because the investor is tracking the index.

B. an active strategy because of the high turnover involved in the strategy.

C. a positive or active strategy, depending on whether the collateral is actively managed or not.

Practice Examination 2
Morning Session Solutions

2014

ANSWERS

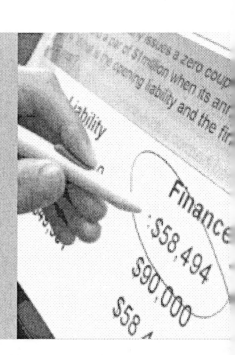

BPP
LEARNING MEDIA

Ethical and Professional Standards

1. **A** Standard IIB – Market Manipulation. The standard covers practices that distort prices or artificially inflate trading volume to mislead market participants. Even though the trading is for the benefit of the funds' investors, it still violates the standard.

    LOS 1b,c and 2a,b,c

2. **B** Standard IIA – Material Nonpublic Information. Edward has no access to material nonpublic information. Standard IIIC – Suitability. Low dividend stocks are unlikely to be suitable for the individual accounts seeking capital stability and stable income.

    LOS 1b,c and 2a,b,c

3. **A** Standard VC – Record Retention. In the absence of regulatory guidance, CFA Institute recommends maintaining records for at least seven years.

    LOS 1b,c and 2a,b,c

4. **B** Standard IA – Knowledge of the Law. The standard requires and understanding of applicable laws and regulations but not a detailed knowledge of all the laws that could potentially govern a member's activities. A failure to report potential violations is less likely to be construed as a violation than a failure to dissociate from unethical conduct.

    LOS 1b,c and 2a,b,c

5. **B** Standard VIIB – Reference to CFA Institute, the CFA Designation, and the CFA Program. Chartered Financial Analyst cannot be used as a noun. The statement that as a CFA charterholder, Elspeth has detailed knowledge of compliance issues is not an exaggeration and does not claim to be superior to others who might also have detailed knowledge.

    LOS 1b,c and 2a,b,c

6. **C** Standard IB – Independence and Objectivity. Employee participation in equity or equity related IPOs should require prior approval. Gifts should be limited to token items. Special cost arrangements should be restricted.

    LOS 1b,c and 2a,b,c

7. **B** Standard ID – Misconduct. Generally, the standard does not cover legal transgressions resulting from acts of civil disobedience in support of personal beliefs. Clay Bell's inebriation and tendency to forget important work raise questions about his professionalism and professional competence. His behavior reflects poorly on him, his firm and the profession.

    LOS 1b,c and 2a,b,c

8. **A** Standard IVA – Loyalty. Undertaking independent practice only includes services that the employer currently makes available, which is not the case for the individuals with assets of less than $10 million. Practice does not include preparations for a new business.

    LOS 1b,c and 2a,b,c

9. **C** Standard IIIA – Loyalty, Prudence and Care. The duty of loyalty is to the client. The beneficiaries are the client.

    LOS 1b,c and 2a,b,c

10.　A　Standard VIIA – Conduct as Members and Candidates in the CFA Program. Members and candidates should not engage in any conduct that compromises the integrity of the CFA examinations. Information that cannot be disclosed to candidates includes details of actual questions on the exam, and broad topic areas and formulas tested or not tested in the exam. All information is confidential until CFA Institute chooses to release it. Patrick Sharpe should not release information and Richard Harper should not ask him to do so.

LOS 1b,c and 2a,b,c

11.　B　Standard VA – Diligence and Reasonable Basis. Pressure of commitments is not a reason to do incomplete research based on a few newspaper articles.

LOS 1b,c and 2a,b,c

12.　A　Standard IIIB – Fair Dealing. The standard states that members and candidates must deal fairly and objectively with clients when making investment recommendations etc. Different levels of service are permitted so long as they are disclosed and available to all clients.

LOS 1b,c and 2a,b,c

13.　A　Standard IIIE – Preservation of Confidentiality. When Maria Santos contacted the charity, she had not been given permission to reveal confidential information about her client at the time.

LOS 1b,c and 2a,b,c

14.　A　Standard VIC – Referral fees. Sanjiv Woods should also have disclosed the referral fee to his employer. Emma Goldsmith should disclose referral fees paid.

LOS 1b,c and 2a,b,c

15.　C　Standard IVC – Responsibilities of Supervisors. On discovery of a violation, the supervisor should increase supervision or place appropriate limitations on the wrongdoer pending the outcome of the investigation.

LOS 1b,c and 2a,b,c

16.　B　Standard VIA – Disclosure of conflicts. Members should disclose any matter that could reasonably be expected to impair their independence and objectivity. The son's shareholding is immaterial while James Mason's shareholding is significant.

LOS 1b,c and 2a,b,c

17.　C　If a member does not accept a proposed disciplinary sanction the matter is referred to a hearing panel.

LOS 1a

18.　A　A GIPS compliant firm may make such a statement to an individual client when reporting the performance of that client's portfolio to that client.

LOS 4a

Quantitative Methods

19. **C**   Semi-annual required return: $1.13^{0.5} - 1 = 0.063$ or 6.3%

Value: $\dfrac{1,000}{0.063} = 15,873$

LOS 5d

20. **C**   There are various ways to work this out. The present value of all the flows discounted at 8.1% comes to approximately zero i.e. the IRR of the flows is 8.1% (more precisely 8.06%).

Time	Flow	Value at time 2 discounted at 8.1%
3 – 12	(3,000)	(20,039)
15	55,000	19,982
		(57)

We have shown the value at time 2. Calculating values at time 0 would make no difference to the answer.

LOS 5e

21. **B**   When deciding between mutually exclusive projects, the project with the highest NPV (which may not have the highest IRR) should be selected.

LOS 6a

22. **C**   Price of T bill: $100 - 5.32 \times \dfrac{70}{360} = 98.9656$

Effective annual yield: $\left(\dfrac{100}{98.9656}\right)^{\frac{365}{70}} - 1 = 5.57\%$

LOS 6f

23. **C**   A normal distribution has a low frequency in both tails and a higher frequency around the median/mean/mode. This means that the cumulative frequency will increase gradually first of all, then increase more rapidly before tailing off to the far right.

LOS 7c

24. **B**   It is possible but less likely for the MAD and standard deviation to be equal, but the MAD cannot exceed the standard deviation.

LOS 7g

25.   **A**   Using a tree:

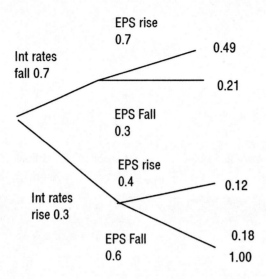

Sinᵢ en, the probability that interest rates fell is $\dfrac{0.12}{0.49+0.12} = 0.197$

Not ₁lso be solved using Bayes's formula, which gives the same calculation as above.

LOS 8a and 8j

26.   **C**   P(0 defaults) + P(1 default) + P(2 defaults)

$$\left(0.85^{10}\right)+\left(0.85^{9}\times0.15\times10\right)+\left(0.85^{8}\times0.15^{2}\times\frac{10!}{8!2!}\right)=0.820$$

LOS 9f

27.   **C**   This is an annuity question, with the annuity starting at t = 8 and ending t = 27.

A = 500,000

r = 6%

N = 20

PV = A $[1-(1/(1+r)^{N}]$ / r

PV = 500,000 [1 − 0.3118] / 0.06

   = \$5,734,961

As the annuity starts in year 8, the present value calculated is at time 7. So we must discount a further 7 years to give PV at time 0.

PV_{0} = 5,734,961 / $(1+0.06)^{7}$

   = \$3,814,076

LOS 5e

28.　**B**　When the sample size is large and the population variance is known, the normal distribution (i.e. the z statistic) can be used. If the population variance is unknown for a large sample, the student t distribution (i.e. the t statistic) should be used.

LOS 10j

29.　**A**　The test is one tailed (is the manager capable of earning a positive alpha), so the critical statistic is approximately 1.65 at the 5% error level (since the sample size is very large, the student t distribution will be very similar to the normal distribution). The null hypothesis is that the manager does not have skill and results are due to chance or worse.

The test statistic is $\dfrac{2.1-0}{12 / \sqrt{100}} = 1.75$

This is greater than the critical statistic, so the null hypothesis is rejected and the pension fund concludes that the manager is skilful.

LOS 11f

30.　**A**　In the first situation, the null hypothesis will be that the customer is not a credit risk. Seeking to avoid the loss of new customers and taking on more bad customers as a result means the company is happier not to reject this null hypothesis i.e. a type II error is more likely to occur and the risk of the type I error (rejecting the null hypothesis incorrectly and rejecting a customer as a bad credit risk) is minimized.

In the second situation, the null hypothesis is that there is no stock market anomaly. The company is happier not to reject the null hypothesis since it does not wish to invest in unprofitable strategies. This means that a type II error is more likely to occur and the risk of a type I error (rejecting the null hypothesis incorrectly and concluding an anomaly exists) is minimized.

LOS 11b

31.　**C**　Elliot Wave Theory has a number of short and long term cycles.

LOS 12g

32.　**A**　Neckline − (Head − Neckline) = 50 − (67 − 50) = 33

LOS 12d

Economics

33.　C　When marginal product starts to decline, it is just past its maximum value. So long as marginal product is positive, total product will increase. So long as average product is below marginal product (which is most likely to be the case since marginal product has just gone past its maximum), average product will increase.

LOS 15b

34.　B　The Fed will conduct open market sales. This reduces the monetary base and the supply of money, causing a rise in interest rates. There is a decrease in the supply of bank loans causing a decrease in supply of loanable funds.

LOS 19h

35.　A　The social cost is due to the deadweight loss and to rent seeking. Perfect price discrimination is where a firm could sell each unit for the highest price anyone is willing to pay for it, which would reduce the consumer surplus to zero. Marginal cost pricing sets price equal to marginal cost, which will maximize the total surplus.

LOS 13d,l and 16a

36.　A　Raising interest rates in the face of a supply shock such as this might cause consumption to fall and unemployment to rise.

LOS 19h

37.　A　When the price of one good increases, demand for the other good increases i.e. the second good is substituted for the first by consumers.

LOS 16b

38.　C　Aggregate hours worked multiplied by labour productivity would result in the potential GDP of an economy. Sustainable growth may be estimated as the growth in labour productivity plus the long term labour force growth rate.

LOS 17j

39.　B　Automatic stabilizers as the name suggests do not require intervention by policy makers.

LOS 19p

40.　B　The firm will produce where price equals average total cost in the long run, giving a zero economic profit. Average total cost will not be at a minimum, unlike perfect competition. The profit maximizing condition is that marginal revenue equals marginal cost, as is always the case.

LOS 16a

41.　A　With loose enforcement, it is as if the rent ceiling does not exist, so the unregulated rent becomes the rent that people pay.

LOS 13k

42.　A　Growth rate = $(240/220)^{0.5} - 1 = 4.45\%$

LOS 17c

43.   C   The increase in money wages will reduce SRAS by increasing costs, making firms willing to supply less at each price level. In the long run, the increase in wages is accompanied by an increase in prices, meaning that there is no impact on LRAS.

LOS 15d,i

44.   A   A change in plant size is a long run decision by effecting long run productive capacity. Staying in the industry (or leaving it) is a long run decision. Shutting down gives the option to recommence production in the short term. A firm will shut down when its variable cost exceeds the price.

LOS 16a,c

Financial Reporting and Analysis

45. **C**   Common size statements can be constructed for the same company over a number of years or for different companies in the same year.

     LOS 10d and 25j

46. **C**   Under the first in first out method, the oldest inventory is assumed to have been sold first. In this scenario, in 2013 12,000 units were sold with a purchase price of $12, and in 2014 the remaining 8,000 units purchased in 2013 are assumed to have been sold first. Then the additional 27,000 units are sold, which have a purchase price of $14. The remaining inventory (33,000 units) are all then assumed to have been bought in 2014 @ $14 giving inventory value of $462,000 (33,000 x 14).

     LOS 29c

47. **A**   The interest costs will start being depreciated in 2013, reducing the 2013 profit compared to if they had been charged as an expense in 2011 and 2012. The value of assets will be higher due to the capitalization of interest, making stockholders' equity higher and reducing the debt to equity ratio.

     LOS 30a

48. **A**   A schedule for the three years 2012, 2013 and 2014 is as follows.

	Dec 31 2012	Dec 31 2013	Dec 31 2014
Balance sheet carrying amount	40,000	20,000	-
Tax base	-	-	-
Temporary difference	40,000	20,000	-
Balance sheet deferred tax liability	30% × 40,000 = $12,000	20% × 20,000 = $4,000	-

     LOS 31d

49. **C**   IFRS requires the effective interest method. US GAAP prefers it but also permits the straight line method.

     LOS 32b

50. **A**   Losses should be recognized immediately, whatever method is used.

     LOS 25b

51. **B**

	$
Net income	800
Increase in receivables (1,200 – 1,100)	(100)
Decrease in inventories (890 – 920)	30
Increase in payables (750 – 710)	40
Decrease in tax liability (200 – 290)	(90)
Depreciation expense	85
Cash flows from operating activities	765

     LOS 27e

52. **A** High management turnover relates to opportunities and disputes with auditors relates to attitudes.

    LOS 33a

53. **A** Under FIFO, in times of rising prices, cost of sales would be lower than LIFO and hence gross profit margin would be higher. Closing inventory would contain the most recently purchased inventory so will be higher in value.

    LOS 29e

54. **A** A qualified report is when there is some limitation or exception to accounting standards. A disclaimer is when the auditors are not able to issue an opinion.

    LOS 22d

55. **B** Increasing inventory turnover indicates lower inventories, so obsolescence is unlikely to be a problem. Paying for purchases more quickly does not affect inventory levels. A company might window dress its accounts to show a lower level of year end inventories for some reason.

    LOS 29h

56. **C** The opening inventory of 50 units is valued at $20 each.

    FIFO ending inventories = $20 \times 25 + 20 \times 22.5 = \$1,400$

    The last 60 units purchased are included in FIFO.

    LIFO ending inventories = $50 \times 20 + 10 \times 22.5 = \$1,225$

    Since the inventory system is periodic (not perpetual), we do a calculation for the whole year, so the units sold are the last units purchased in the year.

    Difference in inventory valuation = $1,400 - 1,225 = \$175$.

    Since we are not given details about the opening inventories in detail, we have to assume that they are valued the same for both methods.

    LOS 29c

57. **A** The depreciation expense will be the same for both depreciation methods when a company is replacing its assets and prices are stable. However, the asset base with straight line depreciation will be higher, meaning that its return on equity will be lower.

    LOS 30c

58. **C** Closing deferred tax liability = $40\% \times \$120,000 = \$48,000$

    Opening deferred tax liability = $30\% \times \$100,000 = \$30,000$

    Deferred tax expense = increase in liability = $18,000

    LOS 31d,e

59. **A** Both actuarial gians and losses and actual return on plan assets are shown in the other comprehensive income and not the profit and loss.

    LOS 32k

60. **A** Both sets of rules encourage use of the direct method but permit the other.

LOS 27c

61. **B** Company B is diversified, giving it more stable revenues and profits. It has high profits, indicating operational efficiency. Its profits are stable, indicating margin stability. The other companies have only two favorable and one unfavorable factor.

LOS 35c

62. **A** Number of days sales $= \dfrac{0.5(670+620)}{5,090} \times 365 = 46.25$

Number of days inventory $= \dfrac{0.5(430+430)}{4,100} \times 365 = 38.28$

Number of days payables $= \dfrac{0.5(520+480)}{4,100} \times 365 = 44.51$

$46.25 + 38.28 - 44.51 = 40.02$

Note that since inventories are constant, COGS = purchases.

LOS 28e

63. **C** Changes to LIFO are accounted for prospectively. Other changes are accounted for retroactively.

LOS 29g

64. **A** Tax base = $750,000 – $150,000 = $600,000

Temporary difference = Carrying amount – Tax base

$= ($750,000 – $75,000) – $600,000$

$= $75,000$

LOS 31c

65. **C** Only unrealized gains on trading securities are recognized in the income statement. Unrealized gains and losses on available-for-sale securities are taken through stockholders equity, in other comprehensive income.

LOS 26f

66. **B** Return on assets $= \dfrac{\text{Net income}}{\text{Total assets}}$. If a company uses a large amount of borrowings, total assets will be very high compared to net income.

LOS 28d

67. **B** The net income for 2012 will be increased by the reversal of the initial impairment (the original impairment would have been charged as an expense, reducing net income in 2011). The assets will have the same value as if the impairment had not occurred, since it has now been reversed out. Return on assets will therefore be higher in 2012.

LOS 30h

68.   C   Add back interest saved: ($1m × 5%) $50,000

Less the increase in tax: (40% × $50,000)   ($20,000)

Additional earnings after conversion $30,000

Diluted EPS = ($20,000,000 + $30,000) / (1,000,000 + 250,000)

= $16.02

LOS 25g

Corporate Finance

69. **B**   Project Y will have a higher NPV than project X for any cost of capital above 12%. It will have a positive NPV up to a cost of capital of 18%.

LOS 36c

70. **C**   Cost of equity = $\dfrac{10 \times 1.03}{172} + 0.03 = 8.99\%$

   WACC = $\dfrac{8.99 \times 100 + 5(1 - 0.3) \times 40}{140} = 7.42\%$

LOS 37a

71. **C** $\dfrac{5,000,000 - 500,000 \times 20 \times 4\% \times (1 - 0.3)}{3,000,000 - 500,000} = 1.888$

LOS 39d

72. **A**   Cost of trade credit if paid on day 20 = $(1 + \text{Discount}/(1 - \text{Discount}))^{(365/\text{No. of days beyond discount period})} - 1$

   Cost of trade credit if paid on day 20 = $(1 + 0.02/0.98)^{(365/10)} - 1 = 109\%$

LOS 40g

73. **B**   Return on assets = net margin × total asset turnover

   Net margin = operating margin × effect of non operating items × tax effect

   ROA = 10 × 1.1 × 0.65 × 1.4 = 10.01%

LOS 28d

74. **B**   In a two-tier board, executive members are on the management board.

LOS 41b

75. **B**   Operating cycle is the amount of time to convert raw materials into cash from a sale = number of days inventory + number of days receivables = 25 + 52 = 77.

LOS 40c

76.   B   The information we know from the question is as follows:

	Original $		Revised $
Sales	350,000	+50%	472,500
Variable costs	?		?
Profit before fixed costs	?		?
Fixed costs	?		?
EBIT	?	+50% × 1.5	?
Interest	?		?
EBT	?	+50% × 1.5 × 2	?
Tax at 30%	?		?
Net income	49,000	+50% × 1.5 × 2	?

Since the tax rate is 30%, the original EBT is $70,000.

Since $DFL = \dfrac{EBIT}{EBT}$ i.e. $2 = \dfrac{EBIT}{70,000}$, EBIT is $140,000.

Since $DOL = \dfrac{Profit\ before\ fixed\ costs}{EBIT}$

i.e. $1.5 = \dfrac{Profit\ before\ fixed\ costs}{140,000}$, Profit before fixed costs = $210,000. Since sales increased by 50%, profit before fixed costs also increased by 50% to $315,000.

Alternatively, having calculated the EBIT of $140,000 as above, we can try each answer in turn to see which is consistent with an original EBIT of $140,000.

In answer B, the new profit before fixed costs is $315,000, so the previous profit before fixed costs must have been $\dfrac{315,000}{1.5} = \$210,000$. Since the EBIT is $140,000, the fixed costs must be $70,000. We now have the whole original income statement so can check that $315,000 is consistent with the DOL given in the question when sales increase by 50%.

LOS 38b

77.   B   Directors with too many board positions will be unable to give adequate time to the company. Cumulative voting is preferable for minority shareholders to obtain board representation.

LOS 41b,c,d

78.   B   Breakeven is where total revenue = total costs and net inciome is zero. Total costs = fixed costs + variable costs + fixed financial costs.

LOS 38e

Portfolio Management

79. **B** The portfolio can be invested for the long term and is not needed to finance current expenses. This indicates high ability to take risk. However, Janet believes that investing is about luck and is concerned about losses, suggesting low willingness to take risk.

 LOS 45d

80. **C** Both the CAL and CML are upward sloping straight lines and both cut the y axis at the risk free rate.

 LOS 44b

81. **A** Most endowments and foundations are established with the intent of having perpetual lives.

 LOS 42b

82. **B** $\sqrt{10^2 0.7^2 + 8^2 0.3^2 + 2 \times 0.7 \times 0.3 \times 48} = 8.66\%$

 LOS 43e

83. **B** The security characteristic line is a regression of the excess return over the risk free rate for the stock against the market's excess return over the risk free rate. Its intercept will be zero on average, but may be positive or negative for any sample of observations. The gradient of the line measures the sensitivity of the security's excess returns to the market's excess returns, i.e. the security's beta.

 LOS 44f

84. **A** The amount of money to invest is relatively small so a mutual fund is most likely to be appropriate.

 LOS 42d

Equity

85. **B** The fundamentals based approach uses expectations. Price to sales multiples assumes that similar companies (as measured by sales) trade on the same ratio of price to sales. This ignores all drivers of value other than sales, such as net margins.

LOS 51h

86. **B** The shakeout phase is after the high growth phase, so there is still growth in sales (albeit slowing down) but increasing competition for market share.

LOS 50g

87. **C** $$25\% = \frac{30\% \times 80 + P - 80}{P}$$

P = $74.67.

This is using the formula in the book. An alternative formula which states that the equity in the position is the stock price – debt would show the calculation as:

$$25\% = \frac{P - 70\% \times 80}{P}; P = 74.67$$

The debt in the position is the 70% of the initial stock price of $80. The equity in the position is the current price – $56 of debt. When this is equal to 25% of the stock price, a margin call is received.

LOS 46f

88. **B** An equal weighted index will have a higher representation for small cap stocks than value weighted or price weighted (unless small cap stocks happen to have smaller stock prices). When small cap stocks do well, the equal weighted index will outperform.

LOS 47d

89. **A** PIPE = private investment in public equity. A public company does a private placement of its shares to institutions. A private equity house would invest in private equity, not public equity.

LOS 49c

90. **C** The semi strong form states that information that is publicly available is incorporated into a security's price. This would make fundamental analysis useless, as it is based on the use of publicly available financial and economic information etc.

LOS 48e

91. **A** A level II ADR does not involves raising capital, whereas a level III permits raising capital on public markets and rule 144A permits raising capital through a private placement.

LOS 49e

92.   **C**   A marketable limit buy order is one that will be at least partly filled by the best offer price. The column with the higher prices is the offer price, as people wish to sell at a higher price. An investor wishing to buy with a marketable limit order would put in a price of 54 or higher.

LOS 46h

93.   **B**   Hedge funds decide which databases they report their returns to, so the constituents of the index prepared based on a database are determined by the constituents, not by the database operator. Hedge fund indexes are typically equally weighted. They are subject to survivor bias because funds with poor performance may stop reporting their returns to the database.

LOS 47j

94.   **A**   There are low barriers to entry, since the high cost of airplanes can be managed through leasing arrangements. High fixed costs mean that airlines will compete for passengers, since each additional passenger means an increase in revenue with relative low increases in costs.

LOS 50e

95.   **C** $$\frac{5\times1.08}{1.09}+\frac{5\times1.08^2}{1.09^2}+\frac{5\times1.08^3}{1.09^3}+\frac{5\times1.08^3\times1.02}{0.09-0.02}\times\frac{1}{1.09^3}=85.597$$

LOS 51e

96.   **B**   The data is examined to create a hypothesis. The hypothesis is then tested on data from the population that has just been examined. This is an invalid statistical procedure.

LOS 48f

Fixed Income

97. **B**   Since LIBOR is constant over the year at 4%, but the compounding intervals are longer for the longer dated LIBOR, LIBOR is expected to fall.

For example, calculating the expected rate for 90 days LIBOR in 90 days time.

$1.01 \times (1 + r) = 1.02$; $r = 0.99\%$ or 3.96%.

LOS 54h

98. **A**   A reserve fund is an example of an internal credit enhancement. An SPV is often used in asset-backed securities but is not itself a credit enhancement tool. Other examples of external credit enhancement are letter of credit and bond insurance.

LOS 52b

99. **C**   The agreement to pay at least the present value of the future scheduled payments means that investor reduces reinvestment risk by receiving a larger present value if interest rates have fallen.

LOS 52f

100. **B**   The change in value for a change in yields of 1% will depend on the bond's current yield to maturity. Yield curve risk refers to non parallel shifts in yield, whereas duration only considers parallel shifts in yield. Duration does not change just because a bond is a credit sector bond rather than a government bond, as it just measures the change in value for a 1% change in yield.

LOS 55b

101. **B**   Bond B has a smaller percentage increase in price for a yield decrease than the percentage decrease in price for a yield increase. This indicates that the relationship is become less convex towards the left, which indicates a callable bond.

LOS 52f

102. **A**   Value of bond at 6% and 5% with four years maturity:

Time	Flows	PV at 6%	PV at 5%
1 – 4	40	138.61	141.84
4	1,000	792.09	822.70
Value		930.70	964.54

The change in value due to the change in discount rate is 964.54 – 930.70 = 33.84

LOS 54a

103. **C**   Bond C is priced at a premium to par, so it will have the highest coupon level. This means it will have the highest amount to reinvest and the highest reinvestment risk.

LOS 54b

104. **C**   This imposes a limit on borrowing and is effectively an agreement not to raise debt.

LOS 52c

105. **B**   Ginnie Mae Pass through securities are backed by the US government, so there is no difference in credit risk.

LOS 56j

106. **C**   Modified duration assumes a linear relationship, so the price change predicted by duration is equal for a rise or fall in price. The actual relationship for an option free bond is that the price rise is greater than the price fall.

LOS 58b

107. **A**   Multilateral agency bond issues are known as supranational bonds.

LOS 53e

108. **B**   This is known as the spot curve or strip curve (or zero curve).

LOS 54g

109. **C**   z spread is unaffected by interest rate volatility, as it assumes zero volatility. It is option adjusted spread (OAS) that is affected by interest rate volatility.

LOS 54j

110. **C**   A call option is of benefit to the issuer, as they can call the debt if interest rates decrease which allows them to retire the existing high coupon debt and issue new debt at a lower rate.

LOS 52f

Derivatives

111. **A**   The company wants the ability to terminate the swap, but only if interest rates rise. An option on a swap (a swaption) will achieve this.

   LOS 61a

112. **B**   The seller of the future exercises delivery options.

   LOS 59e

113. **B**   The put option with the lowest premium will be the lowest strike of 50. The investor will buy the put paying the premium of 6. If the stock price falls below 50, the value of the share is maintained at 50 since it can be sold under the option for this price. This gives a loss of 10 on the share plus the premium of 6 paid for the option = 16 in total.

   LOS 62b

114. **B**   Government regulation and guarantee over losses are characteristics of exchange-traded derivatives.

   LOS 57d

115. **C**   The long position may not pay for the tin and the short position may not deliver the tin, so both sides have default risk.

   LOS 58a

116. **B**   The lower bound for a European put is the higher of zero and the present value of PV (strike - share), i.e. $\dfrac{50}{1.04} - 42 = 6.08$

   LOS 59k

Alternative Investments

117. **A**   A mortgage REIT invests in mortgages and is similar to the risk and return of a fixed income investment. Equity REITs invest in commercial or residential properties and have the risk and return profile similar to equity.

LOS 63d

118. **A**   Investor redemptions are a feature of hedge funds but not a worry for valuation. Poor liquidity and no market prices of the underlying investments are both contributors to valuation issues for hedge funds.

LOS 63d

119. **A**   When prices are low and volatile, producers hedge by selling futures, causing the market to enter backwardation with the futures price below the expected spot price.

LOS 63e

120. **B**   Commodity index strategies are active because of the high turnover.

LOS 63e

The Chartered Financial Analyst® Program

Practice Examination 2
Afternoon Session

2014

The Afternoon Session of Practice Examination 2 consists of 120 multiple choice questions which must be completed in three hours. The topic areas covered are:

BPP
LEARNING MEDIA

Questions 1 through 18 relate to Ethical and Professional Standards

1. Joseph Carmello CFA has read an article in a financial newspaper regarding a study by a leading financial analyst firm. The article reports factual information contained in the study and additional interpretation by the newspaper of this factual information. Joseph Carmello uses the factual information from the newspaper article in a report that he is writing and acknowledges the financial newspaper and the financial analyst firm as his sources of information in his report. The information in the newspaper article turns out to be incorrectly copied from the original study and to be erroneous. With regard to best practice recommended in Standard IC – Misrepresentation, it is *most likely* that Camello has:

   A. violated the standard by not obtaining the original study for review.

   B. not violated the standard because the standard only applies to interpretation and analysis of data rather than factual information.

   C. not violated the standard because he did not know that the factual information had been reported incorrectly by the newspaper.

2. Diane Atkins CFA is an analyst working for an investment firm in London, England. She regularly goes to an exclusive club after work where she can have some dinner, read a magazine and relax over a drink with some friends. One night, she is sitting in a secluded part of the public lounge of the club having a relaxing glass of cognac by herself, when she accidentally overhears a conversation. She recognizes the voices as those of the chief executive officer and chief financial officer of a company that she follows and realizes that they are discussing the potential take-over of another named company. The next day in the office she analyzes the financial statements of both companies in detail together with other information she has gleaned from analysis of the companies in the past. She combines her knowledge of the potential take-over with the other information and comes to a conclusion that the take-over would be extremely beneficial for the company. Accordingly she buys stock in both the potential bidder and potential target. With regard to Standard IIA – Material Nonpublic Information of CFA Institute's Standards of Professional Conduct, it is *most likely* that Atkins has:

   A. violated the standard.

   B. not violated the standard due to her use of the mosaic theory.

   C. not violated the standard because the information about the potential take-over was accidentally overhead in a public lounge.

3. Abigail Hogan earned the right to use the CFA designation 30 years ago and since then has worked in the investment industry until she retired six months ago. She has continued to pay her CFA Institute membership fees and file professional conduct statements with CFA Institute over this time. She has now notified CFA Institute that she is retired and been granted retired status. On her personal cards, she continues to refer to herself as Abigail Hogan CFA. When she gives the card to people, she explains to them that she now has retired status. It is *most likely* that Abigail Hogan has:

   A. not violated CFA Institute Standards of Professional Conduct.

   B. violated CFA Institute Standards of Professional Conduct by using the CFA designation on her card.

   C. violated CFA Institute Standards of Professional Conduct by not explaining in writing on the card that she is retired.

4. Janet Iffe CFA is a manager for the portfolio of a defined benefit pension plan. She has been directed by the plan sponsor to use the plan's brokerage to purchase goods and services for the plan. The sponsor has assured Janet that the goods and services purchased from the brokerage will benefit solely the plan's beneficiaries. Janet is aware that this broker charges higher commissions and does not offer superior service compared to other brokers used by her. Iffe can *most likely* satisfy her duty of loyalty to the client by:

   A. complying with the sponsor's directions without taking further actions.

   B. refusing to act for the sponsor unless he permits the use of Janet's normal brokers who offer lower commissions and no worse service.

   C. complying with the sponsor's directions while disclosing that the directed brokerage may mean that the client is not getting best execution.

5. Trevor Sharpe CFA is the chief investment officer for a university endowment. His friend Michael Jones CFA has recently set up his own private equity firm, the Termite Factory, having previously worked for various private equity investment houses. Trevor wishes to help his friend and, having performed detailed checks and analysis of the Termite Factory and its operations, decides to invest part of the endowment's funds with the Termite Factory. It is *most likely* that Sharpe has:

   A. violated Standard VIA – Disclosure of Conflicts.

   B. violated Standard VA – Diligence and Reasonable Basis.

   C. not violated any CFA Institute Standards of Professional Conduct.

6. The recommended procedures for compliance for Standard IIA – Material Nonpublic Information *least likely* state that there should be:

   A. no overlap of personnel between the investment banking area of a brokerage firm and its sales and research departments.

   B. a prohibition on all types of proprietary activity in a security when a firm comes into possession of material nonpublic information about the security.

   C. a watch list of securities shown only to the few people responsible for compliance to monitor transactions in specified securities where the firm has possession of material nonpublic information about the securities.

7. Standard IIID – Performance Presentation *most likely*:

   A. requires firms to apply GIPS® Standards to ensure compliance with the standard.

   B. permits firms to make brief presentations with only a limited amount of information provided.

   C. permits firms to use representative accounts based on the top quartile of individual accounts in a composite when presenting performance information to individuals.

8. Alicia Johnson CFA is a portfolio manager working for Blighton Investments. She manages a number of individual accounts, including those for her parents. When acquiring shares in equity initial public offerings (IPOs), she allocates shares firstly to her clients other than her parents where the issue is suitable for them. She only allocates shares to her parents if sufficient shares remain after other clients have been satisfied and the issue is suitable for them. Johnson has *most likely*:

    A. violated Standard IVA – Loyalty.

    B. violated Standard VIB – Priority of Transactions.

    C. not violated any CFA Institute Standards of Professional Conduct.

9. David Faust CFA manages a fund which invests in equity securities in illiquid stock markets. He wishes to sell a security which is currently held by the fund but is concerned that the illiquidity of the stock market concerned will result in a disadvantageous price for his fund below the fair price of the security. He decides to work the trade by gradually selling the security so as to minimize adverse market impact and prevent other market participants knowing that a substantial holding is being sold. As a result, he is able to liquidate the fund's holdings eventually at a higher price than he would have otherwise achieved, to the benefit of the investors in the fund. With respect to Standard IIB – Market Manipulation, it is *most likely* that the trading of the security by Faust has:

    A. violated the standard.

    B. not violated the standard because no market manipulation has taken place.

    C. not violated the standard because the trading is for the purpose of benefiting the investors in the fund.

10. Cooperative Investment Management Inc. typically uses teams to make group decisions concerning investment analysis, for which the group is collectively responsible. Jane Way CFA is a member of such a group. Her group has followed the usual process, in which Jane Way has confidence, to come to a consensus view about the impact of a change in interest rates. However, Jane Way is in disagreement with the conclusion of the team. According to CFA Institute Standards of Professional Conduct, Way's best course of action on the publication of the report by the group is *most likely* to be:

    A. declining to be associated with the report.

    B. allowing the report to be published without dissociating from the report.

    C. allowing the report to be published but insist that her name is recorded as dissenting from the consensus view.

11. A recommended procedure of compliance for Standard VIB – Priority of Transactions is *least likely* to be:

    A. strict limits on investment personnel acquiring securities in private placements.

    B. investment personnel only participating in equity initial public offerings (IPOs) with appropriate disclosure.

    C. the establishment of restricted periods when investment personnel are not permitted to trade in specified securities.

12. An investment firm has a statement of ethics and professional conduct that states the following:

"Employees must not engage in any professional conduct involving dishonesty, fraud, or deceit. This requirement applies only to employee's conduct while at work and is not intended to apply to any employee's conduct outside of work."

With respect to standard ID – Misconduct, it is *most likely* that the firm's statement of ethics and professional conduct is:

A. at least as strict as the requirements in the standard.

B. less strict than the standard, which requires that all conduct by employees should be covered.

C. less strict than the standard, which requires that all conduct by employees that reflects adversely on the employee's integrity should be covered.

13. Standard IIIE – Preservation of Confidentiality *most likely* states that members of CFA Institute:

A. must not provide the CFA Institute Professional Conduct Program (PCP) with information that falls under the definition of confidential information for the standard.

B. must provide the CFA Institute Professional Conduct Program (PCP) with information even if it falls under the definition of confidential information for the standard, when permissible under applicable laws.

C. are encouraged to provide the CFA Institute Professional Conduct Program (PCP) with information even if it falls under the definition of confidential information for the standard, when permissible under applicable laws.

14. An action by an employee of an investment firm who is a member of CFA Institute which is *least likely* to be a violation of Standard IVA – Loyalty is:

A. contacting other employees about conducting an employee buyout of the business.

B. taking home copies of computer spreadsheets for personal use that the employee developed while working for the firm and prior to resigning from the firm.

C. being involved in charitable activities outside of work which take up a substantial amount of time without prior discussion with the investment firm's management.

15. Bombady Jones CFA is an equity analyst who works for an investment bank. He specializes in the agricultural sector. He is aware that a new organic fertilizer which causes no harm to wildlife and deters insects and beetles from eating crops is being tested by a company that he follows. He identifies farms at which the fertilizer is being tested, although he is unaware which farms are using the actual new product and which farms are being used as a control group. He speaks to the owners of the farms to obtain details of their results. He also speaks to the company who reports that testing of the product has indicated its success in increasing yields without damaging the environment. After carefully analyzing possible demand, revenues and costs for the new product he forecasts that earnings per share for the company will increase dramatically. In his report, he recommends the company as a strong buy, on the basis that its earnings per share will increase. It is *most likely* that Jones has violated:

A. Standard IIIA – Loyalty, Prudence and Care.

B. Standard VA – Diligence and Reasonable Basis.

C. Standard VB – Communications with Clients and Prospective Clients.

16. Frederick East CFA is a portfolio manager at Western Apex Investment Management, who manages equity portfolios for individual investors. One of Frederick's clients proposes to Frederick that where the portfolio earns a return at least 5% greater than the risk free rate in a year, Frederick can have the use of the client's yacht for two weeks during the summer vacation. Frederick ensures that this offer does not create any conflict of interest in his behavior by treating all his clients fairly and equally when making investment decisions. The next year, all of his equity portfolios, including that belonging to this client, earn a return that is around 7% above the risk free rate. Frederick takes advantage of the client's offer and spends time on his yacht without notifying his employer of the arrangement. It is *most likely* that East has:

A. violated CFA Institute Standards of Professional Conduct relating to compensation.

B. not violated CFA Institute Standards of Professional Conduct because the client's offer represents a gift.

C. not violated CFA Institute Standards of Professional Conduct because the client's offer has not resulted in his disadvantaging any of his clients.

17. Verification of a firm's claim of compliance with the Global Investment Performance Standards (GIPS®) should *most likely* be conducted by:

A. the firm's auditor.

B. the firm's compliance officer.

C. a third party independent of the firm.

18. When local laws and regulations are in conflict with the requirements of the Global Investment Performance Standards (GIPS®), a firm that wishes to claim compliance with GIPS standards must *most likely* follow the:

A. local laws and regulations and cannot claim to be GIPS compliant.

B. GIPS requirements in order to be able to claim to be GIPS compliant.

C. local laws and regulations and disclose how these conflict with the GIPS standards in order to claim compliance.

Questions 19 through 32 relate to Quantitative Methods

19. The stated annual rate of return is 25% on a quarterly compounding basis. The equivalent stated effective annual rate of return is *closest to*:

    A. 24.2%.

    B. 25.5%.

    C. 27.4%.

20. The interest rate that in economic theory reflects the time preference of individuals for current versus future real consumption is *most likely* the:

    A. real risk-free interest rate.

    B. real risk-free interest rate plus a maturity premium.

    C. nominal risk free interest rate plus a default risk premium, liquidity premium and maturity premium.

21. Projects X and Y both have the same cost of capital and give the same negative net present value. Both projects consist of one outflow followed by a series of constant inflows and have the same final maturity. The undiscounted sum of the inflows exceeds the initial outflow for both projects. Project X has a smaller initial outflow than project Y. It is *most likely* that:

    A. both projects have the same internal rate of return.

    B. project X has a higher internal rate of return than project Y.

    C. project Y has a higher internal rate of return than project X.

22. A distribution is positively skewed. It is *most likely* that the distribution's:

    A. mean value exceeds its modal value.

    B. median value exceeds its mean value.

    C. modal value exceeds its median value.

23. A distribution has a finite variance. The proportion of the distribution that lies within 2 standard deviations of its mean is *at least*:

    A. 75%.

    B. 83%.

    C. 95%.

24. There are 6 corporate bonds. 3 bonds are AAA rated, 2 bonds are AA rated and 1 bond is A rated. Three of the bonds are from the utilities sector, 2 bonds are industrials and 1 bond is pharmaceuticals. Assuming that there is no correlation between industry sector and credit rating, the probability of the three bonds from the utilities sector all being AAA rated, the 2 industrials bonds being AA rated and the pharmaceuticals bond being A rated is *closest to*:

    A. 0.008.

    B. 0.017.

    C. 0.050.

25. A bond has a value of $1,000 and a maturity of one year. There is a 5% probability that the bond issuer will default over the year, in which case investors expect to see 30% of their investment being returned to them at the end of the year. The risk free rate of interest for the year is 4%. The lowest default risk premium that a risk neutral investor would expect to receive is *closest to*:

    A. 3.89%.

    B. 5.47%.

    C. 7.05%.

26. An investor does not wish to suffer a return below the risk free rate of 0.5% on any investment. Details of the expected return and standard deviation of returns for three investments are as follows.

Investment	Expected return %	Standard deviation %
A	5.0	4.2
B	7.5	6.5
C	9.5	7.8

    The returns on each investment are normally distributed. The investor is *most likely* to select:

    A. investment A.

    B. investment B.

    C. investment C.

27. A portfolio has a value of $2,000,000, an expected return of 9% and a standard deviation of returns of 8%. The returns are normally distributed. The investor plans to withdraw $80,000 from the portfolio at the end of the year but wishes to keep the initial $2,000,000 value intact.

    Extract from a table giving the cumulative probabilities for a standard normal distribution.

Z	0	0.01	0.02	0.03	0.04	0.05	0.06	0.07	0.08	0.09
0.50	0.692	0.695	0.699	0.702	0.705	0.709	0.712	0.716	0.719	0.722
0.60	0.726	0.729	0.732	0.736	0.739	0.742	0.745	0.749	0.752	0.755
0.70	0.758	0.761	0.764	0.767	0.770	0.773	0.776	0.779	0.728	0.785
0.80	0.788	0.791	0.794	0.797	0.800	0.802	0.805	0.808	0.811	0.813
0.90	0.816	0.819	0.821	0.824	0.826	0.829	0.832	0.834	0.837	0.839
1.0	0.841	0.844	0.846	0.849	0.851	0.853	0.855	0.858	0.860	0.862
1.1	0.864	0.867	0.869	0.871	0.873	0.875	0.877	0.879	0.881	0.883

    The probability that the investor will be able to withdraw the $80,000 without allowing the portfolio value to fall below $2,000,000 is *closest to*:

    A. 0.69.

    B. 0.74.

    C. 0.87.

28. The mean daily return on a stock market index over a period of 20 days was 0.05%. The standard deviation of returns for the stock market index is 2.0%.

Extract from the Student t distribution:

df	p=0.100	p=0.050	p=0.025	p=0.010	p=0.005
18	1.330	1.734	2.101	2.552	2.878
19	1.328	1.729	2.093	2.539	2.861
20	1.325	1.725	2.086	2.528	2.845

Assuming that returns are independent over time and are normally distributed, the mean daily return on the stock market index at the 95% confidence level will lie between:

A. -0.827% and 0.927%.

B. -0.883% and 0.983%.

C. -0.886% and 0.986%.

29. An analyst has developed a hypothesis concerning a possible anomaly in stock market returns based on companies' price to earnings ratio. In order to test this, she takes 12 consecutive years of data up to the present day. For each year, she takes the companies in the index in that year and identifies their stock price at December 31 and the consensus earnings per share forecasts for the specified year available on December 31. She uses this data to conclude on her hypothesis. The analyst has *most likely* created:

A. survivorship bias.

B. time period bias.

C. look ahead bias.

30. The test procedure that is used to test inequality between two variances where the populations are normally distributed is most likely the:

A. t test.

B. F test.

C. χ^2 test.

31. In a head and shoulders pattern used in technical analysis, it is *most likely* that the:

A. rally creating the head has lower volumes than the rally for the left shoulder.

B. neckline is the price at which the left shoulder and right shoulder reach their approximate highest points.

C. rally for the right shoulder is characterized by as high buying enthusiasm as for the rally for the left shoulder.

32. Which of the following chart pattern is an example of a reversal pattern used to signal the end of a trend?

A. Rectangle patterns.

B. Triangle patterns.

C. Head and shoulders pattern.

Questions 33 through 44 relate to Economics

33. When setting an inflation target, a central bank will *most likely* exclude certain items from the relevant broad based price index because they:

    A. do not reflect consumer spending patterns.

    B. give a high level of volatility to the price index.

    C. are suffering price increases in excess of those considered to be normal.

34. Details of three possible industry supply curves as a follows.

    Curve A

    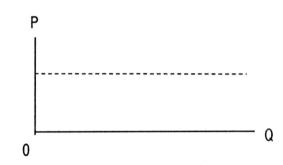

    Curve B

    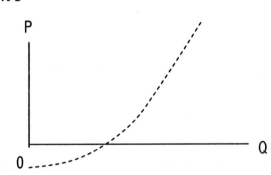

    Curve C

    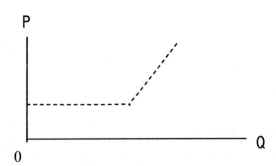

    The curve which *most likely* fits the industry supply curve in perfect competition is:

    A. curve A.

    B. curve B.

    C. curve C.

35. The MXN/USD exchange rate is 13.3254

    The USD/GBP exchange rate is 1.4231

    What is the GBP/MXN cross rate?

    A. 0.0527

    B. 0.0832

    C. 0.2462

36. An increase in real GDP and an increase in financial innovation will *most likely* cause an overall:

    A. increase in demand for money.

    B. decrease in demand for money.

    C. increase or decrease in demand for money, depending on the strength of each factor.

37. In the context of a duopoly, the Nash equilibrium *most likely* states that:

    A. the firms will collude in order to maximize total profits.

    B. each firm will make its best choice of action given the choice of action of the other firm.

    C. the firm that cheats on a collusive arrangement will benefit at the expense of the other firm.

38. Details of the CPI over several years are as follows.

Year	1	2	3
CPI	300	320	340

    It is *most likely* that:

    A. the inflation rate is constant.

    B. the cost of living is rising in real terms.

    C. the CPI is being overstated due to quality changes.

39. The macroeconomic school of thought which believes that the wage rate is sticky and that the economy will normally operate at full employment is *most likely* the:

    A. classical view.

    B. Keynesian view.

    C. monetarist view.

40. An efficiency wage *least likely* describes the wage rate that:

    A. is equal to the marginal revenue product.

    B. a firm pays to attractive more efficient workers.

    C. when paid by most firms gives rise to unemployment.

41. When the government implements a balanced budget, it is *most likely* that aggregate demand will:
    A. increase.
    B. decrease.
    C. stay constant.

42. With perfect price discrimination, the monopolist would *most likely* produce at the point where:
    A. marginal cost equals price.
    B. marginal cost equals average total cost.
    C. average total cost equals marginal revenue.

43. Which of the following least well describes a primary way by which a central bank can manipulate the money supply?
    A. Official reserve requirements.
    B. Open market operations.
    C. Taxation.

44. Where a government reduces taxes by borrowing from the public to make up the lost tax revenue, Ricardian equivalence suggests:
    A. That the reduction in current taxation will have no impact on spending due to individuals anticipating future taxes needed to repay the borrowing.
    B. That the combination of lower taxes plus higher borrowing will lead to inflation.
    C. That lower taxes will balance and higher borrowing will lead to additional spending which will stimulate the economy in the short term.

Questions 45 through 68 relate to Financial Reporting and Analysis

45. An accounting ratio which is *most likely* to be an activity ratio is:

    A. the acid test ratio.

    B. receivables turnover.

    C. return on investment.

46. When selecting an inventory valuation method, International Financial Reporting Standards *most likely* state that a company:

    A. must value all inventories using the same method.

    B. may value different inventories using different methods.

    C. must value all inventories of a similar nature and use using the same method.

47. Under US GAAP, development costs relating to internally developed software where the product is technically feasible and to be sold to customers:

    A. may be capitalized.

    B. must be capitalized.

    C. must not be capitalized.

48. A company acquires a long lived asset at a cost of $300,000 which will be depreciated to a residual value of zero over three years. The tax code states that long lived assets are depreciated on a straight line basis over two years to a zero residual value. If the tax rate is 25%, which of the following is *closest* to the deferred tax liability to be shown in the accounts at the end of the first year?

    A. $nil.

    B. $12,500.

    C. $37,500.

49. A company prepares its accounts under US GAAP. On December 31 2012, the company issued a bond with a face value of $10 million at a price equal to par. The company is making annual repayments of $2 million (including interest) over 6 years, commencing on December 31 2013. The company is using the effective interest rate method to account for the loan. The cash flow that will be recorded in the financing section for the year ended December 31 2013 is *closest to*:

    A. $547,000.

    B. $1,453,000.

    C. $2,000,000.

50. A company has net income of $5,000,000 for the year ended December 31 2013. Details of its share capital are as follows.

At December 31	2013	2012
Common stock ($1 par value)	$2,000,000	$1,500,000
5% preferred stock ($10 par value)	5,000,000	5,000,000

The company did an issue of 500,000 common shares at market price on April 1 2012. In addition the company has $1,000,000 of convertible debt in issue paying a coupon of 6% and with conversion terms of 50 shares per $100 of par value. The tax rate is 30%.

The diluted earnings per share for the year ended December 31 2013 is *closest to*:

A. $2.02.

B. $2.03.

C. $2.12.

---

51. Extracts from a company's financial statements prepared under US GAAP are as follows.

	$
Net income	2,890
Changes in working capital	(510)
Depreciation	400
Cash flow from operating activities	2,780
Cash flow from investing activities	(1,200)
Cash flow from financing activities	900
Increase in cash	2,480

The interest paid in the year was $500, dividends paid were $200 and the tax rate is 30%..

The free cash flow to equity is *closest to*:

A. $2,180.

B. $2,480.

C. $2,680.

---

52. The purpose of a company securitizing its receivables is *least likely* to:

A. record a gain on the sale.

B. create an unsustainable increase in operating cash flows.

C. obtain a tax benefit that can be added to stockholders equity.

---

53. Under International Financial Reporting Standards, it is *most likely* that dividends paid:

A. must be shown as a financing activity.

B. must be shown as an operating activity.

C. may be shown as a financing activity or an operating activity.

54. Which of the following is *not* one of the principal qualitative characteristics that make financial statements useful, according to the IFRS Framework for the Preparation and Presentation of Financial Statements?

   A. Relevance.

   B. Timeliness.

   C. Faithful representation.

55. Extracts from a company's financial statements are as follows.

   Year ended December 31

	2013 $m	2012 $m
Inventories	504	480
Receivables	832	794
Cash and cash equivalents	50	100
Payables	680	640
Short term debt	500	400
Sales	4,805	4,102
Cost of goods sold	3,200	2.500

   The payables turnover ratio for the year ended December 31 2013 is *closest to*:

   A. 4.71.

   B. 4.85.

   C. 4.89.

56. In times of rising prices, it is *most likely* that compared to a company using LIFO accounting for inventories, a company that is following US GAAP and is using FIFO accounting will have a:

   A. higher current ratio and lower cash flow from operating activities.

   B. lower current ratio and the same cash flow from operating activities.

   C. higher current ratio and the same cash flow from operating activities.

57. The impact of a company revaluing its long lived assets upwards is *most likely* to:

   A. reduce the debt to equity ratio and reduce net income.

   B. reduce the debt to equity ratio with no impact on net income.

   C. increase the debt to equity ratio with no impact on net income.

58. An example of a deductible temporary difference for deferred tax purposes is *most likely*:

   A. goodwill created on an acquisition.

   B. royalty income being taxable in the year it is received but recognized as accounting income in a later year.

   C. straight line depreciation of a long lived asset for accounting purposes and accelerated depreciation for tax purposes.

59. Compared to reporting a lease as a capital lease, a company reporting a lease as an operating lease will most likely report in the early years of the lease's life:

A. lower return on capital and lower operating cash flows.

B. higher return on capital and lower operating cash flows.

C. higher return on capital and higher operating cash flows.

60. Extracts from a company's financial statements are as follows.

December 31

	2013 $	2012 $
Cost of long lived assets	3,450	2,780
Accumulated depreciation	1,210	990

The depreciation expense for the year ended December 31 was $250, assets costing $860 were purchased in the year and there was a gain on the sale of long lived assets of $20.

The amount included in investing activities as cash received on the disposal of long lived assets is *closest to*:

A. $100.

B. $140.

C. $180.

61. Under International Financial Reporting Standards, goodwill arising on an acquisition should be:

A. capitalized.

B. capitalized and amortized.

C. not recognized as a separate asset.

62. Extracts from a company's financial statements are as follows.

Year ended December 31

	2013 $m
Current assets	1,200
Noncurrent assets	880
Total assets	2,080
Current liabilities	900
Long term debt	600
Total liabilities	1,500
Preferred stock	200
Common stock	100
Retained earnings	280
Stockholders equity and liabilities	2,080

Current assets includes cash of $120 and current liabilities includes short term debt of $300.

The debt to total capital ratio as at December 31 2013 is *closest to*:

A. 57%.

B. 61%.

C. 72%.

63. A company writes down the value of inventory below its original cost to its net realizable value. If the value of the inventory subsequently increases back to its original cost, the company:

A. must reverse the write down under International Financial Reporting Standards and US GAAP.

B. must not reverse the write down under International Financial Reporting Standards and US GAAP.

C. must reverse the write down under International Financial Reporting Standards but must not reverse the write down under US GAAP.

64. When a company repurchases its debt before its final maturity, any material difference between the repurchase price and the carrying amount of the debt on the balance sheet is *most likely* shown as:

A. other comprehensive income.

B. a separate gain or loss on the income statement.

C. part of operating income or expenses on the income statement.

65. Under International Financial Reporting Standards, minority interests in the balance sheet are shown as part of:

A. liabilities.

B. stockholders equity.

C. a separate category between liabilities and stockholders equity.

66. A company's net profit margin is 5% and its asset turnover is 2. The company has generated a return on equity of 15%. The financial leverage ratio of the company is closest to:

A. 0.7.

B. 1.5.

C. 6.0.

67. A company that follows International Financial Reporting Standards has a long lived asset with a balance sheet carrying value of $10,000,000 and a fair value of $8,100,000. The value in use for the asset is estimated to be $8,000,000. If the asset is sold, $300,000 of expenses would be incurred. The amount of the impairment loss that is recognized in the financial statements is *closest to*:

A. $1.9 million.

B. $2.0 million.

C. $2.2 million.

68. A company writes down some of its inventories below cost to their net realizable value in the year ended December 31 2012. In the year ended December 31 2013, the company reverses out the revaluation. It is *most likely* that, compared to if the write down had not occurred in 2012, the 2012 accounts will have a:

   A. higher gross profit.

   B. higher current ratio.

   C. higher debt to equity ratio.

Questions 69 through 78 relate to Corporate Finance

69. Details of a project are as follows.

Time	Cash flow
0	(100)
1	308
2	(210)
IRR	2% and 106%

The project should be selected for any cost of capital:

A. above 2%.

B. between 2% and 106%.

C. below 2% and above 106%.

70. Details of a company's cost of capital schedule are as follows.

Amount of new debt $m	After tax cost of debt %	Amount of new equity finance $m	Cost of equity %
0 - 2	4.0	0 – 9	8.0
2 – 8	4.7	9 – 20	9.5
>8	5.3	>20	10.9

The company raises finance so as to maintain a debt to total capital ratio of 50%. Which of the following is closest to the *second* breakpoint for the company?

A. $4 million.

B. $9 million.

C. $16 million.

71. When a company declares a dividend, the dividend is *most likely* paid to the registered owner of the shares on the:

A. date of record.

B. ex dividend date.

C. dividend declaration date.

72. A high float factor for a company *most likely* indicates that:

A. the company's checks from customers are taking a long time to clear.

B. the company has a high balance in its bank account relative to its daily transaction level.

C. the company is using a fast system such as electronic payments to make its payments to suppliers.

73. Which of the following is *least* likely to be used in evaluating accounts receivable management?

    A. Review of the aging schedule.

    B. Calculation of the number of days receivables.

    C. Growth in quarterly sales.

74. The primary role of a company's audit committee is *most likely* to:

    A. hire the company's auditors.

    B. ensure that financial information reported to shareholders is complete and accurate.

    C. ensure that the external auditors' priorities are aligned with the interests of shareholders.

75. A company has sales of $800,000, variable costs of $300,000, fixed costs of $100,000 and interest expense of $70,000. The tax rate is 30%. The degree of total leverage is *closest to*:

    A. 1.06.

    B. 1.46.

    C. 1.52.

76. A conventional project has a payback period. It is *most likely* that the project has a:

    A. positive net present value.

    B. discounted payback period.

    C. positive internal rate of return.

77. The pure play method of estimating beta for a stock is *most likely* based on:

    A. building up the beta through analysis of a company's operating risk and financial risk.

    B. the use of a comparable publicly traded stock's beta adjusted for differences in financial leverage.

    C. the regression of the stock's excess returns over the risk free rate against the market's excess returns over the risk free rate.

78. A company wishes to have the flexibility to repurchase its shares in the event of a slide in the stock price. The repurchase method that it will *most likely* find appropriate is:

    A. a Dutch auction.

    B. direct negotiation.

    C. open market purchases.

Questions 79 through 84 relate to Portfolio Management

79. A portfolio consists of many assets, each of which has the same standard deviation. The correlation coefficient for each pair of assets in the portfolio is 0.5. The variance of the portfolio will *most likely* tend towards:

A. zero.

B. 50% of the variance of each asset.

C. the covariance for each pair of assets.

80. Details of three investments are as follows.

Investment	Total risk	β
A	16%	0.8
B	20%	1.1
C	24%	1.5

The market has an expected return of 8% and a standard deviation of returns of 12%. The risk free rate is 2%.

The investment with the *highest* level of *unsystematic* risk is:

A. investment A.

B. investment B.

C. investment C.

81. Reginald Unsworth is an individual with $5 million to invest in a portfolio. He has investment objectives that reflect a moderate to high risk tolerance and return objective. He is financially sophisticated and wishes to maximize the Sharpe ratio of his portfolio. His son is planning to buy a house in the near future so he plans to give $500,000 to his son within the next year. Details of three possible asset allocations are as follows.

Asset class	Allocation A	Allocation B	Allocation C
Stocks	75%	70%	60%
Bonds	20%	20%	30%
Cash	5%	10%	10%
	100%	100%	100%
Expected return	10.0%	9.0%	8.0%
Standard deviation of returns	11.1	10.2	7.5

The risk free rate is 4%. The asset allocation that is *most likely* to be suitable for Jonathan is:

A. allocation A.

B. allocation B.

C. allocation C.

82. An investment policy statement for an individual should *most likely*:
    A. be rewritten each time the individual changes her portfolio manager.
    B. be used at the feedback stage to assess a manager's performance.
    C. specify the tactical asset allocation that will be adopted by the manager.

83. The money weighted return *most likely*:
    A. is different for different investors in the same mutual fund.
    B. can be used to compare different investment opportunities.
    C. measures the actual return on $1 invested over the period in question.

84. Details of three investments are as follows.

Investment	Expected return %	Standard deviation of returns %
A	5%	2%
B	10%	3%
C	15%	5%

A risk neutral investor would *most likely* select:

A. investment A.
B. investment B.
C. investment C.

Questions 85 through 96 relate to Equity

85. Classifying companies into industry groups by means of business cycle analysis *most likely*:

    A. relies on analysis of correlation of historical returns between companies.

    B. gives industry groupings that are similar in different geographical regions.

    C. should not be used to break companies down into two major groupings of cyclical and noncyclical.

86. It is *most likely* that:

    A. a closed end fund trades at net asset value.

    B. a closed end fund can be invested in by new investors after it is set up.

    C. investors in an open end fund can trade their units in the secondary market.

87. The index weighting system that will *most likely* require rebalancing on a regular basis is:

    A. price weighted.

    B. equal weighted.

    C. value weighted.

88. Compared to a global equity index that gives weightings to regions based on market capitalizations, a global equity index that gives weightings to regions based on GDP will have a weighting to emerging markets that is:

    A. lower.

    B. higher.

    C. approximately the same.

89. An analyst wishes to value a company's value to all its investors, based on a cash flow driver of value. The multiple that is *most likely* to be suitable for the investor is:

    A. Enterprise value to sales.

    B. Enterprise value to EBITDA.

    C. Price to (net income + depreciation).

90. An investor believes that it may be possible to earn a positive alpha by investing in low price to earnings stocks. The form(s) of the efficient market hypothesis that the investor appears to believe not to apply are the:

    A. weak form only.

    B. weak form and semi-strong form only.

    C. weak form, semi-strong form and strong form.

91. A global registered share *most likely*:

    A. is used as part of a BLDR program.

    B. is held in a GDR program traded in dollars.

    C. can trade in range of different currencies other than its home currency.

92. An investor wishes to sell a large block of securities in one transaction. This would *most likely* trade in a:

    A. brokered market.

    B. order driven market.

    C. quote driven market.

93. An equal weighted total return index consists of three stocks. Details of stock prices and dividends for each stock are as follows.

Stock	Number of shares in free float	Beginning of period price $	End of period price $	Dividends paid at the end of the period $
X	1,000,000	53.00	55.00	1.00
Y	3,000,000	42.00	39.00	1.00
Z	4,000,000	80.00	90.00	4.00

    If the opening value of the index is 1,000, the end of period value for the index is *closest to*:

    A. 1,061.

    B. 1,086.

    C. 1,106.

94. A chain of supermarkets would *most likely* be classified in the industry sector relating to:

    A. basic materials.

    B. consumer staples.

    C. consumer discretionary.

95. A company has a dividend payout ratio of 60%, an expected growth in earnings per share of 4% per year indefinitely and a beta of 1.2. The risk free rate is 3% and the market risk premium is 5%. The stock's forward P/E ratio is *closest to*:

    A. 8.0.

    B. 12.0.

    C. 12.5.

96. When investors keep track of the gains and losses for individual investments separately from each other, this is *most likely* referred to as:

    A. narrow framing.

    B. mental accounting.

    C. the disposition effect.

Questions 97 through 110 relate to Fixed Income

97. Which of the following is a key motivation for a company seeking debt finance to issue asset-backed securities rather than a corporate bond?

A. Asset-backed securities can have a better credit rating than the issuer.

B. Asset-backed securities need no credit enhancement.

C. Asset-backed securities always attract a AAA credit rating from rating agencies.

98. An investor buys an 8% annual coupon bond with three years to maturity. The bond has a yield to maturity of 9% and is currently priced at 97.36574 per 100 of par value. The bond's Macauley duration is *closest to*:

A. 2.44.

B. 2.52.

C. 2.78.

99. A bond currently has a price of 102.50 and a yield to maturity of 5%. If the yield is moved up or down by 75 basis points, the price moves to 96.35 or to 108.85. The approximate modified duration of the bond is *closest to*:

A. 6.1.

B. 8.1.

C. 8.3.

100. The bond which *least likely* has an embedded option for the issuer is a:

A. convertible bond.

B. mortgage pass through.

C. capped floating rate note.

101. A callable bond has an annual coupon of 5% and a yield to maturity of 4%. Compared to the bond's effective duration, the modified duration of the bond will *most likely* be:

A. lower.

B. higher.

C. the same.

102. A US corporate bond has a maturity of 10 years and is paying a semi annual coupon of 5%. A US Treasury bond with a 10 years maturity has a yield to maturity of 4%. The nominal spread for the corporate bond is 1.2% and the zero volatility spread is 1.0%. The price of $1,000 par value of the corporate bond is *closest to*:

A. $984.56.

B. $984.71.

C. $1,000.00.

103. A repo agreement could be considered *most similar* to a:
    A. certificate of deposit.
    B. syndicated loan.
    C. collateralized loan.

104. The bond whose price will *most likely* fall the most if interest rates increase is:
    A. a fixed rate bond.
    B. an inverse floater.
    C. a floating rate bond.

105. A bond's horizon yield can best be described as:
    A. the internal rate of return between the total return and the purchase price of the bond.
    B. the actual return achieved taking into account changes in reinvestment rate.
    C. an estimation of the reinvestment risk over the time period from purchase to maturity.

106. A bond has a price of 103, an effective duration of 5.2 and a convexity of 40. The new price of the bond if interest rates increase by 50 basis points is *closest to*:
    A. 100.22.
    B. 100.32.
    C. 100.43.

107. A muni bond that is backed by the income from the project that it was used to finance is *most likely* an example of:
    A. appropriation backed bond.
    B. general obligation bond.
    C. revenue bond.

108. Details of spot rates for the next 18 months are as follows.

Period	6 months	12 months	18 months
Spot rate	4%	6%	7%

A company is planning to issue a one year bond with a semi annual coupon of 5% in six months time. The expected yield on which the bond will be issued is *closest to*:
    A. 8.49%.
    B. 9.00%.
    C. 9.20%.

109. The security which is most likely to have the largest increase in price if interest rates fall and interest rate volatility falls is a:
    A. putable bond.
    B. fixed rate bond.
    C. floating rate note with a collar.

110. Eurocommercial paper is *most likely*:

    A. interest bearing.

    B. settled T + 0.

    C. non-negotiable.

Questions 111 through 116 relate to Derivatives

111. Which of the following is *most* likely to occur when a futures margin account falls below the maintenance margin level?

    A. Variation margin is added up to the maintenance margin level.

    B. Variation margin is added up to the initial margin level.

    C. Variation margin is added depending on the price change the following day.

---

112. An investor has a portfolio with a total value of $20 million and an asset allocation of 75% equities and 25% bonds. She wishes to change her allocation to 50% in each asset class and takes out an equity swap in order to achieve this. The swap is based on a rate of 4% fixed ($\frac{actual}{365}$) with quarterly settlement. In the most recent 90 days period, the return on the S & P was 2%. Which of the following is *closest to* the amount that the investor will pay or receive under the swap?

    A. Pay $50,685.

    B. Pay $50,000.

    C. Receive $24,658.

---

113. The purpose of an options market is *least likely* to be:

    A. price discovery.

    B. risk management.

    C. volatility discovery.

114. Details of the profit and loss profile of three positions at expiration are shown below.

Graph A

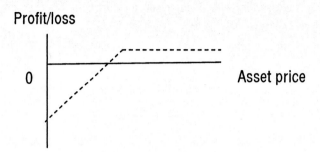

Graph B

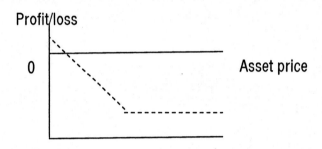

Graph C

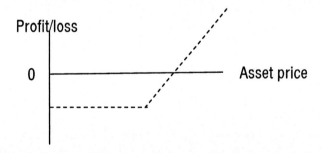

The graph which *most likely* represents a covered call position is:

A. graph A.

B. graph B.

C. graph C.

---

115. A put option with a strike of $132 and an expiration of three months has a value of 9.17. The risk free interest rate is 5% and the stock price is $140. The value of a call option with the same strike and expiration on the same stock is *closest to*:

A. 13.64.

B. 18.77.

C. 23.46.

116. A company plans to borrow $10 million in 92 days time for a 90 days period. The interest rate for the loan is LIBOR + 100 basis points. The company takes out a forward rate agreement (FRA) at a rate of 5%. In 92 days time, LIBOR is 7%. The amount that the company will pay or receive in 90 days time under the FRA is *closest to*:

    A. $49,000.

    B. $50,000.

    C. $74,000.

Questions 117 through 120 relate to Alternative Investments

117. Which of the following is *best* described as an equity investment in real estate open to the public market?

   A. Shares of a real estate investment trust.

   B. Holder of a mortgage-backed security.

   C. Construction lending.

118. Which of the following actions is *least* likely to be sufficient in assessing the risk-return profile of investing in alternative investments?

   A. Detailed review of historic standard deviation, returns and Sharpe ratios.

   B. Measurement of the Sortino ratio allowing for biases for non-normal distributions.

   C. Stress testing and scenario analysis.

119. For an investor in a commodity index it is *most likely* that the return component that is positive will be the:

   A. collateral yield.

   B. spot price return.

   C. convenience yield.

120. An analyst has stated that a difficulty when measuring performance for a venture capital fund is determining valuations of holdings, even at exit. However, this is compensated for by the advantage that meaningful benchmarks are available against which fund managers' performance can be measured. The analyst is *most likely*:

   A. correct in terms of the difficulty but incorrect in terms of the advantage.

   B. incorrect in terms of the difficulty but correct in terms of the advantage.

   C. incorrect in terms of the difficulty and incorrect in terms of the advantage.

The Chartered Financial Analyst® Program

Practice Examination 2
Afternoon Session Solutions

2014

ANSWERS

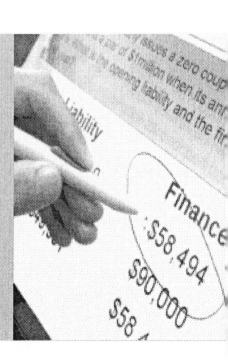

BPP
LEARNING MEDIA

Ethical and Professional Standards

1. **A** Standard IC – Misrepresentation. The standard states that knowingly committing misrepresentations is where the member or candidate either knows or should have known that the misrepresentation has occurred. Best practice is to obtain the original study for review, as this would have prevented the misrepresentation from occurring. The standard covers any untrue statement, omission of a fact or a statement that is otherwise false or misleading.

    LOS 1b,c and 2a,b,c

2. **A** Standard IIA – Material Nonpublic Information. The standard prohibits the use of material nonpublic information. The information is clearly material, involving a takeover, and is not public.

    LOS 1b,c and 2a,b,c

3. **A** Standard VIIB – Reference to CFA Institute, the CFA Designation, and the CFA Program. So long as a member continues to pay the reduced dues and comply with requirements for retired status, she has the right to use the CFA designation.

    LOS 1b,c and 2a,b,c

4. **C** Standard IIIA – Loyalty, Prudence and Care. The manager is obligated to seek best price and best execution and be assured by the client that the goods or services purchased from the directed brokerage will benefit the account beneficiaries. In addition, the manager should disclose that the client may not be getting best execution from the directed brokerage.

    LOS 1b,c and 2a,b,c

5. **A** Standard VIA – Disclosure of Conflicts. Members should disclose to their employer all matters that could reasonably be expected to impair their independence and objectivity. The friendship with Michael Jones represents a potential conflict of interest that should be disclosed to the endowment's officers.

    LOS 1b,c and 2a,b,c

6. **B** Standard IIA – Material Nonpublic Information. A prohibition on all types of proprietary activity is not appropriate e.g. for a firm that is a market maker in a security.

    LOS 1b,c and 2a,b,c

7. **B** Standard IIID – Performance Presentation. Firms are recommended to apply GIPS® Standards. Use of accounts from the top quartile is not representative and cannot be considered fair, accurate and complete. Brief presentations are permitted, but best practice is to include a reference to the fact that limited information has been provided.

    LOS 1b,c and 2a,b,c

8. **B** Standard VIB – Priority of Transactions. Alicia has breached her duty to her parents by treating them differently simply because of the family relationship. As fee paying clients, her parents are entitled to the same treatment as other clients. Alicia has no beneficial interest in the account.

    LOS 1b,c and 2a,b,c

9.   **B**   Standard IIB – Market Manipulation. Working a trade so as to achieve best execution does not constitute misleading other market participants through practices that distort prices or artificially inflate trade volumes.

LOS 1b,c and 2a,b,c

10. **B**   Standard VA – Diligence and Reasonable Basis. Where a member does not agree with the group conclusion, but believes that the consensus opinion has a reasonable and adequate basis and is independent and objective (Jane Way is explicitly stated as having confidence in the process), there is no need to dissociate from the report even if it does not reflect the member's opinion.

LOS 1b,c and 2a,b,c

11. **B**   Standard VIB – Priority of Transactions. There should be limited participation in equity IPOs.

LOS 1b,c and 2a,b,c

12. **C**   Standard ID – Misconduct. The standard requires that members and candidates must not engage in any professional conduct involving dishonesty etc. or commit any act that reflects adversely on their professional reputation, integrity or competence.

LOS 1b,c and 2a,b,c

13. **C**   Standard IIIE – Preservation of Confidentiality. The standard is not intended to prevent members from cooperating with the PCP. When permissible under applicable laws, members should consider the PCP as an extension of themselves and are encouraged to cooperate with investigations into the conduct of others.

LOS 1b,c and 2a,b,c

14. **A**   Standard IVA – Loyalty. An employee buyout ultimately depends on the approval of the employer and is therefore consistent with the standard. Work done for the employer cannot be used personally without permission. Where an employee undertakes extensive work outside of his employment which could compromise his ability to fulfill his employment duties, he should discuss this with the employer.

LOS 1b,c and 2a,b,c

15. **C**   Standard VB – Communications with Clients and Prospective Clients. Bombady Jones has not distinguished between facts and opinions by stating that earnings per share will increase. This represents his view rather than a fact.

LOS 1b,c and 2a,b,c

16. **A**   Standard IVB – Additional Compensation Arrangements. Frederick East should disclose full details of this additional compensation arrangement with his employer and obtain written consent from all parties involved.

LOS 1b,c and 2a,b,c

17. **C**   The verifier must be an independent third party, which would include but is not limited to the firm's auditor.

LOS 3c

18. **C**   Local laws must be followed but this must be disclosed to be GIPS compliant, where the laws conflict with GIPS.

LOS 4c

Quantitative Methods

19. **C**   The quarterly interest rate is $\dfrac{25\%}{4} = 6.25\%$

The effective annual rate is $1.0625^4 - 1 = 27.44\%$

LOS 5c

20. **A**   The question specifies real consumption, so the nominal risk free rate is irrelevant. The real risk free rate is the single-period interest rate for a completely risk free security and represents the time preference for current versus future real consumption.

LOS 5b

21. **C**   Consider two projects with a cost of capital of 20%.

Time	Project X	Project Y
0	(10,000)	(20,000)
1	11,000	23,000
NPV at 20%	(833)	(833)
IRR	10%	15%

If both projects had the same *positive* NPV, project X would have the higher IRR.

LOS 6b

22. **A**   A normal distribution has the same mean, median and mode. If one very high value is added to this distribution, the mode will not be affected. The median will move fractionally to the right, so it will be higher than the mode. The mean will be affected most by the extremely high value and will be the highest of the three.

LOS 7j

23. **A**   According to Chebyshev's inequality: $1 - \dfrac{1}{2^2} = 0.75$

LOS 7h

24. **B**   The number of different ways in which the bonds can be put into the categories is given by the general formula for labeling problems.

$$\frac{6!}{3!2!1!} = 60$$

There is a 1 in 60 chance that three particular bonds will be AAA rated, two particular bonds will be AA rated and one particular bond will be A rated. i.e. a probability of 0.017.

LOS 8o

25. **A** $1000(1 + r) \times 0.95 + 300 \times 0.05 = 1000 \times 1.04$

$r = 0.0789$ or 7.89%. This gives a default premium over the 4% risk free rate of 3.89%.

LOS 8l

26. **C** Calculating the safety first ratio for each investment:

    Investment A: $\dfrac{5-0.5}{4.2} = 1.071$

    Investment B: $\dfrac{7.5-0.5}{6.5} = 1.076$

    Investment C: $\dfrac{9.5-0.5}{7.8} = 1.15$

    Investment C has the highest value, meaning that a return of less than 0.5% has the lowest probability of arising for investment C compared to the other two investments.

    LOS 9n

27. **B** The portfolio needs to increase in value by $80,000 to avoid the opening capital level being breached after the $80,000 is withdrawn. This is a return of 4%. The z score for 4% is $\dfrac{9-4}{8} = 0.625$. The related probability for this z score is between 0.732 and 0.736.

    LOS 9l

28. **A** Since the population is normally distributed and its standard deviation is known, the z statistic of 1.96 for a 95% interval estimate can be used.

    Interval estimate $= 0.05 \pm 1.96 \times \dfrac{2.0}{\sqrt{20}} = 0.05 \pm 0.877$

    i.e. -0.827% to 0.927%

    If we had been given the standard deviation of the sample (which is much more likely in practice and probably in questions too), we would have used the t statistic with 19 degrees of freedom of 2.093 instead of 1.96.

    LOS 10j

29. **B** There is no survivorship bias, since the data is based on the companies in the index in each year in question. There is no look ahead bias since the earnings per share forecasts are available on the same date as the stock price. A 12 year period is somewhat short for testing for an anomaly.

    LOS 10k

30. **B** The χ^2 test is used for a test concerning a single variance and the t test is used to test means.

    LOS 11i

31. **A** The neckline is the low point after the left shoulder and before the right shoulder. High buying enthusiasm implies high volumes, and volumes are lower for the right shoulder.

    LOS 12d

32. **C** Both triangle and rectangle patterns are forms of continuation patterns that predict the resumption of a market trend.

    LOS 12d

Economics

33. **B** The objective of the index is to identify underlying inflation and highly volatile items (e.g. fuel) will potentially distort the underlying pattern.

    LOS 18f

34. **C** The industry supply curve is the sum of the curves for the individual firms. It becomes flat at the shutdown price, where price equals variable cost. Below this price, some firms shutdown and industry supply becomes perfectly elastic.

    LOS 13c

35. **A** GBP/MXN = $[(MXN/USD) \times (USD/GBP)]^{-1}$

    $$= (13.3254 \times 1.4231)^{-1}$$

    $$= 0.0527$$

    LOS 21e

36. **C** An increase in real GDP increases wealth, so people hold more money as they spend more. An increase in financial innovation generally reduces demand for money as other means of spending etc. become available.

    LOS 19c

37. **B** With the Nash equilibrium, each firm makes its best choice given what the other does. With the possibility of cheating on a collusive agreement, both firms have to cheat to avoid being exploited by the other firm.

    LOS 16f

38. **C** The percentage increase in the CPI is falling, so the inflation rate is falling. It is not possible to draw conclusions about changes in the real cost of living from inflation data in isolation. Improvements in quality lead to higher prices, but this increase in price is not due to inflation, leading to the CPI being upwardly biased.

    LOS 18f

39. **C** Both the Keynesian view and monetarist view are that the wage rate is sticky. The classical view and the monetarist view both believe that the economy is self regulating and will normally operate at full employment.

    LOS 18c

40. **A** The efficiency wage is a wage above the competitive equilibrium paid by a firm to attract the best workers. If many firms offer an efficiency wage, this will increase supply of labor, causing unemployment. Setting marginal revenue product equal to the wage rate (not just an efficiency wage) will maximize profits.

    LOS 15j

41. **A** In a balanced budget, government spending = government income through taxes. Each $1 of government spending increases aggregate demand more than each $1 of taxes reduces aggregate demand, giving an overall increase in aggregate demand.

 LOS 19k

42. **A** With perfect price discrimination, price = marginal revenue, so the monopoly firm will produce where marginal cost = marginal revenue = price.

 LOS 16a

43. **C** Central banks have three primary ways of manipulating the money supply. Open market operations; its official policy rate and manipulation of official reserve requirements.

 LOS 19f,g

44. **A** Ricardian equivalence is named after David Ricardo. The reality of whether spending increases will depend upon the correct anticipation of future taxation needed to repay the borrowing.

 LOS 19j

Financial Reporting and Analysis

45. **B** Activity ratios measure the use of a balance sheet item to generate sales.

LOS 28b

46. **C** Inventories of a similar nature and use must be valued using the same method. Inventories that are different in nature and use may be valued using different methods from each other.

LOS 29b

47. **B** IFRS permit development costs such as software to be capitalized so long as they satisfy certain criteria. Such software development costs must be capitalized under US GAAP but other development costs must not be capitalized.

LOS 30b

48. **B** A schedule of temporary differences:

	Balance sheet carrying amount	Tax base	Temporary difference
Long lived asset	200,000	150,000	50,000

Deferred tax liability $= 50,000 \times 0.25 = \$12,500$

LOS 31d

49. **B** The effective interest rate is the IRR of the cash flows, which is 5.47%

Time	Flow	PV at 5.47%
0	(10,000,000)	(10,000,000)
1-6	2,000,000	10,000,000
		-

Of the $2,000,000 repaid in year 1, 5.47% × 10,000,000 (= $547,000) is interest and the rest is capital (= $1,453,000). The capital is shown as a financing flow.

LOS 32b

50. **A** Weighted average of shares $= 1,500,000 + \dfrac{9}{12} \times 500,000 = 1,875,000$

Shares issued on conversion of debt $= \dfrac{1,000,000}{100} \times 50 = 500,000$

Diluted earnings per share $= \dfrac{5,000,000 - 5\% \times 5,000,000 + 70\% \times 6\% \times 1,000,000}{1,875,000 + 500,000} = 2.018$

LOS 25g

51. **C**

	$
Cash flow from operating activities	2,780
Investing activities	(1,200)
Financing activities (excluding dividend)	1,100
Free cash flow to equity	2,680

LOS 27i

52. **C** When receivables are sold, it creates a one-off benefit to operating cash flows. The sale proceeds may be higher than the book value of the receivables, giving a gain.

LOS 34b

53. **C** There is the option of showing dividends paid as operating or financial activities. US GAAP requires classification as a financing activity.

LOS 27c

54. **B** Timeliness is a desirable feature of financial information, but is not one of the principal qualitative characteristics.

LOS 24d

55. **C** Purchases = Cost of sales + ending inventories − closing inventories = 3,200 + 504 − 480 = 3,224.

Average payables = 0.5(680 + 640) = 660

Payables turnover $= \dfrac{3,224}{660} = 4.885$

LOS 28e

56. **A** In times of rising prices, FIFO gives a higher inventory value since it includes the latest items purchased in inventories. This gives it a higher current ratio. However, it will be paying higher taxes due to its higher profits, meaning that it will have lower cash flow from operating activities.

LOS 29h

57. **A** Total assets and stockholders equity will increase, reducing the debt to equity ratio. The higher carrying value of the long lived asset will give a higher depreciation expense, reducing net income.

LOS 30g

58. **B** Deductible temporary differences result in a deferred tax asset, whereas taxable temporary differences result in a deferred tax liability. When income is taxed now but only recognized in future periods for accounts purposes, we need to reduce the income statement tax charge in this year and increase the income statement tax charge in the later year, to match the accounting recognition of the income and its related tax charge.

LOS 31f

59. **B** Operating cash flows are lower for an operating lease because the whole lease rental is charged as an operating cost, whereas the rental is split into a depreciation element and interest element for a capital lease. The operating lease means that no assets are recognized on balance sheet whereas the capital lease will recognize the leased asset. This means that the operating lease will report higher return on capital in the earlier years.

LOS 32h

60. **C** Cost of assets sold:

	$
Closing cost	3,450
Opening cost	(2,780)
Additions	(860)
Cost of assets sold	(190)

Accumulated depreciation of assets sold:

	$
Closing depreciation	1,210
Opening depreciation	(990)
Depreciation expense	(250)
Assets sold	(30)

Carrying value of assets sold = 190 − 30 = $160

Since they were sold for a gain of $20, the sale proceeds must be $180.

LOS 27e

61. **A** Goodwill is viewed as having an indefinite life, so it is not amortized but is subject to annual impairment reviews.

LOS 26e

62. **B** $$\frac{600+300}{600+300+200+100+280} = 60.8\%$$

LOS 28d

63. **C** US GAAP treats the write down as establishing a new base cost for the inventory, so it cannot be revalued above this. IFRS require reversal back to original cost if the value subsequently rises to this level.

LOS 29f

64. **B** The gain or loss will be recorded in the income statement. If material, it is disclosed separately.

LOS 32c

65.　B　IFRS require that minority interest is shown as part of stockholders equity. US GAAP require that it is shown as a separate category.

LOS 26g

66.　B　ROE = Net margin × asset turnover × financial leverage

15% = 5% × 2 × financial leverage

Financial leverage = 1.5

LOS 28d

67.　B　The impairment loss is measured as the excess of the carrying amount of the asset over its recoverable amount. The recoverable amount is the higher of value in use and fair value – costs to sell. Recoverable amount is the higher of $8 million and 8.1 – 0.3 = $7.8 million. The impairment loss is therefore 10 – 8 = $2 million.

LOS 30h

68.　C　The write down will be charged as part of cost of goods sold, increasing costs and reducing profit. The inventory will be lower, reducing the current ratio. The lower profit will give lower stockholders equity, increasing the debt to equity ratio.

LOS 29h

Corporate Finance

69.   **B**   The project has a negative NPV at 0%, indicating that it starts with a negative NPV, which first becomes positive (at 2%) and then turns negative again (at 106%).

LOS 36c

70.   **C**   The first breakpoint occurs when $2 million of debt is raised, meaning $4m of total capital is raised. The second breakpoint is when $8 million of debt is raised, which gives total capital raised of $16 million. The third breakpoint is when $9 million of equity is raised, which gives a breakpoint of $18 million.

LOS 37k

71.   **A**   The company pays the dividend to whoever is in the shareholders' register on this date, regardless of who is the beneficial owner of the shares.

LOS 39b

72.   **A**   The float factor measures how long it takes checks from customers to clear after being deposited.

LOS 40f

73.   **C**   Growth in quarterly sales can be achieved without good credit control/accounts receivable procedures.

LOS 40f

74.   **B**   Hiring the auditors and ensuring that their priorities are aligned with shareholder interests are also roles of the audit committee, to the end of ensuring that financial information reported is accurate, complete etc.

LOS 41e

75.   **C**   Given the information in the question, we can prepare the income statement and then increase sales by an arbitrary number (say +100%) and see what the increase in EBT is (or net income, since the 30% tax rate does not have any effect on leverage).

	Original $		Revised $
Sales	800,000	+100%	1,600,000
Variable costs	300,000	+100%	600,000
Profit before fixed costs	500,000		1,000,000
Fixed costs	100,000		100,000
EBIT	400,000		900,000
Interest	70,000		70,000
EBT	330,000		830,000

EBT increases by 152%. Since sales increased by 100%, the DTL is 1.52.

Alternatively:

$$DOL = \frac{\text{Profit before fixed costs}}{\text{EBIT}} = \frac{500,000}{400,000} = 1.25$$

$$DFL = \frac{\text{EBIT}}{\text{EBT}} = \frac{400,000}{330,000} = 1.212$$

$$DTL = 1.25 \times 1.212 = 1.52$$

LOS 38b

76.   **C**   Since the project has a payback period, its undiscounted cash inflows must at least equal its initial cost. This indicates that the IRR is most likely to be positive (or zero if the cash inflows = initial outflow). However, the discounted cash flows will not necessarily be equal to or more than the initial cash outflow.

LOS 36d

77.   **B**   The pure play method is used to estimate the beta of a project or stock that is not publicly traded, so the beta of a comparable traded stock is used as the starting point.

LOS 37h

78.   **C**   Open market purchases give the most flexibility.

LOS 39c

Portfolio Management

79. **C** Where each asset has the same standard deviation and each pair of assets has the same correlation coefficient, the variance of the portfolio of N assets is given by $\sigma_p^2 = \dfrac{\sigma^2}{N} + \dfrac{N-1}{N}\rho\sigma^2$. Where N is very large, $\dfrac{\sigma^2}{N}$ becomes very small and $\dfrac{N-1}{N}\rho\sigma^2$ is virtually equal to $\rho\sigma^2$, which is the covariance between each pair of securities.

    LOS 43e

80. **C** We need to calculate the systematic risk of each investment, using the formula $\beta\sigma_m$ and then calculate the unsystematic risk, using the formula $\sigma_i^2 = \sigma_s^2 + \sigma_u^2$.

Investment	Systematic risk	Unsystematic risk
A	$0.8 \times 12 = 9.6\%$	$\sqrt{16^2 - 9.6^2} = 12.8\%$
B	$1.1 \times 12 = 13.2\%$	$\sqrt{20^2 - 13.2^2} = 15.0\%$
C	$1.5 \times 12 = 18.0\%$	$\sqrt{24^2 - 18^2} = 15.9\%$

    LOS 44b,e

81. **C** Asset allocation A has insufficient liquidity ($500,000 or 10% of the portfolio will be needed in cash in the next year). Allocations B and C both fit this criterion.

    The other criterion is the Sharpe ratio.

    Asset allocation A: $\dfrac{10-4}{11.1} = 0.54$

    Asset allocation B: $\dfrac{9-4}{10.2} = 0.49$

    Asset allocation C: $\dfrac{8-4}{7.5} = 0.53$

    Asset allocation C has a higher Sharpe ratio than allocation B.

    LOS 45g

82. **B** The IPS relates to the client not the manager, so a good IPS does not need to be rewritten just because the manager changes. The IPS may specify a medium to long term strategic asset allocation, but is unlikely to specify the tactical asset allocation (if there is to be active TAA), since this will change in response to market conditions. At most it will specify acceptable ranges around the strategic asset allocation. The manager's performance must be assessed by reference to the clients objectives and constraints and the strategic benchmark.

    LOS 45b

83.   **A**   The money weighted return will be different for different investors because they invested money at different points in time. It cannot be used to compare investment opportunities very easily because of differences in scale and timing of cash flows. The time weighted return measures the return of $1 invested over the whole period.

            LOS 43a

84.   **C**   A risk neutral investor is indifferent to risk, so she will select the investment with the highest return.

            LOS 43d

Equity

85. **B**   Although the business cycle might be at different stages in different geographical regions, this is not to say that different companies will be viewed as cyclical or noncyclical. The use of correlations of historical returns is a statistical technique, not a business cycle approach.

LOS 50b

86. **B**   Closed end funds are traded in the secondary market (typically at a discount to asset value) so new investors can buy stock/units in the secondary market. Investors trade units in an open end fund with the fund itself.

LOS 48b

87. **B**   As the market capitalizations of companies change, the equal weighted index will always need rebalancing back to equal weights. The value weighted (market capitalization weighted) index will automatically have the correct proportions. The price weighted approach involves holding one share in each stock, so it will not need rebalancing.

LOS 47d

88. **B**   Emerging markets contribute a far higher amount to world GDP than they do to world equity market capitalization.

LOS 47c

89. **B**   Since the analyst is interested in all investors, we need enterprise value rather than equity price. Since the analyst wants a cash flow based approach, we use the better proxy for cash flow = EBITDA (earnings before interest, tax, depreciation and amortization).

LOS 51i

90. **B**   The price to earnings ratio is publicly available information.

LOS 48d

91. **C**   A global registered share is registered in different stock markets and trades in the currency of that stock market.

LOS 49e

92. **A**   A large block of securities would be harder to trade in a quote driven or order driven market due to its size. The broker will find a buyer who is willing to take the whole position.

LOS 46j

93. **A** The return on an equal weighted index is the mean of its constituent's returns, since each stock is equally weighted in the index.

Stock X: $\dfrac{55+1}{53} - 1 = 5.66\%$

Stock Y: $\dfrac{39+1}{42} - 1 = -4.76\%$

Stock Z: $\dfrac{90+4}{80} - 1 = 17.50\%$

Mean return = $\dfrac{5.66 - 4.76 + 17.50}{3} = 6.13\%$

$1,000 \times 1.0613 = 1,061$

LOS 47e

94. **B** Supermarkets sell staple goods for consumers.

LOS 50b

95. **B** Cost of capital = $3 + 1.2 \times 5 = 9\%$

$P/E = \dfrac{0.6}{0.09 - 0.04} = 12.0$

LOS 51h

96. **B** Separate mental accounts are maintained for each investment.

LOS 48g

Fixed Income

97. **A** Asset-backed securities do require credit enhancement and do not necessarily attract a AAA rating – it depends on the level of credit enhancement.

   LOS 52b

98. **C** The bond's Macauley duration is a weighted average of the times to the receipt of cash flows. The weights are the shares of the full price corresponding to each coupon and principle payment.

Period	Cash flow	Present value	Weight	Period x Weight
1	8	7.339449	0.0753006	0.0753006
2	8	6.733439	0.0690831	0.138166
3	108	83.395815	0.855616	2.566848
		97.468703		2.7803146

   LOS 55b

99. **B** $$\frac{108.85 - 96.35}{2 \times 102.50 \times 0.0075} = 8.13$$

   LOS 55b

100. **A** A convertible bond is converted into stock at the option of the investor, not the borrower.

   LOS 52f

101. **B** The bond is priced above par, suggesting that it is relatively close to its call price. Effective duration allows for the risk of call so will give a lower percentage increase in price for the bond than its modified duration, which assumes the cash flows are not affected by changes in interest rates. A lower increase in price means a lower duration for effective duration compared to modified duration.

   LOS 55b,c

102. **A** The bond will have a semi annual coupon of $25. The yield to maturity will be 5.2% (4% + nominal spread since we are using the yield to maturity, not spot rates) i.e. 2.6%.

Time	Flows	PV at 2.6%
1 – 20	25	386.07
20	1,000	598.49
Value		984.56

   LOS 54i

103. **C** A repo is effectively a collateralized loan, with the gilt providing the collateral for the borrowing.

LOS 53h

104. **B** When interest rates rise, the coupon on an inverse floater will fall, reducing the bond's value.

LOS 52a

105. **A** Horizon yield is an annualized holding period return calculated as the difference between the purchase price and the total return.

LOS 55j

106. **C** Price change due to duration = $5.2 \times 0.005 \times 100 = -2.6\%$

Price change due to convexity = $40 \times 0..5^2 \times 100 = 0.1\%$

Overall price change = $-2.6 + 0.1 = -2.5\%$

New price = $103(1 - 0.025) = 100.43$

LOS 55b, k

107. **C** Revenue bonds are backed by the revenue from the project that the bond was used to finance, such as a toll or bridge.

LOS 56j

108. **A** The forward rates for the second six months and the third six months area calculated as follows.

Second six months: $1.02(1+r) = 1.03^2$; r = 4% for six months.

Third six months: $1.03^2(1+r) = 1.035^3$; r = 4.5% for six months.

Value of the bond on issue:

$$\frac{2.5}{1.04} + \frac{102.5}{1.04 \times 1.045} = 96.717$$

The IRR of the bond's flows is 4.247%

Time	Flows	PV at 4.247%
0	(96.72)	(96.72)
1	2.5	2.40
8	102.5	94.32
Value		-

This is quoted as $4.247 \times 2 = 8.49\%$

LOS 55c

109. **B**   The decline in interest rate volatility will reduce the value of the put option in the putable bond, restricting its price rise compared to the option free fixed rate bond. The FRN has a floor which will mean that it becomes a fixed rate note when the floor is reached, but not before.

LOS 52f

110. **A**   Eurocommercial paper is interest bearing, as opposed to US commercial paper that is issued at a discount.

LOS 52a

Derivatives

111. **B**   A locked limit is when the price of transaction is outside the daily price limits, so the transaction cannot take place.

   LOS 59d

112. **A**   The existing allocation is $15 million equity and $5 million debt. The target allocation is $10 million equity and $10 million debt. The swap will need to have a notional principal of $5 million where the investor is paying the equity return and receiving the bond return.

   Amount receivable/(payable): $5,000,000 \times \left(4\% \times \dfrac{90}{365} - 2\% \right) = (50,685)$

   LOS 61b

113. **A**   Options markets do not reveal information about the underlying price of an asset, but information about expected volatility for the asset's price.

   LOS 57d

114. **A**   A covered call gives the same profile as a short put. The investor owns the asset, which makes losses as the asset price falls and profits as the asset price rises. The investor also writes an out of the money call on the asset, which makes a constant profit (equal to the premium) is the asset price falls and an increasing loss if the asset price rises. Combining the asset and the short call to give a covered call gives increasing losses (reduced by the premium received) as the asset price falls and a constant profit (equal to the increasing profit on the asset less the increasing loss on the call option) as the asset price rises.

   LOS 62a,b

115. **B**   Using put call parity:

   $$c = 9.17 + 140 - \dfrac{132}{1.05^{0.25}} = 18.77$$

   LOS 60m

116. **A**   The company will buy the FRA with a notional principal of $10 million and receive compensation since LIBOR is above the FRA rate. The discounted value of the compensation in 90 days time is:

   $$10,000,000 \times \dfrac{1 + (7\% - 5\%) \times \dfrac{90}{360}}{1 + 7\% \times \dfrac{90}{360}} = \$49,140$$

   LOS 58g

Alternative Investments

117. **A**   Mortgage-backed security is a debt type investment, and construction lending is a debt instrument for the private market.

   LOS 63d

118. **A**   Alternative investments are illiquid and standard deviations may not be reliable because they are based on estimated values rather than transacted values. Better to consider downside risk.

   LOS 63g

119. **A**   The collateral return is the return on the cash used as margin to take the long futures exposure. It is the return on T bills or other more actively managed short term cash investments.

   LOS 63d

120. **C**   The valuation of an investment at exit is objectively determined by the sale price of the investment. It is only prior to exit that there is a valuation problem. Meaningful benchmarks are not readily available for assessing venture capital fund performance.

   LOS 63e

Practice Examination 3
Morning Session

2014

The Morning Session of Practice Examination 3 consists of 120 multiple choice questions which must be completed in three hours. The topic areas covered are:

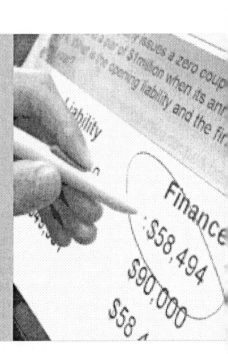

BPP
LEARNING MEDIA

Questions 1 through 18 relate to Ethical and Professional Standards

1. A recommended compliance procedure in Standard VIB – Priority of Transactions is *most likely* to be a:
   A. prohibition on participation in equity initial public offerings (IPOs) and private placements by employees.
   B. limitations on participation in equity initial public offerings (IPOs) and a prohibition on participation in private placements by employees.
   C. limitations on participation in equity initial public offerings (IPOs) and restrictions on participation in private placements by employees.

2. Jack Jones CFA offers equity marketing services to public companies and companies that wish to have their securities publicly traded. He is approached by SilverService Inc. which wishes the investing public to recognize more fully the underlying value of its stock. Jack Jones disseminates e mails and creates an internet site that describes itself as an independent provider of analysis on quoted companies. He uses the e mails and internet site to provide analysis on several companies, including SilverService Inc., releasing a number of speculative statements about SilverService's prospects and recommending the company for investment. This increases public awareness of SilverService Inc. and its stock price increases substantially.

   Jones has *most likely* violated:
   A. Standard IIB – Market Manipulation only.
   B. Standard VA – Diligence and Reasonable Basis only.
   C. Standard IIB – Market Manipulation and Standard VA – Diligence and Reasonable Basis.

3. Monica Jersey CFA is a portfolio manager with Maryland Investment Management. One of her clients is Joseph Murray. Joseph Murray has a large salary but a small asset base and wishes his portfolio to generate a steady rate of return with low volatility in order to meet his children's educational expenses. Murray has noted that low dividend high growth small cap stocks are expected to perform well in the foreseeable future by a large number of analysts and has asked Jersey to include such stocks as a significant proportion of the overall portfolio.

   In order to comply with CFA Institute's Standards of Practice, Jersey should *least likely*:
   A. implement the client's instructions.
   B. refrain from implementing the client's instructions.
   C. seek an affirmative statement from the client that suitability is not a consideration.

4. Marcus Garvey CFA works for an investment bank and is advising a client on its public issue of securities. Garvey has reason to believe that the financial information being prepared by the client is incomplete and inaccurate in certain respects. He discusses this with the investment bank's legal adviser who points out that Garvey is not certain that the information is incomplete and inaccurate and it would be difficult for anyone to prove that Garvey was involved in the dissemination of such information even it were the case. In order to comply with CFA Institute's Standards of Professional Conduct, Garvey should *most likely*:

    A. take no further action.

    B. report the situation to his supervisor.

    C. notify the local regulator of his belief concerning the financial information.

5. A composite has been existence for 13 years and the firm has been claiming compliance with GIPS standards since the composite was created. The minimum number of years of investment performance that must now be presented for a GIPS compliant presentation is:

    A. 5 years.

    B. 10 years.

    C. 13 years.

6. Irmina Ishan CFA is an equity analyst who has just completed writing an investment report on a pharmaceutical company. She notes in the report that a key risk for the company is the fact that many of its products are approaching the end of their patent period. She recommends that the company as a sell, stating that the fact that its cash flow will fall in future years as a result of competitive pressures from generic products means that it will be unable to maintain its current level of dividends without increasing debt levels. Ishan arranges for the report to be sent to all of her firm's clients by e mail. As is standard practice in the firm, the report is first sent to larger clients and then to smaller clients.

    Ishan has *most likely* violated:

    A. Standard IIIB – Fair Dealing and Standard VB – Communication with Clients and Prospective Clients.

    B. Standard IIIB – Fair Dealing but not Standard VB – Communication with Clients and Prospective Clients.

    C. Standard VB – Communication with Clients and Prospective Clients but not Standard IIIB – Fair Dealing.

7. Rodney Smith CFA has read a report in a highly reputable newspaper on a study produced by an investment house. The newspaper report summarizes the main findings of the study. Smith tries to obtain the study directly from the investment house but is unable to do so. He uses the newspaper report in his own research work which is then published. In order to follow best practice under CFA Institute's Standards of Practice, Smith should *most likely* cite the:

    A. newspaper report only.

    B. study produced by the investment house only.

    C. newspaper report and the study produced by the investment house.

8. George Buchanan CFA works for Opoco Investment Management. Opoco Investment Management has a policy that when employees resign, they are put on 'gardening leave', such that they remain in the employment of the company until their notice period is served but they are required not to attend the office. George Buchanan is planning to resign and to use his knowledge of Opoco Investment Management's clients' names in order to identify their contact details through using internet sources, trade directories and the like.

    Buchanan is *most likely*:

    A. not permitted to do this at any time.

    B. permitted to do this after he has served his notice period.

    C. permitted to do this after he has handed in his resignation.

9. Ruth Jacobs CFA is the compliance officer for Veritable Investment Management. She has prepared a compliance procedure regarding voting of proxies which states the following.

    "The firm has a duty to vote proxies in an informed and responsible manner. Proxies have economic value to the firm's clients. As a result, the firm votes all important proxies but will not vote routine proxies where a cost benefit analysis suggests that voting is not necessary."

    The compliance statement prepared by Jacobs *most likely*:

    A. does not violate CFA Institute's Standards of Professional Conduct.

    B. violates CFA Institute's Standards of Professional Conduct, which state that all proxies should be voted.

    C. violates CFA Institute's Standards of Professional Conduct, which state that each proxy should be voted only after full consultation with the client on the issue being decided.

10. Michael Lucey is a CFA candidate who has just sat level I of the CFA examination program. He is an active user of internet chat forums dedicated to discussing the CFA program and the day after the exam discusses some particularly challenging questions on a forum with other candidates, where they compare their answers to these questions.

    Philip Weeks CFA has been a marker for the CFA level III exam in the past. He is now offering training courses for the CFA examinations. When potential students contact him, he explains that as a marker in the past, he has a good understanding of the way in which the questions are written and as a result can offer an improved course through imparting this understanding to his students.

    It is *most likely* that:

    A. Lucey and Weeks have both violated CFA Institute's Standards of Practice.

    B. Lucey has violated CFA Institute's Standards of Practice but Weeks has not violated the Standards.

    C. Weeks has violated CFA Institute's Standards of Practice but Lucey has not violated the Standards.

11. When a CFA charterholder supervises a large number of employees, Standard IVC – Responsibilities of Supervisors *most likely* states that the supervisor:

    A. may delegate supervisory duties and responsibilities.

    B. may not delegate supervisory duties and responsibilities.

    C. may delegate supervisory duties but not delegate supervisory responsibilities.

12. Laura Marks CFA works very hard as an investment adviser and likes to unwind in the evening with some friends. She regularly gets intoxicated in these evening drinking sessions. Stephen Flaherty CFA is an investment adviser who regularly has to work late in the office. To compensate himself for this, he charges his evening meal in a restaurant as expenses. It is *most likely* that CFA Institute Standards of Professional Conduct ID – Misconduct has been violated by:

A. Marks but not by Flaherty.

B. Flaherty but not by Marks.

C. neither Marks nor Flaherty.

13. A goal of the GIPS Executive Committee is *most likely* to:

A. promote the interests of investment firms.

B. promote government regulation on a global basis.

C. encourage global competition among investment firms.

14. Francis Xavier CFA is an employee at NAC Investment Management, a division of NAC Banking Corporation. He is somewhat dissatisfied with the firm as he feels that NAC Banking Corporation has not honored commitments that it made to the employees at NAC Investment Management. Xavier is considering two courses of action. He is considering setting up his own investment advisory boutique and to this end approaches the relevant regulatory authority to register this new firm. However, he would prefer to continue working at NAC Investment Advice as an independent entity. To this end, he approaches other employees with a view to leading an employee buyout of the firm from its owner.

Xavier has *most likely* violated Standard IVA – Loyalty:

A. by registering the new firm but not by approaching other employees about a possible employee buyout.

B. by approaching other employees about a possible employee buyout but not by registering the new firm.

C. neither by registering the new firm nor by approaching other employees about a possible employee buyout.

15. It is a requirement of the GIPS standards that assets should be valued at:

A. cost.

B. fair value.

C. market value.

16. When information received from a client is outside the scope of the confidential relationship between the client and adviser and does not involve illegal activities, the *most effective* compliance procedure to ensure compliance with Standard IIIE – Preservation of Confidentiality is to:

A. avoid disclosing any information except to authorized fellow employees.

B. establish if the information is background material which, if disclosed would enable the adviser to improve service to the client.

C. identify the context in which the information was disclosed and whether the information is relevant to the work being done by the adviser.

17. John Salako CFA has a high net worth individual as a client. The individual has a high level of risk tolerance and wishes to hold a diversified portfolio that offers the prospect of high returns. Salako recommends to his client that he invests in a portfolio of hedge funds, comprising 10% of his overall portfolio. One of the hedge funds in the portfolio follows a highly leveraged long short strategy which has yielded high but volatile returns since the fund's inception. Prior to investing, Salako established that the fund principals have a good reputation in the industry and the fees, although high, are in line with the industry. However, within a month of Salako investing in the fund, it reports dramatic losses with suspicions of fraudulent activity by one of the fund managers.

    Salako has *most likely* violated:

    A. Standard IIIC – Suitability but not Standard VA – Diligence and Reasonable Basis.

    B. Standard VA – Diligence and Reasonable Basis but not Standard IIIC – Suitability.

    C. neither Standard IIIC – Suitability nor Standard VA – Diligence and Reasonable Basis.

18. Catherine de la Rue CFA is an investment analyst who works in a developing country where there are very few securities laws. In particular, there are no laws prohibiting trading or causing others to trade on material nonpublic information. De la Rue has accidentally been given some information concerning a significant new contract that has been won by a company which has not yet been made public. De la Rue *most likely*:

    A. may act on this information.

    B. must not act on this information.

    C. must act on this information in order to satisfy her fiduciary duties to her clients in the developing country.

Questions 19 through 32 relate to Quantitative Methods

19. An actuary wishes to establish whether an equity manager is skilful or not to an error level of 1%. She analyzes 100 monthly returns of the manager and identifies that his mean outperformance over his benchmark is 1.2%, with a standard deviation of 5.5%. The actuary will *most likely*:

   A. make a type I error.

   B. make a type II error.

   C. reject the null hypothesis.

20. A 182 days T-bill has a quoted yield of 9.15%. A 182 days certificate of deposit has a quoted yield of 9.20%. A bond with 182 days to maturity has a quoted yield of 9.25%. An investor seeking to maximize the yield on investment on an equivalent annual basis will *most likely* invest in the:

   A. T-bill.

   B. corporate bond.

   C. certificate of deposit.

21. In technical analysis, a point and figure chart:

   A. requires selection of a reversal size.

   B. represents time on the horizontal axis.

   C. cannot use a logarithmic scale on the vertical axis.

22. An analyst is measuring the annual standard deviation of returns for a stock market series. He assumes that returns are independent over time and identifies the return on the series for five months as follows.

Month 1	Month 2	Month 3	Month 4	Month 5
2.1%	3.2%	-0.5%	1.5%	4.3%

   The annual standard deviation for the stock market series is *closest to:*

   A. 5.6%.

   B. 6.3%.

   C. 21.8%.

23. A regulatory organization dealing with the media industry is about to make a ruling on the appropriateness of companies owning multiple interests in different media such as broadcasting and newspapers. One company which will suffer from a negative ruling is A2B Inc. and an analyst believes that A2B Inc.'s stock price reflects a 60% probability of a negative ruling being published. Another company which will suffer from a negative ruling is Z2Y Inc. The same analyst believes that Z2Y Inc.'s stock price reflects a 40% probability of a negative ruling arising. The investment strategy which will *most likely* profit given the analyst's views is:

   A. sell A2B and sell Z2Y.

   B. buy A2B and sell Z2Y.

   C. sell A2B and buy Z2Y.

24. When the probability of estimates close to the value of the population parameter increases as the sample size increases, the point estimate is referred to as:

    A. efficient.

    B. unbiased.

    C. consistent.

25. A, B and C are discrete random variables with the possible outcomes A = (5,9,13), B = (2,7,21) and C = (3,7,22). Probability functions for each variable, f(A), g(B) and h(C) are as follows.

    f(5) = 0.3 f(9) = 0.8 f(13) = -0.1

    g(2) = 0.1 g(7) = 0.4 g(21) = 0.4

    h(3) = 0.2 h(7) = 0.3 h(22) = 0.5

    The function which *most likely* satisfies the conditions for a probability function is:

    A. function A.

    B. function B.

    C. function C.

26. If the annual inflation rate is 5%, the number of years that it will take for prices to double is *closest to*:

    A. 14 years.

    B. 17 years.

    C. 20 years.

27. An analyst is measuring returns on large cap, medium cap and small cap stocks. Large cap stocks are categorized as having a value of 3, medium cap stocks are categorized as having a value of 2 and small cap stocks are categorized as having a value of 1. The measurement scale being used by the analyst is *most likely*:

    A. ordinal.

    B. nominal.

    C. interval.

28. A stock has a price of $100. In any year, the stock price may increase by 10%, with a probability of 0.6, or fall by 8%, with a probability of 0.4. An investor who owns the stock has sold a call option at a strike price of $105 and bought a put option at a strike price of $85. Both options are European options exercisable at the end of the third year. The probability that the investor will *not* sell the share under either of the options is *closest to*:

    A. 0.096.

    B. 0.192.

    C. 0.288.

29. The students t distribution will *most likely* be used for a sample where the sample size is:

    A. large and the population is nonnormal with a known variance.

    B. small and the population is normal with an unknown variance.

    C. small and the population is nonnormal with an unknown variance.

30. An analyst has estimated that the probability that small cap stocks will outperform the Russell 3000 index is 20% and that medium cap stocks will outperform the Russell 3000 index is 40%. The probability that either small cap or medium cap stocks will outperform the Russell index is *closest to*:

    A. 0.08.

    B. 0.52.

    C. 0.60.

31. The F-distribution would *most likely* be used for a statistical test concerning:

    A. a single variance.

    B. inequality of variances.

    C. a paired comparison test.

32. A father wishes to give his daughter $100,000 and plans to save $500 each month, starting immediately. If the interest rate at which he can invest the money is 6% (APR), the number of months before he will have the required sum available is *closest to*:

    A. 138 months.

    B. 139 months.

    C. 140 months.

Questions 33 through 44 relate to Economics

33. In a market for a good, where Government imposes a per-unit tax on sellers and not on buyers of the good, it is *most likely* that compared to when there are no taxes, the quantity of the good demanded will:

    A. increase.

    B. decrease.

    C. stay constant.

34. A central bank for a country that has a high inflation rate but without a well functioning market for bonds and overnight loans would *most likely* adopt:

    A. an inflation rate targeting rule.

    B. an exchange rate targeting rule.

    C. a monetary base instrument rule.

35. For an industry in perfect competition with economies of scale, the long run impact on the market price for the industry's good of a shift in demand to the right is *most likely* that the price will:

    A. fall.

    B. rise.

    C. stay the same.

36. When own-price elasticity of demand is 1 on a straight line demand curve, it is *most likely* that:

    A. demand is perfectly elastic.

    B. total revenue is at its highest value.

    C. an increase in price will lead to less elasticity.

37. A factor which is *least likely* to cause a leftward shift in the demand for money curve is:

    A. a decrease in real GDP.

    B. an increase in interest rates.

    C. an increase in the use of credit cards.

38. For a firm that is maximizing its profit, it is *most likely* that its:

    A. marginal product will be equal to its marginal cost.

    B. marginal revenue product will be equal to its marginal cost.

    C. wage rate will be equal to its marginal cost multiplied by its marginal product.

39. A firm that wishes to minimize its average variable cost will *most likely* produce to the point where marginal product:

    A. becomes negative.

    B. equals average product.

    C. reaches its highest value.

40. Which of the following factors has been the *most* influential in affecting economic growth in developed countries?

    A. Technology.

    B. Labor.

    C. Capital.

41. In monopolistic competition, it is *most likely* that in the long run:

    A. economic profit will be zero.

    B. there will be no excess capacity.

    C. price will be equal to marginal cost.

42. An increase in the net tax rate is *most likely* to have which of the following impacts?

    A. Increase in aggregate demand.

    B. Decrease in disposable income.

    C. Increase in marginal propensity to consume.

43. A monopolist will *most likely* produce at the point on its demand curve which is:

    A. elastic.

    B. inelastic.

    C. unitary elastic.

44. Within the income approach to calculating GDP, which of the following is *least* likely to be added to be a component of national income?

    A. Interest income.

    B. Rent.

    C. Exports less imports.

Questions 45 through 68 relate to Financial Reporting and Analysis

45. Extracts from the financial statements for the year ended December 31 2013 of a company that uses US GAAP are as follows.

	2013 $	2012 $
Total assets	9,540	8,470
Total liabilities	5,420	4,640
Stockholders equity	4,120	3,830
Net income	690	550

The net income is after charging income taxes at a rate of 30%.

The return on equity if the financial statements are *closest to*:

A. 17.4%.

B. 18.9%.

C 19.9%.

46. A company issues a bond with a five year bullet maturity and a 9% annual coupon at a price of 104. The nominal value of the bond is $100 million and the issue proceeds are $104 million. There are issue costs of $1 million. The net proceeds are used to redeem short term debt. Compared to the financial statements prepared under International Financial Reporting Standards, the financial statements prepared under US GAAP after the issue and the redemption of the short term debt will *most likely* have a lower:

A. current ratio.

B. asset turnover.

C. debt to equity ratio.

47. In one year, a housebuilding company capitalizes interest costs on borrowings related to the construction of houses. Thereafter, no further interest is capitalized and the houses have not yet been sold. Compared to if it had not capitalized such interest costs, in subsequent years the company will *most likely* have:

A. lower net income and the same current ratio.

B. higher financial leverage and lower fixed asset turnover.

C. lower inventory turnover and lower return on total capital.

48. A long lived asset that is to be disposed of by means of a distribution to the owners of the company through a spin-off will *most likely*:

A. be transferred into current assets.

B. be left at book value in the balance sheet.

C. result in a profit or loss being recorded on the disposal of the asset.

49. A company has a tax burden of 0.4, an interest burden of 0.7 and operating margins of 25%. The company's net margin is *closest to*:

    A. 4.5%.

    B. 7.0%.

    C. 10.5%.

50. A company has an accrual of $2,000 relating to rent expense as at December 31 2012 and a prepayment of $1,500 relating to rent expense as at December 31 2013. In the year ended December 31 2013, the company paid cash of $15,000 relating to rent. The rent expense for the year ended December 31 2013 is *closest to*:

    A. $11,500.

    B. $14,500.

    C. $15,500.

51. Comfy Inc. manufactures and sells cushions. In the year ended December 31 2012, it manufactured 410,000 cushions, of which 10,000 cushions were rejected on their completion and had to be scrapped. This was considered to be abnormal wastage. The raw materials for the cushions had a cost of $3.00 per cushion. However, Comfy Inc. received a discount from this price of 10% for bulk purchases and received a further discount of 5% (based on $3.00 per cushion) for prompt settlement of invoices. Labor costs relating to the manufacture of the cushions were $2 million and factory overheads, which included $300,000 for rent, were $3 million. The overhead costs of the warehouse where the cushions are stored were $80,000, including $50,000 of rent. In the year, 380,000 cushions were sold. The total for costs above which should be expensed in the year ended December 31 2012 is *closest to*:

    A. $5,826,696.

    B. $5,827,598.

    C. $5,830,598.

52. An analyst has calculated the following ratios for a company.

Inventory turnover	5.2
Payables turnover	5.9
Receivables turnover	4.9

    The company's cash conversion cycle is *closest to*:

    A. 75 days.

    B. 83 days.

    C. 87 days.

53. A company has purchased $10,000,000 of fixed assets in exchange for the issue of $10,000,000 of new debt issued. This will *most likely* be shown in the cash flow statement as a:

    A. supplementary note.

    B. net cash flow of zero in financing activities.

    C. cash outflow in investing activities and a cash inflow in financing activities.

54. Compared to the completed contract method, the financial statements of a company using the percentage of completion method in the first year of a long term contract will *most likely* have a lower:

    A. current ratio.

    B. asset turnover.

    C. debt to equity ratio.

55. Changes in the basic elements (assets, liabilities, equity, income and expenses) within financial statements are *most likely* portrayed in the:

    A. balance sheet.

    B. income statement.

    C. cash flow statement.

56. Extracts from the notes to the financial statements of a UK company that prepares its accounts using International Financial Reporting Standards are as follows.

	£
Retirement obligations	3,400,560
Plan assets	3,110,660
Unrecognized loss	450,000

    The balance sheet liability that would be shown in the financial statements in respect of pensions if the company were following US GAAP would be *closest to*:

    A. £289,900.

    B. £739,900.

    C. £3,400,560.

57. A company has a low number of days sales in inventory. This *most likely* indicates:

    A. the risk of obsolescent inventories.

    B. a just in time system of inventory management.

    C. the company is more likely to be selling luxury products than staple products.

58. Mathey SA is a French company that sells bath salts. At January 1 2013, it had inventories of 100,000 packets of bath salts, each of which cost €5.00. Details of its sales and purchases of bath salts over the first three months of 2013 are as follows.

Date	Quantity	Price €
24 January	40,000 sold	34.00
29 January	30,000 purchased	6.00
5 February	60,000 sold	34.00
29 February	45,000 purchased	7.00
14 March	10,000 sold	34.00

Mathey SA uses a perpetual inventory system and the FIFO method of valuing inventories. The gross profit for the three months ended March 31 2013 is *closest to*:

A. €3,174,000.

B. €3,180,000.

C. €3,280,000.

59. A company wishes to report high growth in earnings per share in the next year. In order to achieve this, it will *most likely*:

A. increase the expected useful life of the asset and revise the expected residual value of the asset upwards.

B. increase the expected useful life of the asset and revise the expected residual value of the asset downwards.

C. change its depreciation method from straight line to an accelerated method and revise the expected residual value of the asset downwards.

60. An item that is *least likely* to be treated as other comprehensive income under US GAAP is:

A. unrealized losses on derivatives contracts accounted for as hedges.

B. unrealized gains on marketable equity securities held for trading purposes.

C changes in the funded status of a company's defined benefit pension plan.

61. Extracts from the cash flow statement for the year ended December 31 2013 of a company that uses US GAAP are as follows.

	$
Net income	5,240
Increase in working capital	1,110
Depreciation expense	670
Cash flow from operating activities	4,800
Capital expenditure	690
Cash paid to acquire short term investments	100
Cash flow from investing activities	790
Dividends	1,000
Debt repaid	3,000
Cash flow from financing activities	4,000
Increase in cash	10

The reinvestment coverage ratio for the year ended December 31 2013 is *closest to*:

A. 6.1.

B. 7.0.

C 7.6.

62. The three conditions in the fraud triangle described in the Statement on Auditing Standards 'Consideration of Fraud in a Financial Statement Audit' *most likely* include:

A. rationalization.

B. communication.

C. organizational structure.

63. A portfolio manager specializes in the selection of value stocks, specifically those with high book to price ratios. The analyst wishes to avoid selecting stocks of companies that have excessive risk of financial weakness. A screening criterion that the analyst would *most likely* use to manage this risk would be:

A. debt to capital.

B. earnings growth.

C. negative net income.

64. Company X prepares its accounts under International Financial Reporting Standards and Company Y prepares its accounts under US GAAP. On January 1 2012, both companies have issued debt with a five year maturity at a premium to par with exactly the same terms. Company Y is not using the preferred method under US GAAP for calculating its interest expense. It is *most likely* that in the financial statements for the year ended December 31 2013, company X will have a higher:

A. debt to equity ratio than company Y.

B. interest coverage ratio than company Y.

C. cash flow from financing activities than company Y.

65. Company X is leasing an asset to company Y for a period of 6 years. The asset has an expected useful life of 10 years. The value of the leased asset is $500,000 and the lease payments over the next 6 years have a present value of $480,000. After the lease period expires, company Y has the option to purchase the asset for $20,000. Company X is not reasonably certain that company X will make all the required payments under the lease. Both companies prepare their financial statements using US GAAP.

It is *most likely* that the lease will be classified as:

A. a capital lease by company X and by company Y.

B. an operating lease by company X and by company Y.

C. an operating lease by company X and a capital lease by company Y.

66. Details of percentage changes over a year taken from a company's financial statements are as follows.

Revenue	+15%
Net income	+20%
Total assets	+15%
Operating cash flow	-5%

It is *most likely* that:

A. net margins have decreased.

B. the quality of earnings is falling.

C. the level of working capital has fallen.

67. Extracts from a company's balance sheet are as follows.

	$
Cash	1,050
Receivables	3,800
Inventories	2,500
Current assets	7,350
Long lived assets	4,240
Total assets	11,590
Payables	2,160
Short term bank loans	800
Current liabilities	2,960
Long term bonds	4,200
Deferred tax liability	1,100
Total liabilities	8,260
Stockholders equity	3,330
	11,590

The company's debt to capital ratio is *closest to*:

A. 54%.

B. 56%.

C. 60%.

68. An analyst wishes to analyze a company's solvency. The ratio that she would *least likely* calculate is the:

    A. cash ratio.

    B. financial leverage ratio.

    C. fixed charge coverage ratio.

Questions 69 through 78 relate to Corporate Finance

69. A 260 days T-bill is trading on a yield of 3%. The price of the T-bill is *closest to*:
    A. 97.00.
    B. 97.83.
    C. 97.86.

70. A company has a debt to equity ratio of 40% in market value terms and a weighted average cost of capital of 8.3%. It is considering diversifying its operations by investing in new business areas. One possible investment is in a private company. The beta of a public company with a debt to equity ratio of 20% that is in the same business area as the private company is 1.4. The required return for debt investors in the private company is 5% and the tax rate is 30%. The company plans to finance the acquisition using its existing debt to equity ratio. The market risk premium is 5% and the investing company uses a risk free rate of 4%. The weighted average cost of capital that should be used to assess the new investment is *closest to*:
    A. 8.3%.
    B. 8.5%.
    C. 9.5%.

71. In a two tier board system, it is *most likely* that the supervisory board consists of:
    A. only executive management.
    B. only independent and non executive directors.
    C. both executive management and independent and non executive directors.

72. A conventional project generates a constant annuity. It has a discounted payback period of 4 years. It is *most likely* that the:
    A. profitability index is greater than 1.
    B. payback period is greater than 4 years.
    C. accounting rate of return is less than the cost of capital.

73. A company has made the following statement.

    "The company has a policy of returning excess cash to shareholders through the most efficient means possible. The company has recently sold one of its major operating divisions for cash and is using the proceeds to pay down remaining balance sheet debt and to finance a dividend to shareholders. This dividend will be paid in four installments over the next year."

    The dividend being paid is *most likely* referred to as:
    A. regular.
    B. special.
    C. liquidating.

74. Details of a company's budget income statement are as follows.

	$
Revenue	500,000
Operating costs	250,000
Operating income	250,000
Interest expense	80,000
Income before tax	170,000

The company's degree of operating leverage at the budget activity level is 1.6. The operating margin that the company will need to generate in order to break even at the income before tax level is *closest to*:

A. 24.2%.

B. 27.8%.

C. 32.4%.

75. A company, Trading Inc, has a $2.80 cumulative preferred stock in issue. The number of preferred shares in issue is 324,000. If the price of the preferred stock is $55, which of the following is *closest* to the cost Treding Inc's cost of preferred stock?

A. 5.09%.

B. 4.50%.

C. 2.80%.

76. A company's audit committee should *most likely* have:

A. all of its members independent of management.

B. a majority of its members independent of management.

C. a majority of executive directors and a strong independent chairman.

77. A company wishes to repurchase shares. The method that is *most likely* to result in a transfer of value to selling shareholders from shareholders who do not sell is:

A. a Dutch auction.

B. direct negotiation.

C. open market purchases.

78. A company which is solely financed by equity will pay a dividend of $1.50 a share in one year's time. The dividend is expected to grow by 3% each year for an indefinite period. The stock price is $30. The company is considering an investment of $100 million in a project in the same business area as its existing operations. The project will generate cash flows of $5 million at the end of the first year, thereafter increasing by 4% a year indefinitely. The investment will be financed by a new stock issue, with issue costs of 4% of the gross issue proceeds. The net present value of the investment is *closest to*:

A. $18,812,000.

B. $20,833,000.

C. $21,000,000.

Questions 79 through 84 relate to Portfolio Management

79. Details of total risk and unsystematic risk (measured in standard deviations) for three investments are as follows.

Investment	Total risk %	Unsystematic risk %
A	20	10
B	25	18
C	30	25

The investment with the highest expected return is *most likely* to be:

A. investment A.

B. investment B.

C. investment C.

80. A portfolio perspective to investing *least likely*:

A. helps avoid disastrous outcomes.

B. improves the risk return trade-off.

C. always provides downside protection.

81. The investment policy statement for an individual investor will *most likely* not specify:

A. rebalancing policy.

B. tactical asset allocation.

C. strategic asset allocation.

82. An investor who wishes to calculate the mean return over time on a constant dollar investment at the beginning of each period will *most likely* use the:

A. harmonic mean.

B. geometric mean.

C. arithmetic mean.

83. A closed-end fund that has a share price that tracks its net asset value is *most likely*:

A. a mutual fund.

B. a no load fund.

C. an exchange traded fund.

84. The beta of a security for the capital asset pricing model is *most likely* identified by:

A. calculating the security's systematic risk as a proportion of market risk.

B. calculating the slope of the regression line when the security's returns are regressed against stock market returns.

C. dividing the product of the security's unsystematic risk and its correlation with market returns by the market's total risk in standard deviations.

Questions 85 through 96 relate to Equity

85. The strong form of the efficient market hypothesis would *most likely* be tested by means of:

    A. an event study.

    B. a serial correlation test.

    C. examination of abnormal profits from trading on private information.

86. A shareholder with a minority interest in the shares of a company who wishes to have board representation will *most likely* prefer voting rights to be:

    A. proxy.

    B. statutory.

    C. cumulative.

87. A company has a retention ratio for its profits of 45%, an expected growth rate in dividends of 3.7% and a forward price to earnings ratio of 22.9. The company's cost of equity is *closest to*:

    A. 5.7%.

    B. 6.1%.

    C. 6.3%.

88. A public company wishes to raise money in the next six months in order to finance the expansion of existing manufacturing facilities and to invest in new manufacturing facilities. The source of finance that is *least likely* to be appropriate is:

    A. commercial paper.

    B. new equity shares.

    C. long term bank loan.

89. The Barclays Capital Global Aggregate Bond Index *most likely*:

    A. consists only of government bond issues.

    B. is comprised of a varying number of bond issues.

    C. does not have a minimum issue size for inclusion in the index.

90. Government industry classification systems *most likely*:

    A. distinguish between large and small companies.

    B. include both for-profit and not-for-profit organizations.

    C. disclose information about specific businesses and companies.

91. A mutual fund that is only permitted to invest in public equities traded in secondary markets is *most likely* permitted to invest in:

    A. a stock index futures contract.

    B. a single stock futures contract.

    C. the common stock of a public company traded only through dealers.

92. The index weighting scheme that *most likely* has the highest transaction costs for investors is:
    A. price weighted.
    B. equal weighted.
    C. market capitalization weighted.

93. Global depositary receipts are *most likely*:
    A. denominated in US dollars.
    B. issued in all major stock markets worldwide.
    C. securities that represent ownership in global registered shares.

94. When calculating a company's enterprise value using a multiplier model, the fundamental variable that is *least likely* to be suitable is:
    A. sales.
    B. earnings before tax.
    C. earnings before interest, tax, depreciation and amortization.

95. The stage of the industry life cycle where prices are *most likely* to be high is the:
    A. growth stage.
    B. mature stage.
    C. embryonic stage.

96. An investor who believes that a stock that has earned high returns in the recent past will probably continue to earn high returns in the future is *most likely* exhibiting:
    A. narrow framing.
    B. gambler's fallacy.
    C. the disposition effect.

Questions 97 through 110 relate to Fixed Income

97. A provision that provides the issuer with the right to repurchase its bonds from the bondholder at a pre-determined price prior to the bond's maturity date is referred to as a:

   A. call provision.

   B. put provision.

   C. make whole provision.

98. If the US Federal Reserve wishes to increase interest rates, it would *most likely*:

   A. reduce bank reserve requirements.

   B. use verbal persuasion to influence bankers.

   C. conduct open market purchases of Treasury securities.

99. A bond has the following schedule for coupon payments.

Years	Coupon rate
2012 – 2014	1%
2015 – 2016	3%
2017 – 2020	5%

   The market rate of interest for bonds of a similar type is 2.5%. The bond is *most likely* referred to as:

   A. a step-up note.

   B. a deferred coupon bond.

   C. an accrued interest bond.

100. An analyst has stated that floating rate securities have interest rate risk due to their margin over LIBOR but not due to changes in market interest rates. The analyst is *most likely* correct in respect of:

   A. the margin but not changes in market interest rates.

   B. changes in market interest rates but not the margin.

   C. both the margin and changes in market interest rates.

101. An investor has a liability to meet in two years time of $110,250 and $100,000 to invest today in order to achieve this. Yields to maturity are currently 5% and the yield curve is flat. The investor uses his funds to purchase a bond with a maturity of three years and an annual coupon of 5%. Immediately after he purchases the bond, there is a parallel downward shift in yields to a level of 4%. Thereafter, yields are unchanged. The investor will *most likely* find that after two years he has:

   A. assets equal to liabilities.

   B. a deficit of assets under liabilities.

   C. a surplus of assets over liabilities.

102. The Macauley duration of a fixed income security:

A. cannot exceed its final maturity.

B. will always indicate a negative slope.

C. is the first derivative of the price yield function.

103. Debt securities that are privately placed under a Rule 144A offering in the US *most likely*:

A. cannot be sold on until two years after the original placement.

B. can only be sold on after they have been registered with the SEC.

C. can only be traded among large institutions as defined under rule 144A.

104. A bond with a maturity of three years and an annual coupon of 2% is priced at 91.83. A bond of comparable credit quality and liquidity with a maturity of three years and an annual coupon of 4% will have a price that is *closest to*:

A. 97.28.

B. 98.32.

C. 99.14.

105. The special redemption price of a callable bond issue is *most likely* set at:

A. par.

B. a premium to par.

C. the price which ensures that the yield on call is equal to the bond's original yield to redemption on its issue.

106. The purpose of Tranches and support Tranches in a mortgage-backed security is *most likely* to reallocate:

A. credit risk.

B. prepayment risk.

C. credit risk and prepayment risk.

107. The yield to worst for a fixed income security *most likely*:

A. gives the worst possible yield over the investment horizon.

B. cannot be calculated for a mortgage backed security with prepayment risks.

C. ignores potentially different exposures to investment risk in different scenarios.

108. A bond pays a coupon of 6%. The next coupon is due in 55 days time, at which time the bond will have one year to its maturity. The previous coupon was paid 127 days ago. The bond is trading on a yield to maturity of 5%. The clean price of the bond is *closest to*:

A. 101.10.

B. 102.28.

C. 103.19.

109. Details of US dollar LIBOR are as follows.

3 months	5.0%
6 months	6.3%
9 months	7.1%
12 months	8.5%

The expected rate for 3 months LIBOR in 3 months time is *closest to*:

A. 5.7%.

B. 7.5%.

C. 8.4%.

110. When assessing the risk of a bond, the impact of parallel shifts in yield is considered in the:

A. Macauley duration approach.

B. full valuation approach.

C. Macauley duration approach and the full valuation approach.

Questions 111 through 116 relate to Derivatives

111. In a currency swap, the notional principle is *most likely*:
    A. never exchanged.
    B. always exchanged.
    C. sometimes exchanged.

112. A trader purchased a T-bill futures contract when the IMM index was quoted at 96.43. He sold the contract when the IMM index was quoted at 97.12. The profit on the trader's position is *closest to*:
    A. $431.
    B. $1,725.
    C. $6,900.

113. A stock is currently priced at $180. It will have a price at the end of one period of either $200, with a probability of 60%, or $160, with a probability of 40%. An investor buys the stock and sells it forward at a price of $186. The interest rate for one period is 6%. At the end of the period, the investor will have an overall expected profit or loss *closest to*:
    A. $5.00 loss.
    B. $2.00 profit.
    C. $6.00 profit.

114. Details of option prices for European put options on a share where the current stock price is $120 are as follows.

	Expiration date		
Strike price	March	June	September
118	10.11	14.15	21.05
120	11.14	15.20	20.92
125	13.94	17.97	20.83

The option whose price is *most likely* inconsistent is the:
    A. June 120.
    B. March 118.
    C. September 125.

115. A covered call is *most similar* to a:
    A. short put.
    B. short call.
    C. long call and short put.

116. A forward contract *most likely*:
    A. represents a contingent claim.
    B. is marked to market to control credit risk.
    C. can be settled by physical delivery or cash settlement.

Questions 117 through 120 relate to Alternative Investments

117. Which of the following alternative investments is *most likely* to provide an inflation hedge?
    A. Real estate.
    B. Private equity.
    C. Hedge funds.

118. An example of an event driven hedge fund would *most likely* be a:
    A. managed futures fund.
    B. distressed securities fund.
    C. convertible bond arbitrage fund.

119. Adding commodities to a portfolio *most likely*:
    A. reduces short run risk and long term inflation exposure.
    B. increases short run risk and reduces long term inflation exposure.
    C. reduces short run risk and has no impact on long term inflation exposure.

120. Global REIT indexes *most likely*:
    A. exhibit smoothed returns.
    B. have a high correlation with the stock market.
    C. have a high correlation with the bond market

Practice Examination 3
Morning Session Solutions

2014

ANSWERS

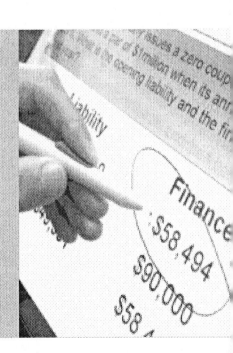

BPP
LEARNING MEDIA

Ethical and Professional Standards

1. **C** Standard VIB – Priority of Transactions. There should be limited participation in equity IPOs and restrictions on private placements.

    LOS 2b

2. **C** Standard IIB – Market Manipulation and Standard VA – Diligence and Reasonable Basis. Disseminating such speculative statements under the guise of an independent website represents information based manipulation. There is no reasonable basis for recommending the company.

    LOS 2b

3. **A** Standard IIIC – Suitability. When the adviser knows that an unsolicited request is unsuitable, the adviser should either refrain from making the trade or seek an affirmative statement from the client that suitability is not a consideration.

    LOS 2b

4. **B** Standard IA – Knowledge of the Law. Seeking legal advice does not absolve a member from the requirement to comply with laws and regulations. Given the information, the best course of action is to take the matter forward by reporting to his supervisor and establishing whether a wrongdoing has occurred.

    LOS 2b

5. **B** Initially, the firm could present five years of performance, adding on one year for each additional year up to 10 years.

    LOS 4a

6. **A** Standard IIIB – Fair Dealing states that all clients should be treated fairly. Always favoring larger clients in terms of sending out research reports is unfair. Standard VB – Communication with Clients and Prospective Clients states that members should distinguish between fact and opinion. It is Irmina's opinion that the cash flow will fall, rather than an observable fact.

    LOS 2b

7. **C** Standard IC – Misrepresentation. If using a newspaper, best practice is to obtain the original study and cite only the author of that study. If the original study is not obtained (which contains a risk of relying on second hand information), both the intermediary and the original should be cited.

    LOS 2b

8. **B** Standard IVA – Loyalty. Using knowledge of client names to contact them after leaving employment is permitted. However, during the notice period, members should not do anything that could harm their employer.

    LOS 2b

9. **A** Standard IIIA – Loyalty, Prudence and Care. A cost-benefit analysis may show that voting all proxies will not benefit the client.

    LOS 2b

10.   A   Standard VIIA – Conduct as Members and Candidates in the CFA Program. Specific details of questions may not be disclosed until released by CFA Institute. Those involved in the exam setting process must not release information on the exam questions, deliberations on the exam process and scoring of questions.

LOS 2b

11.   C   Standard IVC – Responsibilities of Supervisors. Delegation of supervisory duties does not relieve a supervisor of supervisory responsibility.

LOS 2b

12.   B   Standard ID – Misconduct. The standard is not designed to cover a member's personal life except to the extent that any misconduct would reflect adversely on their professional reputation, integrity or competence. Claiming personal living costs as a business expense is dishonest.

LOS 2b

13.   C   The goals of the GIPS Executive Committee include promoting investor interests and fostering the notion of self regulation.

LOS 3a

14.   C   Standard IVA – Loyalty. Preparations for starting a new business are permitted while still employed. An employee lead buyout would ultimately depend on the owner's approval so does not breach any duty of loyalty.

LOS 2b

15.   B   GIPS Fundamentals of Compliance paragraph 0.A.13

LOS 4a

16.   A   Standard IIIE – Preservation of Confidentiality. The simplest, most conservative and most effective way to comply with the standard is not to disclose information except to authorized fellow employees working with the client.

LOS 2b

17.   C   The client is prepared to take risk and wishes to have a diversified portfolio. Salako's due diligence on the fund suggests no problems and seemed to be at an appropriate level.

LOS 2b

18.   B   Standard IA – Knowledge of the law and Standard IIA – Material Nonpublic Information. The Standards are stricter than local laws and must be applied. The Standards prohibit acting on material nonpublic information.

LOS 2b

Quantitative Methods

19. **B** Null hypothesis: the manager is not skilful i.e. the excess return is not significantly different from zero. $\mu = 0$

Alternative hypothesis: the manager is skilful i.e. $\mu = 0$

One tailed test at the 1% error level gives a critical value of 2.33 (since the sample size is very large, the normal distribution and the student t distribution are almost the same).

Standard error: $\dfrac{5.5}{\sqrt{100}} = 0.55$

Test statistic: $\dfrac{1.2 - 0}{0.55} = 2.18$

The test statistic is less than the critical statistic, meaning that the null hypothesis cannot be rejected. There may be a type II error i.e. not rejecting the null hypothesis when it should have been rejected.

LOS 11b

20. **A** T-bill:

Price $= 100 - 9.15 \times \dfrac{182}{360} = 95.374$

Yield $= \dfrac{100 - 95.374}{95.374} = 4.85\%$

EAR $= 1.0485^{\frac{365}{182}} - 1 = 9.96\%$

Certificate of deposit:

Yield $= 9.20 \times \dfrac{182}{360} = 4.65\%$

EAR $= 1.0465^{\frac{365}{182}} - 1 = 9.544\%$

Corporate bond:

Semi-annual yield $= 9.25 \times \dfrac{1}{2} = 4.625\%$

EAR $= 1.04625^2 - 1 = 9.49\%$

(Calculations were done using unrounded numbers).

LOS 6f

21. **A** A point and figure chart moves along the horizontal axis when there is a change in the direction of the price movement, rather than by reference to time. Specifying the price movement that represents a change in direction (i.e. a reversal) is necessary as a result. The vertical axis could be based on a linear or logarithmic scale, depending on how you wish to view the data.

LOS 12b

22. **B**

x	$x - \bar{x}$	$(x - \bar{x})^2$
2.1	-0.02	0.0004
3.2	1.08	1.1664
-0.5	-2.62	6.8644
1.5	-0.62	0.3844
4.3	2.18	4.7524
$\sum x = 10.6$	$\sum(x - \bar{x}) = 0$	$\sum(x - \bar{x})^2 = 13.168$

$$\bar{x} - \frac{10.6}{5} = 2.12$$

$$\sigma^2 = \frac{13.168}{5 - 1} = 3.292$$

Annualized σ^2 = $3.292 \times 12 = 39.504$

Annualized $\sigma = \sqrt{39.504} = 6.285$

LOS 7g

23. **B**

	True probability of negative ruling	
	60%	40%
A2B	Fairly valued	Undervalued
Z2Y	Overvalued	Fairly valued

A2B is undervalued if the actual probability of the negative event is 40%, since its stock price reflects a 60% probability of the event arising.

Z2Y is overvalued if the actual probability of the negative event is 60%, since its stock price reflects a 40% probability of the event arising.

In both scenarios, A2B dominates Z2Y.

LOS 8a

24. **C** Unbiased is that its expected value equals that of the parameter. Efficient is where no other unbiased estimator has a sampling distribution with a smaller variance.

LOS 10g

25. **C** All probabilities must lie between 0 and 1 and the function must sum to 1. Only C satisfies both these conditions.

LOS 9b

26.   **A**   Trying each answer in turn: $1.05^{14} = 1.98$.

Alternatively, $\ln(1.05)x = \ln(2)$

$x = 14.2$

LOS 5f

27.   **B**   The data is being categorized but not ranked.

LOS 7a

28.   **C**   The possible outcomes are:

Up up up: Final stock price $= 100 \times 1.1^3 = 133.10$

Up up down: Final stock price $= 100 \times 1.1^2 \times 0.92 = \$111.32$

Up down down: Final stock price $= 100 \times 1.1 \times 0.92^2 = 93.10$

Down down down: Final stock price $= 100 \times 0.92^3 = 77.87$

The only stock price after three years where neither option is exercised is \$93.10.

The probability of this stock price arising is $0.4^2 \times 0.6 \times \dfrac{3!}{2!1!} = 0.288$

LOS 9g

29.   **B**   Where the variance is unknown and the population is normally distributed, the student t distribution is used for a small sample or a large sample, since the sample variance will be used as an estimate for the population variance.

LOS 10i

30.   **B** $0.2 + 0.4 - 0.2 \times 0.4 = 0.52$.

This approach uses the addition rule for events that are not mutually exclusive.

LOS 8e

31.   **B**   The F test is used when comparing the variances of two populations. A paired comparison test would use the normal (or students t distribution) while a single variance test would use the chi-squared distribution.

LOS 11i

32.   **A**   Using the annuity formula for the value at time n of an annuity from time 1 to n:

$$FV_n = A\left(\frac{(1+r)^n - 1}{r}\right)$$

Since the first annuity payment is at time 0 rather than at time 1, this needs to be adjusted by multiplying the right side of the equation by $(1 + r)$.

$$100,000 = \frac{1.05 \times 500 \times \left(1.005^n - 1\right)}{0.005}$$

$$\frac{100,000 \times 0.005}{500 \times 0.005} + 1 = 1.005^n$$

$$\ln\left(\frac{100,000 \times 0.005}{500 \times 0.005} + 1\right) = \ln\left(1.005\right)n$$

$n = 138.48$

Alternatively, each answer could be tried out in turn using the annuity formula.

LOS 5e

Economics

33. **B** The supply curve will shift upwards and to the left due to the additional tax suffered by the supplier. This will cause the equilibrium point to be at a higher price and lower quantity.

    LOS 13d and 13j

34. **B** The absence of an overnight loans market and bonds market makes it difficult to target inflation through a monetary based or inflation based rule. By fixing the exchange rate with a country with stable inflation, inflation can be linked to that country's inflation rate.

    LOS 19k

35. **A** The impact of economies of scale is to reduce the cost of production as industry output increases. This will have the impact of reducing price as demand shifts to the right.

    LOS 15d and 15f

36. **B** Demand is completely price elastic for a horizontal demand curve. As price increases, elasticity increases. Total revenue reaches its maximum when elasticity = 1.

    LOS 13m

37. **B** An increase in interest rates will cause a decrease in the quantity of real money demanded, rather than a shift in the demand curve.

    LOS 19d

38. **C** $MR \times MP = MRP$; $MC \times MP = W$

    For profit maximization, $MR = MC$ and $MRP = W$

    LOS 15f

39. **B** When marginal product equals average product, marginal cost will equal average variable cost. This will give the minimum average variable cost.

    LOS 15d

40. **A** Technological advances make it possible to produce more/better quality goods with the same labor and capital resources.

    LOS 17l

41. **A** Price will equal average total cost in the long run, giving zero economic profit. Since each firm has a downward sloping demand curve, price will exceed marginal cost. Each firm will produce below its efficient scale, giving rise to excess capacity.

    LOS 16b

42. **B** Increases in the tax rate are used in fiscal policy to reduce aggregate demand. They have the impact of reducing disposable income but do not directly impact the marginal propensity to consume.

    LOS 19o

43. **A** Marginal revenue becomes zero at the point of unitary elasticity. The monopolist will produce at the point where marginal revenue equals marginal cost. This will be to the left of where marginal revenue is zero, i.e. on the elastic portion of the demand curve.

LOS 16b

44. **C** National income is income received from all factors of production in generating output, including interest income and rent. Exports less imports is a component of the expenditure approach to calculating GDP.

LOS 17d

Financial Reporting and Analysis

45. **A**   Opening stockholders' equity: 3,830

Closing stockholders' equity: 4,120

Net income: 690

Return on equity = 690/[1/2(3830 + 4120)

= 17.4%

LOS 28b

46. **B**   The issue costs are shown as a deferred charge (an asset) under US GAAP whereas they are deducted from the liability under IFRS. This means that US GAAP will report higher assets and higher total debt. This will give lower asset turnover, a higher debt to equity ratio and (assuming part of the deferred charge is included in current assets) a higher current ratio.

LOS 32e

47. **C**   The interest costs will be capitalized as part of inventories. In subsequent years, so long as the inventories have not been sold, current assets, total assets and stockholders equity will be higher. Profit before interest will be the same and total capital will be higher. Inventory turnover will therefore be lower (Cost of goods sold ÷ average inventories) and return on total capital will be lower (profit before interest ÷ debt and equity).

LOS 30a

48. **B**   The asset will be left as an asset held for use until disposal without being shown at fair value. On the spin off, the asset will be removed from the accounts at book value, giving no profit or loss.

LOS 30i

49. **B** $0.4 \times 0.7 \times 25 = 7.0\%$

LOS 28d

50. **A**

	$
Cash paid in 2013	15,000
Less: amount relating to 2012	(2,000)
Less: amount relating to 2014	(1,500)
Rent expense for 2013	11,500

LOS 27e

51. B The warehouse costs and the discount for prompt payment are not allocated to inventories but taken directly to the income statement. Materials, labor and factory overhead are spread over the items to which they relate. The 10,000 spoiled items are charged directly to the income statement as abnormal wastage. Of the 400,000 good cushions, the costs of 380,000 are charged to cost of goods sold and 20,000 are taken to inventory. Overall, $\frac{390}{410}$ of material, labor and factory costs are charged to the income statement as either goods sold or abnormal waste.

	$
Material costs (410,000 × $3 × 90%)	1,107,000
Labor	2,000,000
Factory costs	3,000,000
Total manufacturing costs	6,107,000
Manufacturing costs charged against income $(6,107,000 \times \frac{390}{410})$	5,809,098
Warehouse costs	80,000
Discount for prompt payment (410,000 × $3 × 5%)	(61,500)
Total costs charged	5,827,598

LOS 29a

52. B Days inventory: $\frac{365}{5.2} = 70.2$

Days receivables: $\frac{365}{4.9} = 74.5$

Days payables: $\frac{365}{5.9} = 61.9$

$70.2 + 74.5 - 61.9 = 82.8$

LOS 28b

53. A No cash flows have taken place, so nothing is put in the cash flow statement itself at all. However, the notes will disclose details of the transaction.

LOS 27b

54. C A company using the percentage of completion method will recognize sales, profits and receivables in the first year in proportion to the work done. In contrast, a company using the completed contract method will carry forward all costs to date as inventories, not recording sales and profits or receivables. The higher stockholders equity due to recognition of profits will give the percentage of completion method a lower debt to equity ratio. The receivables recognized will give a higher current ratio than recognizing inventories at cost. The sales recognition could give either a lower or higher asset turnover, depending on the ratio of sales to assets. However, since the increase in assets is only the uplift from inventories at cost to receivables including a profit margin, it is likely that asset turnover will increase.

LOS 25b

55. **C** Changes in the five basic elements (assets, liabilities, equity, income and expenses) are portrayed in the cash flow statement and statement of changes in equity.

   LOS 27e

56. **A** Under US GAAP the funded status of the plan is shown on balance sheet (i.e. its liabilities minus its assets). 3,400,560 – 3,110,660 = £289,900.

   LOS 32k

57. **B** A high inventory turnover/low number of days sales in inventory indicates low inventories, which does not suggest a risk of obsolescent inventories. A just in time system will give lower inventories. Companies selling luxury products tend to have lower inventory turnover than companies selling staple products.

   LOS 29h

58. **B**

	€	€
Sales (110,000 × €34)		3,740,000
Cost of goods sold		
Opening inventories (100,000 × €5)	500,000	
Purchases (30,000 × €6 + 45,000 × €7)	495,000	
Closing inventories (45,000 × €7 + 20,000 × €6)	(435,000)	
		(560,000)
Gross profit		3,180,00

   LOS 29d

59. **A** Increasing the useful life will reduce the depreciation expense in the next year, since the depreciation expense is being spread over a greater number of years. Increasing the expected residual value will reduce the depreciation expense in the next year, since less depreciation will be charged in total. Changing to double-declining balance will increase the depreciation expense in the next year.

   LOS 30c

60. **B** All gains and losses on securities held for trading purposes go through the income statement.

   LOS 25l

61. **B** Reinvestment coverage ratio: $\dfrac{\text{Cash flow from operations}}{\text{Cash paid for long term assets}} = \dfrac{4,800}{690} = 6.96$

   LOS 27i

62. **A** The three conditions are incentives/pressures, opportunities and attitudes/rationalizations.

   LOS 33c

63. **A** Financial weakness is measured by debt levels.

   LOS 35d

64.   **B**   Company X is using the effective interest rate method (required under IFRS and preferred under US GAAP) while company Y is using the straight line method to calculate the interest expense. Since the debt has been issued at a premium to par, the amount of the premium credited against the interest expense for the year will be the same each year for company Y, but will be larger in the earlier years and smaller in the later years for company X. This will make the interest expense lower for company X and reduce the liability for company X by more. This will give company X a higher interest coverage ratio and a lower debt to equity ratio. It will have no impact on cash flows.

LOS 32b

65.   **C**   The lease contains a bargain purchase option, so the lessee (company Y) treats it as a capital lease. The revenue recognition requirements are not met, so the lessor (company X) treats it as an operating lease.

LOS 32g

66.   **B**   The fall in operating cash flows despite an increase in net income indicates that earnings quality may have fallen. Net income has risen at a faster rate than revenues, indicating that profitability has increased. The negative cash flow suggests that a large part of net income is not cash flow based, which will probably be reflected in current assets or current liabilities. Working capital has probably increased as a result.

LOS 28a

67.   **C** $\dfrac{800 + 4,200}{800 + 4,200 + 3,330} = 60.0\%$

LOS 28b

68.   **A**   The cash ratio is considered as a liquidity ratio rather than a solvency ratio.

LOS 28b

Corporate Finance

69. **B** $100 - 3 \times \dfrac{260}{360} = 97.83$

The quoted yield on T-bills is on a discount basis.

LOS 40e

70. **C** The equity beta to use in the WACC calculation is as follows.

$$\beta_A = 1.4 \times \dfrac{1}{1 + 0.7 \times \dfrac{20}{100}} = 1.228$$

$$\beta_E = 1.228 \times \left(1 + 0.7 \dfrac{40}{100}\right) = 1.5718$$

The cost of equity is calculated as:

k = 4 + 1.5718 x 5 = 11.859%

$$\text{WACC} = \dfrac{11.859 \times 100 + 5 \times 0.7 \times 40}{140} = 9.47\%$$

LOS 37a and 37i

71. **B** The supervisory board is independent and non executive. The management board consists of executive management.

LOS 41b

72. **A** The only way that the profitability index would not be greater than 1 is if the net present value is exactly zero, which is highly unlikely. The payback period will be shorter than the discounted payback period, as it does not discount the cash flows. Since there is a discounted payback period and the project generates a constant annuity, the accounting rate of return should exceed the cost of capital.

LOS 36d

73. **C** The company has sold part of its business for cash and the proceeds are being distributed. This is a liquidating dividend.

LOS 39a

74. **B** If the company breaks even after interest expense, its profit before interest must be $80,000. Operating profits have fallen by $\dfrac{250,000 - 80,000}{250,000} = 68\%$. Since the DOL is 1.6, sales have fallen by $\dfrac{68}{1.6} = 42.5\%$. Revised sales are therefore 500,000 x 57.5% = $287,500. The operating margin is $\dfrac{80,000}{287.500} = 27.8\%$

LOS 38d

75. **A** Cost of preferred stock = $2.80/$55 = 5.09%

LOS 37a

76. **A** The audit committee is ideally 100% independent directors as it is designed to oversee the financial accounts prepared by the executive management.

LOS 41f

77. **B** A company will use direct negotiation with a limited number of shareholders and will possibly offer a high price to give them an incentive to sell. Open market purchases will be at the market price, so will not cause a transfer of value. In a Dutch auction, shareholders who wish to sell their shares will bid to sell them, specifying the minimum price they are prepared to receive. The company will take the lowest price possible given the competitive bids that are submitted.

LOS 39c

78. **B** Cost of capital: $\dfrac{1.50}{30} + 0.03 = 0.08$ or 8%

Capital raised: $\dfrac{100,000,000}{0.96} = \$104,166,667$ (this gives a net $100 million after paying 4% issue costs).

NPV: $\dfrac{5,000,000}{0.08 - 0.04} - 104,166,667 = \$20,833,333$

LOS 36d

Portfolio Management

79. **B**   The investment with the highest systematic risk will have the highest expected return. Calculating each investments' systematic risk in variances:

A: $20^2 - 10^2 = 300$

B: $25^2 - 18^2 = 301$

C: $30^2 - 25^2 = 275$

LOS 44c

80. **C**   Covariance patterns can change in an unfavorable way for the investor, meaning that all markets fall at the same time.

LOS 42a

81. **B**   Strategic asset allocation and how the portfolio will be rebalanced to restore the strategic asset allocation over time are more likely to be specified than tactical asset allocation.

LOS 45b

82. **C**   The arithmetic mean assumes that the amount invested at the beginning of each period is the same, whereas the geometric mean assumes a buy and hold approach, where the closing value at the end of one period is the opening value at the beginning of the next period.

LOS 43a

83. **C**   ETFs are closed ended, but because of their structure their share prices trade close to net asset value, unlike closed end mutual funds.

LOS 42e

84. **A** $\beta = \dfrac{\sigma_{systematic}}{\sigma_{market}} = \dfrac{\rho_{security,market}\,\sigma_{total}}{\sigma_{market}}$.

The characteristic line is based on a regression of the security's excess returns over the risk free rate against the market's excess returns over the risk free rate (it is the market model that calculates beta by regressing security returns against market returns).

LOS 44e

Equity

85. **C**   The strong form of the EMH states that it is not possible to make profits from nonpublic information, in addition to public information and market information.

LOS 48d

86. **C**   Proxy voting is when a shareholder's vote is cast by someone else on his or her behalf. Statutory voting is one share one vote. Cumulative voting is where shareholders can direct their total voting rights to specific candidates, so in a vote for four directors, a shareholder with one share could direct four votes to one candidate.

LOS 49b

87. **B** $$22.9 = \frac{0.55}{k - 0.037}$$

k = 0.061

Note that the payout ratio is 55% since the retention ratio is 45%.

LOS 51e

88. **A**   An investment in long term manufacturing facilities should be matched with long term financing.

LOS 46a

89. **B**   The Barclays Capital Global Aggregate Bond Index includes government bonds, corporate bonds and securitized issues. There is a minimum issue size for inclusion. The number of bonds in the index varies over time.

LOS 47i

90. **B**   Government classification systems generally do not disclose information about specific companies or businesses, do not distinguish between different types of business and include both for-profit and not-for-profit organizations in their data.

LOS 50b

91. **C**   Trading through dealers represents a secondary market.

LOS 46c

92. **B**   Equal weighting requires more rebalancing as the different returns on each security in the index for each period will result in the weights moving away from equal weightings. This gives higher transaction costs.

LOS 47f

93. **A**   The most common currency of denomination is US dollars, although other currencies such as the euro are also used. GDRs are issued outside of the US, so are not issued in all major stock markets worldwide. Global registered shares are shares that are registered on different exchanges worldwide that trade in the currency of each exchange.

LOS 49d

94. **B** Earnings before tax is after charging the interest expense. Since enterprise value includes both debt and equity, the fundamental variable should be before charging interest.

LOS 51i

95. **C** At the embryonic stage, prices are higher as it is a new product. In the growth phase, prices fall as economies of scale are achieved and distribution channels are opened. At the mature phase, there is little growth and prices are lower due to saturation of demand.

LOS 50h

96. **B** The gambler's fallacy is that recent outcomes affect investors' estimates of future probabilities.

LOS 48g

Fixed Income

97.   A   A call provision allows the issuer to redeem early at a predetermined time and price.

      LOS 52f

98.   B   Reducing reserve requirements and purchasing Treasury securities from banks will both increase the funds available to banks for lending and cause interest rates to fall. Verbal persuasion is less frequently used but is the only possible answer.

      LOS 53e

99.   A   A deferred coupon bond pays a zero coupon for a number of years and then a higher coupon for the remainder of its life. A step-up note has a coupon rate that increases over time.

      LOS 52a

100.   A   The constant margin means that the value of a floating rate note may change if the required margin changes, so there is risk in respect of the margin. Once LIBOR has been fixed for the next period, there is a risk that LIBOR will change before the next reset date, giving additional interest rate risk.

      LOS 55i

101.   C   The investor needs to have assets with a value of $110,250 after 2 years. This will be made up of reinvested coupons (reinvested at the available yield to maturity of 4%) and the present value at time 2 of the bond maturing at time 3 (discounted at its yield to maturity of 4%). This comes to a final value at time 2 of:

$$5,000 \times 1.04 + 5,000 + \frac{105,000}{1.04} = 111,160$$

He has a surplus of assets over liabilities.

Alternatively, we can note that the duration of the bond is probably more than 2 years while the duration of the liability is 2 years. A fall in interest rates should give a greater increase in the bond's value than the liabilities present value.

      LOS 55a

102.   C   The duration of a highly leveraged security can exceed its final maturity. Certain securities will have a price change that is positive for an increase in interest rates and negative for a decrease in interest rates, indicating a positive slope. The description of duration as the first derivative of the price yield function is a correct interpretation of duration, although operationally meaningless.

      LOS 55b

103.   C   Securities placed under a rule 144A offering can be traded amongst large institutions without being registered with the SEC.

      LOS 49d

104.   **A**   The yield of the 2% coupon bond is 5%.

Time	Flow	PV at 5%
0	(91.83)	(91.83)
1	2	1.905
2	2	1.814
3	102	88.11
		-

The price of the 4% coupon bond discounted at a yield of 5% is:

$$\frac{4}{1.05} + \frac{4}{1.05^2} + \frac{104}{1.05^3} = 97.28$$

LOS 54a

105.   **A**   The special redemption price is usually par, which gives the issuer and incentive to redeem the bond at the special redemption price rather than the general redemption price which may be above par.

LOS 52f

106.   **B**   So long as prepayments stay within a particular range, the amortization schedule for capital for a Tranche should be reasonably certain, reducing prepayment risk. This risk is taken on by the support Tranche, which has an uncertain schedule for amortization.

LOS 52e

107.   **C**   The yield to worst does not give an accurate indication of the potential yield/return over the investment horizon, as it assumes that all coupons can be reinvested at the specified yield. It ignores the different reinvestment assumption for each yield calculated in identifying the yield to worst. It can be calculated for MBS based on prepayment assumptions.

LOS 54f

108.   **A**   The full price is:

$$\frac{3}{1.025^{55/182}} + \frac{3}{1.025^{155/182}} + \frac{1033}{1.025^{255/182}} = 103.19$$

Accrued interest is:

$$3 \times \frac{127}{182} = 2.09$$

Clean price is: 103,19 − 2.09 = 101.10

LOS 54a

109. **B** Current 3 months LIBOR: $\dfrac{5.0}{4} = 1.25\%$

Current 6 months LIBOR: $\dfrac{6.3}{2} = 3.15\%$

Expected 3 months LIBOR in 3 months time: $\dfrac{1.0315}{1.0125} - 1 = 0.018765$

Expressed as an annual figure: $1.8765 \times 4 = 7.47\%$

LOS 54h

110. **C** The Macauley duration approach only allows for parallel shifts. The full valuation approach allows for parallel and nonparallel shifts.

LOS 58

Derivatives

111. **C**   The notional principal is typically exchanged but there are some scenarios when it is not exchanged.

        LOS 61b

112. **B**   The price has moved by 97.12 − 96.43 = 0.69 or 69 basis points. This gives a profit of 69 × $25 = $1,725.

        LOS 59f

113. **A**   The final value of the opening stock price is $180 × 1.06 = $191. The investor has agreed to sell the share for $186, so he suffers a loss of $5.

        LOS 58d

114. **C**   The September column is inconsistent as it shows the price of the put option falling as the strike price increases. All the other prices appear consistent with one another (and were in fact calculated using the Black Scholes Merton model with consistent assumptions).

        LOS 63l

115. **A**   A covered call is a long stock position + a short call. This gives a profit/loss graph which has the same shape as a short put.

        LOS 61a

116. **C**   A forward contract is not exchange traded and is not usually marked to market, unlike futures contracts. It represents an obligation rather than a contingent claim. Forward contracts may be settled through delivery of the underlying asset or by cash settlement, depending on the nature of the underlying and the terms of the contract.

        LOS 57c

Alternative Investments

117. **A**   Real estate has the potential to provide an inflation hedge if rents can be adjusted quickly for inflation.

LOS 63a and 63d

118. **B**   A managed futures fund is a sub-group of global macro funds and convertible bond arbitrage is a technique used by a market neutral fund.

LOS 63d

119. **A**   Long only commodities investing provides a natural hedge for long term inflation exposure. Commodities tend to perform better at the times in the business cycle when financial assets perform less well.

LOS 63d

120. **B**   Global REITs are quoted investment vehicles in real estate (real estate investment trusts). They tend to be highly correlated with the stock market rather than the bond market, and returns are volatile rather than smooth.

LOS 63d

Practice Examination 3
Afternoon Session

2014

The Afternoon Session of Practice Examination 3 consists of 120 multiple choice questions which must be completed in three hours. The topic areas covered are:

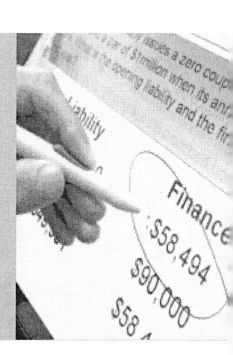

BPP
LEARNING MEDIA

Questions 1 through 18 relate to Ethical and Professional Standards

1. Robert Joslyn CFA is an equity analyst who has just joined a new firm. He wishes to make an immediate impact and as soon as he joined the firm he obtained copies of his research reports from his previous firm, which were all available publicly. He used these reports to prepare research reports for his new firm. In his reports for his new firm, he explicitly states that the research report is based on his previous work for his old firm and refers to the research reports that he used.

   Joslyn has *most likely* violated:

   A. Standard IC – Misrepresentation.

   B. Standard IVA – Loyalty.

   C. Standard VC – Record Retention.

2. Pelham Johnson CFA works for a commercial bank which has significant banking relationships with a client, Tiles Inc. Johnson's supervisors at the bank have made it clear to Johnson that the relationship with Tiles Inc. should not be compromised in any way. Tiles Inc. has requested that Johnson replies to a request for a credit reference for Tiles Inc.

   In the view of Johnson, the amount of credit concerned is probably beyond the ability of Tiles Inc. to borrow safely. Johnson states in his credit reference for Tiles Inc. that the bank has no reason to believe that Tiles Inc. would be unable to repay the amount to be borrowed, although the amount concerned is more than they would usually consider for Tiles Inc. to borrow.

   Johnson has *most likely*:

   A. violated Standard IB – Independence and Objectivity.

   B. violated Standard IIA – Material Nonpublic Information.

   C. not violated CFA Institute's Standards of Professional Conduct.

3. When the CFA Institute Professional Conduct Program (PCP) asks a member to cooperate in an investigation by releasing confidential information about a client where there is no legal requirement not to disclose such information, Standard IIIE – Preservation of Confidentiality states that the member:

   A. must disclose the information to the PCP.

   B. must not disclose the information to the PCP without the client's authorization.

   C. is encouraged to cooperate with the investigation by the PCP by disclosing the information.

4. The best compliance procedure for an investment firm to ensure compliance with Standard IIID – Performance Presentation is *most likely* to:

   A. take reasonable efforts to ensure investment performance information is fair, accurate and complete.

   B. include disclaimers to investment performance information that fully explain the performance results being reported.

   C. ensure that investment performance information is in compliance with CFA Institute's Global Investment Performance Standards (GIPS®).

5. Malcolm Greenslade CFA is a buy-side equity analyst for his firm. He often has a financial interest in securities on which he makes recommendations and these holdings are always disclosed to his employer. Prior to releasing recommendations on securities, he typically completes his own trading in the security so as to avoid a problem with his own trades being completed at the same time or just after trades for his employer's clients. He discloses details of his trading in monthly reports to his employer, as he is required to do under company procedures.

    Greenslade has *most likely*:

    A. not violated CFA Institute's Standards of Practice.

    B. violated CFA Institute's Standards of Practice by his trading.

    C. violated CFA Institute's Standards of Practice by only disclosing his trading in his monthly reports, not at the time it occurred.

6. Janice Derring CFA is an analyst who covers the technology sector. She has just completed a detailed report on a company in the sector which was very well received by her supervisor, the investing public and the company itself. She is subsequently contacted by the company and invited to meet the chief financial officer to discuss the company's business in more detail. The company offers to arrange for her transport to their headquarters by its own private jet. She accepts the offer and visits the company. After the meeting, the chief financial officer invites her to an extremely expensive restaurant before her return and she again accepts this invitation. On her return to the office, she discloses the fact that she used the private jet and was invited to an expensive restaurant by the chief financial officer to her supervisor.

    Derring has *most likely* violated:

    A. Standard IB – Independence and Objectivity and Standard IVB – Additional Compensation Arrangements.

    B. Standard IVB – Additional Compensation Arrangements but not Standard IB – Independence and Objectivity.

    C. Standard IB – Independence and Objectivity but not Standard IVB – Additional Compensation Arrangements.

7. Julian Forbes CFA set up an investment business which subsequently failed due to a stock market crash depriving him of clients. The failure caused him to suffer personal bankruptcy. It is *most likely* that the personal bankruptcy:

    A. reflects adversely on the integrity and trustworthiness of Forbes.

    B. is not viewed as misconduct in CFA Institute's Standards of Professional Conduct.

    C. is grounds for a complaint to be filed against Forbes under the Professional Conduct Program.

8. Harry McNuff CFA is a portfolio manager who works for Brazen Investment Management. A number of his family members have accounts with Brazen Investment Management and pay the same fee rates as other clients of the firm. The firm has obtained an allocation of shares in an oversubscribed issue and is deciding how these should be allocated among the accounts for which they are suitable, including McNuff's own account. The shares should *most likely* be allocated on a pro rata basis to all clients for which they are suitable:

    A. including McNuff and his family member accounts.

    B. except for McNuff forgoing sales to himself and to his family member accounts.

    C. including the family member accounts, but with McNuff forgoing sales to himself.

9. The compliance procedure which is *most likely* to be consistent with Standard VIA – Disclosure of Conflicts with regard to stock ownership by employees is to:

   A. prohibit employees from holding securities in companies that they recommend to clients or that clients hold.

   B. require sell-side employees to disclose any beneficial ownership interest in a security that the employee is recommending.

   C. require sell-side employees to disclose any materially beneficial ownership interest in a security that the employee is recommending.

10. Michel du Baton CFA attends an analysts meeting held by Rugged Outdoors Inc, where the chief financial officer of Rugged Outdoors Inc. informs the analysts that the company's earnings will be significantly lower than expected in the next quarter as a result of a poor reception for the company's latest outdoor equipment range. After the meeting, du Baton telephones his office and informs a portfolio manager to sell off holdings in Rugged Outdoors Inc. immediately.

    Lucy Jones CFA is an analyst who was not invited to the meeting by Rugged Outdoors Inc. because of her outspoken reports on the company in the past. Before the meeting, she has been analyzing Rugged Outdoors Inc.'s financial statements in detail and has noted that a number of retailers are reporting a significant downturn in sales for their key ranges, which include Rugged Outdoor ranges. As a result of her analysis, she concludes that Rugged Outdoors Inc.'s stock price is overvalued and recommends that the stock be sold. Standard IIA – Material Non-public Information has *most likely* been violated by:

    A. neither du Baton nor Jones.

    B. du Baton but not by Jones.

    C. Jones but not by du Baton.

11. Johnson Investment Management, which has adopted CFA Institute's Standards of Professional Conduct as part of its compliance procedures, has an arrangement with Smith Brokers. In the arrangement, Smith Brokers refers prospective accounts to Johnson Investment Management. In exchange, Johnson Investment Management makes available its in house research to Smith Brokers and directs trades from the referred accounts to Smith Brokers.

    Johnson Investment Management should *most likely* disclose to its clients that are referred by Smith Brokers the fact that it:

    A. makes available its in house research to Smith Brokers.

    B. directs trades from the referred accounts to Smith Brokers.

    C. makes available its in house research to Smith Brokers and directs trades from the referred accounts to Smith Brokers.

12. Raymond Osmond CFA is the chief investment officer of a banking group. The group has an insurance subsidiary for which the investment policy statement states that it is mandated to invest primarily in highly liquid government and corporate bonds which are investment grade. Osmond has decided that the portfolio of the insurance subsidiary should have a more diversified base and has consequently invested in some private equity. The private equity investments have low correlations with the existing investments in the portfolio, offer attractive returns and have a lock up period of five years, after which an exit strategy will be implemented. Osmond has *most likely* violated:

    A. Standard IIIA – Loyalty, Prudence and Care and Standard IIIC – Suitability.

    B. Standard IIIA – Loyalty, Prudence and Care but not Standard IIIC – Suitability.

    C. Standard IIIC – Suitability but not Standard IIIA – Loyalty, Prudence and Care.

13. Recommended compliance procedures for Standard IIA – Material Nonpublic Information *most likely* include:

    A. the issuance of press releases by companies prior to analysts meetings and conference calls.

    B. a prohibition on an analyst from a research department providing assistance to the investment banking department of a firm.

    C. a prohibition on all types of proprietary activity in a security when a firm is in possession of material non-public information about the security.

14. When a supervisor leans that an employee has violated the law, the action taken by the supervisor that is *most likely* consistent with Standard IVC – Responsibilities of Supervisors is to:

    A. obtain the employee's assurances that the violation will not be repeated.

    B. report the misconduct to the chief executive officer and warn the employee not to repeat the violation.

    C. place limits on the employee's activities pending the outcome of any investigation into the violation.

15. Marianne Morrison CFA is a portfolio manager with a number of individual clients. One of her clients has recently died, setting up a trust with her assets. The terms of the trust are that her husband, who is 50 years old, will receive income from the trust for the remainder of his life and the assets of the trust will pass to her only child on her husband's death. Morrison is now responsible for managing the trust assets. She identifies the financial and general circumstances of the husband and child, prepares an investment policy statement and prepares capital market expectations. As inflation is expected to be around 5% per annum for the foreseeable future, she decides to invest the portfolio assets in AAA rated US nominal Treasury bonds, to generate sufficient income for the husband while avoiding credit risk for the principal value of the portfolio.

    Morrison has *most likely*:

    A. violated Standard III – Duties to Clients.

    B. violated Standard VI – Conflicts of Interest.

    C. not violated CFA Institute's Standards of Professional Conduct.

16. Abby Salinger has just completed all three levels of the CFA examinations at the first attempt and received confirmation of receiving the CFA designation from CFA Institute. She is interviewed by her firm's in house magazine editor for the purpose of an article on her successful completion of the program. Salinger states that she is very happy to have passed the exams and become a CFA Charterholder, as it will help her future career development and has made her better at valuing equity securities. Salinger has *most likely:*

    A. not violated CFA Institute's Standards of Practice.

    B. violated CFA Institute's Standards of Practice by stating that passing the exams has made her better at valuing equity securities.

    C. violated CFA Institute's Standards of Practice by stating that passing the exams will help her future career development and has made her better at valuing equity securities.

17. Compliance with GIPS standards *most likely:*

    A. is applied on a composite-wide basis.

    B. must be verified by an independent third party.

    C. does not address every aspect of performance measurement.

18. Following an investigation of a member under the Professional Conduct Program, it is *most likely* that a cautionary letter:

    A. may be rejected or accepted by the member.

    B. represents the conclusion of the inquiry by the PCP.

    C. is issued by the Hearing Panel that investigated the matter.

Questions 19 through 32 relate to Quantitative Methods

19. In technical analysis, Bollinger Bands *least likely*:

    A. are wider apart for more volatile securities.

    B. reduce the amount of trading that is required.

    C. are commonly used as part of a contrarian strategy.

20. An annuity of $250 a year commences immediately and stops at the end of 30 years. The interest rate is 7% (APR), with continuous compounding. The present value of the annuity series is *closest to*:

    A. $3,025.

    B. $3,275.

    C. $3,352.

21. If the natural logarithm of a stock price is normally distributed then it is *least likely* that the:

    A. stock price is lognormally distributed.

    B. stock returns are normally distributed.

    C. natural logarithm of stock prices exhibits a positive skew.

22. The reinvestment rate used when calculating the net present value and internal rate of return for a project is:

    A. internally determined for both the net present value approach and the internal rate of return approach.

    B. externally determined for the net present value approach and internally determined for the internal rate of return approach.

    C. internally determined for the net present value approach and externally determined for the internal rate of return approach.

23. When a distribution exhibits positive excess kurtosis, it is *most likely* that compared to the normal distribution it will:

    A. have a lower peak.

    B. have a greater probability of large negative values.

    C. be less likely to reflect the distribution of returns on an equity market series.

24. An analyst estimates that the probability of the GDP growth rate increasing is 40%. If the GDP growth rate increases, he estimates that the probability of an industry's sales increasing is 70%. If the GDP growth rate does not increase, he estimates that the probability of the industry's sales increasing is 20%. The industry's sales actually decline. The probability that the GDP growth rate increased is *closest to*:

    A. 0.20.

    B. 0.27.

    C. 0.60.

25. Stock X has an expected return of 5% and a standard deviation of 8%. Stock Y has an expected return of 7% and a standard deviation of 9%. The stock returns are normally distributed and are independent of each other. The probability that a portfolio consisting of 50% in stock X and 50% in stock Y will have a return of less than -6% is *closest to*:

    A. 0.5%.

    B. 2.5%.

    C. 5.0%.

26. The stock market index earns a return of 5.4% in year 1, 8.1% in year 2 and 9.8% in year 3. The mean annual growth rate in the value of a portfolio that is tracking the stock market is *closest to*:

    A. 7.54%.

    B. 7.75%.

    C. 7.77%.

27. An analyst is researching into whether stocks with high book to price ratios offer superior risk adjusted returns. He identifies all the stocks in the Russell 3000 as at 31 March 2012 and breaks them into two categories, being high book to price and low book to price stocks at this date on the basis of their financial statements for the year ended 31 December 2011. He then analyzes the returns on these stocks over a 20 years period.

    The analyst's approach is *most likely* subject to:

    A. survivorship bias.

    B. time period bias.

    C. look ahead bias.

28. The time preferences of individuals for current versus future real consumption is reflected by the:

    A. real risk free rate.

    B. nominal risk free rate.

    C. nominal risk free rate + maturity premium.

29. A pension fund wishes its equity manager to have a monthly standard deviation of returns of no more than 5%. It has been using the manager for the past two years, over which time the monthly standard deviation has been 5.5%. The test statistic for the relevant statistical test is *closest to*:

    A. 19.

    B. 28.

    C. 29.

30. In technical analysis, an ascending triangle *most likely* arises when the trend line connecting high prices:

    A. and low prices are both rising.

    B. are rising and the trend line connecting low prices are horizontal.

    C. are horizontal and the trend line connecting low prices are rising. ♦

31. In its first year of existence, an equity mutual fund that tracks the stock market index performs very well and as a result, a large amount of funds are invested at the end of the year. In the second year, there is a stock market crash. The money weighted return on the fund over the two years is *most likely*:

   A. lower than the time weighted return.

   B. higher than the time weighted return.

   C. lower or higher than the time weighted return, depending on the amount of new money invested compared to the fund's size.

32. A higher p value for a statistical test *most likely*:

   A. will be caused by a larger sample size.

   B. reflects a higher significance level for the test.

   C. indicates a higher chance of a type II error arising.

Questions 33 through 44 relate to Economics

33. Within the theory of consumer choice, the assumption that a consumer could never have so much of a good that they would refuse more is best known as the assumption of:

    A. non-satiation.

    B. transitive preferences.

    C. complete preferences.

34. When supply of a good by a firm is perfectly inelastic, it is *most likely* that:

    A. the firm has done something internally to merit a high market price.

    B. a tax on the good will have no impact on efficiency.

    C. the whole of the income received by the owner of the factor is the amount required to induce the owner to offer the good for use.

35. The purpose of price discrimination is *most likely* to:

    A. increase total surplus.

    B. improve market efficiency.

    C. convert consumer surplus into economic profit.

36. When a government increases the quantity of money to boost aggregate demand, giving rise to anticipated inflation over time, the long run impact on real GDP is *most* likely that it will persist:

    A. at potential GDP.

    B. above potential GDP.

    C. below potential GDP.

37. In a country where more women are looking for work and the number of young people going to college is increasing, it is *most likely* that the labor force activity ratio will:

    A. increase.

    B. decrease.

    C. increase or decrease, depending on the relative strength of the two factors.

38. The role of the Central Bank *least likely* includes:

    A. monopoly supplier of currency.

    B. setting fiscal policy.

    C. lender of last resort.

39. In perfect competition, firms will *most likely* shut down a plant when:

    A. average revenue is less than average total cost.

    B. average revenue is equal to average variable cost.

    C. average revenue is less than average variable cost.

40. The US Federal Reserve has conducted open market purchases of government securities. The *most likely* impact of this is to:

   A. increase the inflation rate.

   B. increase the federal funds rate.

   C. decrease the supply of loanable funds.

41. In the long run, the main influence on aggregate demand is *most likely* the:

   A. rate of technological change.

   B. wealth and substitution effects.

   C. growth rate in the quantity of money.

42. Which of the following is *least likely* to be a desirable attribute of a tax policy?

   A. Simplicity in establishing any tax liability.

   B. Fairness of the policy should take president over efficiency of tax revenue generation.

   C. A fairness to ensure people in similar situations pay the same taxes.

43. The Nash equilibrium in a duopoly *most likely* predicts that in the long run the two firms will:

   A. be subject to regulatory pricing rules.

   B. act as if they are in a competitive industry.

   C. collude so as to maximize their joint profits.

44. Which of the following is *most likely* to give rise to an unstable equilibrium?

   A. Both demand and supply curve have a negative slope and the supply intersects demand from above.

   B. Both demand and supply curve have a negative slope and the supply intersects demand from below.

   C. Supply curve has a positive slope, demand curve has a negative slope and supply curve intersects from above.

Questions 45 through 68 relate to Financial Reporting and Analysis

45. Extracts from the financial statements for the year ended December 31 2013 of a company that uses US GAAP are as follows.

	2013 $	2012 $
Current assets (excluding cash)	1,700	1,450
Long lived assets	3,380	3,290
Total assets	5,080	4,740
Accounts payable	890	720
Net income	560	420
Cash outflows from investing activities	600	420

The cash flow from operating activities for the year ended December 31 2013 is *closest to*:

A. $480.

B. $990.

C. $1,150.

46. It is *most likely* that for the lessee, compared to an operating lease, a finance lease will have a lower:

A. current ratio.

B. financial leverage ratio.

C. net margin in the later years of the lease.

47. When a company changes it inventory valuation method from LIFO to FIFO, the change should be accounted for:

A. prospectively.

B. retrospectively.

C. as a cumulative adjustment in the year of the change.

48. The feature of financial statements which is *least likely* to be one of the principal characteristics that make financial information useful according to the IFRS Framework for the Preparation and Presentation of Financial Statements is:

A. going concern.

B. relevance.

C. comparability.

49. A company has incurred significant research costs in relation to its future product development. The company has the policy of capitalizing all costs where there is permitted. Compared to the company's asset turnover under US GAAP, its asset turnover under International Financial Reporting Standards will *most likely* be:

   A. lower.

   B. higher.

   C. the same.

50. A company prepares its financial statements under International Financial Reporting Standards. It has just issued debt with a par value of $10 million at a price of $9.6 million. The debt has a maturity of five years and pays an annual coupon of 2%. Issue costs were $0.1 million. The value of the liability at the end of the first year is *closest to*:

   A. $9,572,000.

   B. $9,594,000.

   C. $9,676,000.

51. Compared to the use of straight line depreciation, use of the double declining balance method by a US company will *most likely* result in:

   A. taxes with a lower present value.

   B. higher asset turnover in each year of the asset's life.

   C. a lower return on stockholders equity in the later years of the asset's life.

52. Jumbo Inc. is a US company that sells jacuzzis. At September 30 2013, it had inventories of 400 jacuzzis, each of which cost $250. Details of its sales and purchases of jacuzzis over the next three months of 2013 are as follows.

Date	Quantity	Price $
4 October	50 sold	400
30 October	80 manufactured	280
5 November	60 sold	420
28 November	50 manufactured	310
1 December	30 sold	450

   Jumbo Inc. uses the LIFO method of valuing inventories. The difference between the inventory values using the perpetual system and using the period system of recording inventory is *closest to*:

   A. zero.

   B. $1,800.

   C. $2,100.

53. A company buys a fixed asset on 1 January 2013 for $50,000 which has an expected useful life of 5 years and a zero salvage value. The company plans to depreciate the asset using the straight line method of depreciation. For tax purposes, the asset is to be depreciated over 4 years using straight line depreciation. In the first year of the asset's life, the income tax rate is 40%. During the second year, the tax rate changes to 30%. The income statement for the year ended 31 December 2014 will show deferred tax *closest to*:

   A. $500.

   B. $750.

   C. $1500.

54. Extracts from a company's financial statements are as follows.

	2013	2012
	$	$
Sales	22,900	18,400
Cost of goods sold	11,900	9,570
Receivables	5,700	4,600
Inventories	1,200	800
Payables	920	800

   It is *most likely* that the company is:

   A. building up obsolescent inventories.

   B. expanding sales through favorable credit terms.

   C. taking advantage of payment discounts offered by suppliers.

55. Sinan plc has just acquired 100% of the share capital of Henry plc for a total of £5,000,000. Details of Henry plc's balance sheet at the date of the acquisition is as follows.

	Book value £	Fair value £
Tangible assets	3,000,000	3,500,000
Liabilities	1,000,000	800,000
Stockholders equity	2,000,000	

   In addition, Sinan plc has established that Henry has identifiable intangible assets with an indefinite life that have a value of £800,000.

   The goodwill recorded by Sinan plc as a result of the acquisition is *closest to*:

   A. £700,000.

   B. £1,500,000.

   C. £2,300,000.

56. International Financial Reporting Standards *most likely* require full provision for:

   A. deferred tax liabilities.

   B. deferred tax liabilities and assets.

   C. deferred tax liabilities and assets except those not expected to crystallize in the foreseeable future.

57. Details of inventories for a company are as follows.

Inventory category	X $	Y $	Z $
Balance sheet value	5,000	6,000	7,000
Cost	7,000	9,000	11,000
Net realizable value	5,500	10,000	6,000

The revised total balance sheet value for inventories under International Financial Reporting Standards is *closest to*:

A. $20,000.

B. $20,500.

C. $21,500.

58. A company purchases a fixed asset on 1 January 2012 for $40,000. The asset is to be depreciated at a rate of 10% per year for accounts purposes and 15% per year for tax purposes. During 2013, the company accrued interest income of $5,000, which will be received during 2014. The interest income is taxed in the year that it is received. The income tax rate is 30%. Net temporary differences as at 31 December 2013 are *closest to*:

A. $3,000.

B. $5,000.

C. $7,000.

59. A long lived asset has a balance sheet carrying value of $32,000. The undiscounted value of the expected future cash flows is $34,000 and the present value of the expected future cash flows is $30,000. The asset could be sold for $31,000, with sale costs of $3,000. Under US GAAP, the asset will suffer a writedown in its balance sheet value of:

A. zero.

B. $2,000.

C. $4,000.

60. Company P owns an asset which it is going to lease to company Q, the lease starting on 1 January 2013. The machine was constructed by company P at a cost of $20,000. The lease consists of four annual payments of $6,500, commencing on 1 January 2013 and ending on 1 January 2016. The salvage value of the asset at the end of the lease is expected to be zero. The interest rate for the lease is 7%. The lease receivable that will be included in company P's financial statements as at December 31 2013 is *closest to*:

A. $11,800.

B. $14,400.

C. $18,300.

61. Under International Financial Reporting Standards, deferred tax on revaluation of property is *most likely*:

    A. not recognized.

    B. recognized in stockholders equity in the year of the revaluation.

    C. recognized in the income statement in the year of the revaluation.

---

62. Extracts from a company's financial statements are as follows.

	2013	2012
	$	$
Sales	20,500	19,100
Cost of goods sold	12,100	10,900
Receivables	3,200	2,900
Payables	2,900	2,612
Inventories	1,100	1,000

    The company's payables turnover is *closest to*:

    A. 4.21.

    B. 4.39.

    C. 4.43.

---

63. When a company changes its estimate of the useful life of a fixed asset, the change will *most likely* be accounted for on a:

    A. cumulative basis.

    B. prospective basis.

    C. retrospective basis.

---

64. A company has the following stockholders equity as at December 31 2013 and 2012.

	2013	2012
	$	$
Common stock ($0.1 par value)	10,000,000	9,000,000
Convertible redeemable 5% preferred stock ($10 par value)	5,000,000	5,000,000
Retained earnings	130,000,000	110,000,000
Stockholders' equity	145,000,000	124,000,000

    On 1 April 2013, the company issued 10 million common shares at full price. The conversion terms for the preferred stock are 2 shares for each $10 par value. The company paid a common dividend in the year of $5,000,000.

    The diluted earnings per share for the year ended December 31 2013 is *closest to*:

    A. $0.250.

    B. $0.254.

    C. $0.256.

65. Extracts from the cash flow statement for the year ended December 31 2013 of a company that uses US GAAP are as follows.

	$
Net income	9,030
Increase in working capital	2,432
Depreciation expense	3,400
Cash flow from operating activities	9,998
Capital expenditure	5,090
Cash flow from investing activities	5,090
Dividends	4,000
Shares repurchased	6,500
New debt issued	5,400
Cash flow from financing activities	5,100
Decrease in cash	192

Net income includes tax paid of $4,500 at a rate of 30% and interest expense of $3,200.

The free cash flow to the firm for the year ended December 31 2013 is *closest to*:

A. $5,592.

B. $7,148.

C. $8,108.

66. Cash payments related to trading securities on a short term basis for a property company will *most likely* be reflected in the cash flow statement by:

A. financing ouflows.

B. operating outflows.

C. investing outflows.

67. Extracts from a company's financial statements are as follows.

	2013 $	2012 $
Sales	15,210	14,594
Operating income	2,792	2,570
Interest expense	595	650
Income before tax	2,197	1,920
Tax at 30%	659	576
Net income	1,538	1,344
Total assets	10,500	9,290
Total liabilities	7,380	6,001
Stockholders equity	3,120	3,289

An analyst wishes to calculate return on assets. She is particularly concerned to be able to compare across companies with different capital structures and different tax rates. The return on assets for the company that she will calculate will be *closest to*:

A. 20%.

B. 28%.

C. 49%.

68. In times of rising prices and constant inventory levels, compared to a company using the FIFO method of inventory valuation, a company using the LIFO method of inventory valuation will have a:

    A. lower gross margin and higher cash flows.

    B. lower gross margin and the same cash flows.

    C. higher gross margin and the same cash flows.

Questions 69 through 78 relate to Corporate Finance

69. A company has been offered credit terms by its suppliers of 1/10 net 40. Its rate of interest on its bank overdraft is 10% (daily compounding). The company can also borrow by issuing 30 days commercial paper at a discount of 10%. The company should *most likely*:

   A. pay its suppliers early, financing this with an overdraft.

   B. pay its suppliers at the end of the normal credit period.

   C. pay its suppliers early, financing this with commercial paper.

70. A US investor is estimating the cost of equity to be used for appraising an investment in a foreign company, called Virgilio, in the country Bucolia. The currency of Bucolia is the franc. The investor has identified the following data to assist her in identifying an appropriate country risk premium when estimating the cost of equity of Virgilio.

US government bond yield	2%
Bucolian government bond yield	5%
US equity risk premium	4%
Bucolia equity risk premium	8%
Annualized standard deviation of Bucolia's equity index	25%
Annualized standard deviation of Bucolia's franc denominated government bonds	10%
Annualized standard deviation of Bucolia's US dollar denominated government bonds	15%

   The country risk premium to be used when estimating the cost of equity for Virgilio is *closest to*:

   A. 4%.

   B. 5%.

   C. 7%.

71. When considering whether a person is qualified to be appointed to the board as an independent director, the factor that is *most likely* favorable is that the potential board member:

   A. is qualified as legal counsel.

   B. is now retired and previously worked at the company in senior management.

   C. holds a large number of directorships in other companies in a range of industries.

72. Projects X and Y are mutually exclusive. Details of cash flows for each project are as follows.

Time	Project X	Project Y
0	(5,000)	(20,000)
1	3,000	12,000
2	2,500	7,000
3	2,000	6,000
IRR	25%	14%

The discount rate at which an investor would be indifferent as to which project he would select is *most likely*:

A. between 5% and 10%.

B. between 14% and 25%.

C. above 25%.

73. Shareholder X sells her shareholding in a company to shareholder Y two days after the company has declared a dividend on the stock. Shareholder Y holds the shares until they go ex dividend and then sells them to Shareholder Z before the payment date. The dividend will *most likely* be paid by the company to:

A. shareholder X.

B. shareholder Y.

C. shareholder Z.

74. Details of three graphs plotting the relationship between the degree of operating leverage (DOL) and sales quantity are as follows.

Graph A

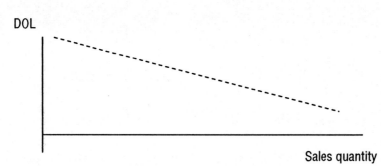

Graph B

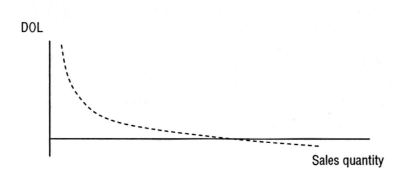

Graph C

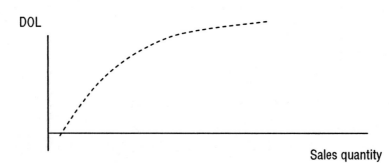

The graph which *most likely* depicts the correct relationship is:

A. graph A.

B. graph B.

C. graph C.

75. Which of the following capital budgeting methods has historically been popular amongst small to middle sized firms?

A. Profitability index.

B. Average accounting rate of return.

C. Payback period.

76. Commercial paper with a committed back-up line of credit *most likely*:

A. is issued by smaller weak borrowers.

B. requires collateral to be attractive to investors.

C. is priced on the basis of money market interest rates.

77. Details of a company's income statement at two different levels of activity are as follows.

	Level I	Level II
Sales	400,000	600,000
Operating costs	230,000	340,000
Profit	170,000	260,000

At a sales level of $500,000, the company's fixed costs increase by a total of $20,000.

The company's degree of operating leverage at level I of activity is *closest to*:

A. 1.06.

B. 1.29.

C. 1.39.

78. A company has 100 million shares in issue with a stock price of $20.00. It is planning to raise new share capital at the current stock price to invest in a project with immediate initial cash outflows of $200 million and giving a constant annuity of $20 million per year indefinitely, starting one year later. The cost of capital for the company is 8%. The amount by which the stock price will increase after the new investment is made is *closest to*:

A. $0.05.

B. $0.45.

C. $2.50.

Questions 79 through 84 relate to Portfolio Management

79. The market risk premium is 4% with a standard deviation of 20%. The risk free rate is 2%. A stock has a total risk of 30% and unsystematic risk of 20%. The expected return on the stock is *closest to*:

   A. 6.0%.

   B. 6.5%.

   C. 8.0%.

80. The investor with a short term time horizon is *most likely* to be:

   A. a bank.

   B. an individual.

   C. an endowment.

81. When a risk budgeting policy is applied to equity managers in an investment program, it is *most likely* that compared to the risk allocated to equities in total when measured in variances, the sum of the individual risks of the equity managers will be:

   A. lower.

   B. higher.

   C. the same.

82. Details of the risk and expected return of two asset classes are as follows.

Asset class	Stocks	Bonds
Expected return %	8.2	4.5
Standard deviation %	11.5	6.2

   The correlation coefficient for the two asset classes is 0.6.

   The standard deviation of an equally weighted stocks/bonds portfolio is *closest to*:

   A. 6.5%.

   B. 8.0%.

   C. 9.0%.

83. When investors have heterogenous expectations, the efficient frontier of risky assets *most likely*:

   A. indicates a non-linear relationship between return and risk.

   B. contains all portfolios which have the minimum risk for a given level of return.

   C. includes the market portfolio that can be combined with the risk free asset to produce efficient portfolios.

84. Asset classes should *most likely*:

   A. be mutually exclusive.

   B. have high correlations with each other.

   C. contain heterogenous securities within each class.

Questions 85 through 96 relate to Equity

85. The use of the comparable price to earnings ratio method to value a company *least likely*:

    A. is based on the law of one price.

    B. reflects the future earnings prospects for the stock.

    C. requires the selection of an appropriate benchmark value for the multiple.

86. The Russell 3000 index has outperformed the Russell 1000 index over the most recent period. It is *most likely* that for an investor tracking the Russell 3000 index:

    A. a price weighted index will outperform an equal weighted index.

    B. a market capitalization weighted index will outperform a price weighted index.

    C. an equal weighted index will outperform a market capitalization weighted index.

87. The interest rate on a loan which an investor obtains from her broker in order to finance the purchase of a security is *most likely* referred to as the:

    A. repo rate.

    B. margin rate.

    C. call money rate.

88. A private investor holds an equity portfolio designed to fund her living expenses in her retirement, which she manages actively. She believes that the price of oil is going to increase and invests in an oil company which she believes to be underpriced, selling shares in other sectors to finance the purchase. The investor's motivation for the trade is *most likely* described as:

    A. saving.

    B. hedging.

    C. information.

89. Convertible preferred stock *most likely*:

    A. has a less volatile stock price than the underlying common stock.

    B. gives shareholders a lower dividend than the company's ordinary shares.

    C. do not allow shareholders the opportunity of sharing in the profits of the company.

90. An industry will *least likely* have low rates of return if there:

    A. are high barriers to entry.

    B. is a high level of capacity.

    C. is a high degree of fragmentation among competitors.

91. Dividend displacement of earnings *most likely* indicates that:

    A. the P/E ratio is inversely related to the dividend payout ratio.

    B. a higher payout ratio for a company may imply a slower growth rate in dividends.

    C. a company with a high rate of return on investment should pay high dividends to maximize its stock price.

92. Hedge fund indices *most likely*:

    A. are biased towards the performance of hedge funds that are outperforming.

    B. exhibit substantial overlap between the constituents for different index providers.

    C. have their constituents determined by the index providers rather than the constituents.

93. The future dividends from a stock trading in an efficient market have been accurately forecast by the market. An investor believes that the stock price is lower than the stock's intrinsic value and the difference is greater than the transaction costs that would be incurred in trading the stock. It is *most likely* that the investor has:

    A. underestimated the stock's risk.

    B. identified a profitable trading opportunity.

    C. established that the market is less efficient than originally thought.

94. The industry that is *least likely* to have a high degree of concentration is:

    A. oil services.

    B. confections and candy.

    C. branded pharmaceuticals.

95. An increasing return on equity for a company *most likely*:

    A. is a positive sign for investors.

    B. can reflect the impact of increasing financial leverage.

    C. can be caused by net income decreasing at a faster rate than stockholders equity.

96. The forms of the efficient market hypothesis that are *most likely* contradicted by abnormal profits from momentum based trading are the:

    A. weak form only.

    B. weak form and semi strong form.

    C. weak form, semi-strong form and strong form.

Questions 97 through 110 relate to Fixed Income

97. When there is negative convexity, the modified duration approach to estimating the change in the price of bond will:

A. always overestimate the new price.

B always underestimate the new price.

C. underestimate the new price for a fall in yields and overestimate the new price for a rise in yields.

98. The type of municipal tax-backed debt that *most likely* has the highest credit risk is:

A. pre-refunded bonds.

B. appropriation-backed obligations.

C. unlimited general obligation debt.

99. A service company has received a rating downgrade and the price decreases on its fixed rate bond. The price decrease is *most likely* caused by:

A. an increase in the bond's credit spread.

B. a decrease in the bond's liquidity spread.

C. a decrease in the bond's underlying benchmark rate.

100. When performing credit analysis on a high yield issuer, which of the following would be considered the weakest source of liquidity?

A. Asset sales.

B. Equity issuance.

C. Working capital.

101. A characteristic of US commercial paper is:

A. they are aimed at retail investors.

B. they usually pay a higher coupon as they are not asset backed.

C. they can be sold in the open market prior to maturity.

102. A bond's prospectus states that the issuer has the right to redeem all or any part of the notes. The redemption price is set at present value of the future coupon and principle payments discounted at the relevant Treasury bond rate plus 100 basis points.

The call provision used above is *most likely* referred to as a:

A. special call provision.

B. sinking fund provision.

C. make whole provision.

103. If a yield curve is normal, it is *most likely*:

    A. flat.

    B. positively sloped.

    C. negatively sloped.

104. The yield to maturity for a Treasury security with a maturity of two years is 4.8%. Treasury spot rates for six month periods over the next two years are 2.2%, 3.0%, 4.4% and 4.9%. The nominal spread for two year corporate bonds is 0.5%, and the zero volatility spread is 0.4%. The price of a two year bond with a semi annual coupon of 6% and a maturity of two years is *closest to*:

    A. 101.31.

    B. 101.42.

    C. 101.50.

105. An analyst is considering the impact of volatility risk for bonds. The analyst should *most likely* conclude that:

    A. bonds with higher durations have higher volatility risk than bonds with lower durations.

    B. bonds with embedded options have higher volatility risk than bonds without embedded options.

    C. bonds with higher durations and with embedded options have higher volatility risk than bonds with lower durations and with embedded options.

106. The Treasury yield curve is *most likely* constructed using:

    A. Treasury STRIPS.

    B. all Treasury securities.

    C. on the run Treasury securities.

107. The use of modified duration to estimate the new price of an option free bond for a specified small change in yields in both directions will give:

    A. the same error for the fall in the yield and the increase in the yield.

    B. a greater error for the fall in the yield than the increase in the yield.

    C. a greater error for the increase in the yield than the fall in the yield.

108. A bond has a maturity of three years, an annual coupon of 6% and a price of 99.47. A year later, the price of the bond is 100.92. The change in value over the year due to the change in the yield is *closest to*:

    A. 0.17.

    B. 1.11.

    C. 1.28.

109. An analyst has stated that modified duration measures the risk of a bond due to changes in market interest rates. The analyst is *most likely*:

    A. correct.

    B. incorrect because duration does not measure yield curve risk.

    C. incorrect because duration does not measure interest rate risk.

110. Agency bonds are *most likely* issued by:

    A. Freddie Mac.

    B. The European Investment Bank.

    C. The State of Carlifornia.

Questions 111 through 116 relate to Derivatives

111. A protective put will *most likely*:

A. have a higher cost for a lower strike price.

B. restrict capital gains if the stock price rises.

C. give a higher value than a covered call if stock prices fall.

112. The role of an options market is *least likely* to be:

A. price discovery.

B. risk management.

C. improving market efficiency.

113. The IMM quote for a Eurodollar futures contract is *most likely* calculated as:

A. 100 + add-on interest.

B. 100 – add-on interest.

C. 100 – discount interest.

114. A party who has entered into a swap where he is making the fixed payment *most likely*:

A. will never have to make a variable payment.

B. may have to make a variable payment in an equity swap.

C. may have to make a variable payment in a currency swap.

115. Given that the stocks included in the S & P 500 index pay dividends, it is *most likely* the case that:

A. a forward contract based on the S & P 500 price only index does not have an arbitrage free value.

B. it is important that a hedging forward contract is based on the total return S & P 500 index rather than the price index.

C. investors with portfolios consisting of non dividend paying stocks outside of the S & P 500 index can still use forwards based on the index to hedge their exposures.

116. A European call option has a strike price of $39. The underlying asset price is $42. The risk free rate of interest for the period to expiration is 5%. The minimum value for the call option is *closest to*:

A. $2.86.

B. $3.00.

C. $4.86.

Questions 117 through 120 relate to Alternative Investments

117. Which of the following is *least likely* to be a reason for investing in real estate as part of a balanced portfolio containing equities, fixed income and alternative investments?

   A. increased long term total returns.

   B. increased diversification.

   C. increased liquidity.

118. It is *most likely* that hedge fund indexes:

   A. have a volatility of returns that is understated.

   B. aim to include all hedge funds of a specified strategy.

   C. can avoid survivorship bias by excluding the previous results of defunct funds from the index.

119. Angel investing capital is usually provided at which stage of financing?

   A. Formative stage.

   B. Later stage.

   C. Mezzanine stage.

120. Venture capital investing is *most likely* suitable for a:

   A. bank.

   B. university endowment.

   C. pension plan with a high proportion of retired lives.

Practice Examination 3
Afternoon Session Solutions

2014

ANSWERS

BPP
LEARNING MEDIA

Ethical and Professional Standards

1. **C** Standard VA – Record Retention. The member must recreate the supporting records at his new firm in order to use his historical recommendations or research reports created at his old firm.

   LOS 2b

2. **A** Standard IB – Independence and Objectivity. Investors can reasonably expect reports to be straightforward and transparent, without use of subtle and ambiguous language.

   LOS 2b

3. **C** Standard IIIE – Preservation of Confidentiality. The standard is not intended to prevent members from cooperating with an investigation by the PCP.

   LOS 2b

4. **C** Standard IIID – Performance Presentation. Although compliance with GIPS is not required to comply with the standard, it is the best method of ensuring compliance.

   LOS 2b

5. **B** Standard VIB – Priority of Transactions. Since he knows his recommendations when completing his own trading, he is breaching the standard by giving his own transactions priority.

   LOS 2b

6. **C** Standard IB – Independence and Objectivity. Special cost arrangements (e.g. use of private jets) should be avoided. However, the invitations would not be viewed as additional compensation.

   LOS 2b

7. **B** Standard ID – Misconduct. Personal bankruptcy may not reflect on the integrity or trustworthiness of the person declaring bankruptcy, unless the circumstances indicate fraudulent or dishonest behavior. There is no indication of this being the case here.

   LOS 2b

8. **C** Standard IIIB – Fair Dealing. Family member accounts which are managed similarly to the accounts of other clients of the firm should not be excluded from buying shares.

   LOS 2b

9. **C** Standard VIA – Disclosure of Conflicts. Prohibition on ownership is overly burdensome and discriminates against employees. Immaterial interests do not constitute a potential conflict of interest.

   LOS 2b

10. **B** Standard IIA – Material Non-public Information. An analysts meeting is selective disclosure, so the information is still considered to be non-public. Lucy Jones is using the mosaic theory to build up a pattern of information about the company and has not relied on material non-public information.

LOS 2b

11. **C** Standard VIC – Referral Fees. All types of referral fee must be disclosed.

LOS 2b

12. **A** Standard IIIA – Loyalty, Prudence and Care and Standard IIIC – Suitability. A highly illiquid investment is not suitable for the insurance company which has mandated investing primarily in highly liquid investments. The chief investment officer if breaching his duty to the subsidiary.

LOS 2b

13. **A** Standard IIA – Material Non-public Information. Analysts may provide limited assistance to investment banking under strictly controlled circumstances. A prohibition on all proprietary trading is not appropriate.

LOS 2b

14. **C** Standard IVC – Responsibilities of Supervisors. Relying on employee assurances or reporting the action up the chain of command is insufficient.

LOS 2b

15. **A** Standard IIIA – Loyalty, Prudence and Care and Standard IIIC – Suitability. Marianne has a duty to the income beneficiary and the remainderman to balance their interests. Investing exclusively in income generating bonds without capital growth means that the real value of the capital will fall over time. This favors the income beneficiary over the remainderman.

LOS 2b

16. **B** Standard VIIB – Reference to CFA Institute, the CFA Designation and the CFA Program. Stating that the CFA designation and the skills that the CFA program cultivates are assets for future career development is permitted. It is not permitted to suggest that CFA charterholders have superior investment performance.

LOS 2b

17. **C** Compliance is on a firm-wide basis. Verification is strongly recommended, not required.

LOS 4a

18. **B** The Hearing Panel is only convened if the member rejects a disciplinary sanction proposed by the Designated Officer. A cautionary letter concludes the investigation and is not accepted or rejected by the member.

LOS 1a

Quantitative Methods

19. **B**   With Bollinger Bands, a common strategy is to sell stocks that have hit the higher band and buy stocks that have hit the lower band i.e. a contrarian strategy. This gives rise to a larger number of trades. A more volatile security would have a wider range between its bands.

   LOS 12e

20. **B**   Using the annuity formula for the present value of an annuity from time 1 to time n.

$$PV = A \times \frac{1}{r}\left(1 - \frac{1}{(1+r)^n}\right)$$

   The effective annual rate is $e^{0.07} - 1 = 0.072508$.

$$PV = 250 + 250 \times \frac{1}{0.072508}\left(1 - \frac{1}{1.072508^{30}}\right) = 3,275.67$$

   Note that the series starts immediately (at time 0) and then continues for a further 30 payments (to the end of the 30th year), so n = 30 and an additional \$250 needs to be added to the present value of the annuity from time 1 to time 30.

   LOS 5e

21. **C**   The distribution of stock prices will have a positive skew if they are lognormally distributed.

   LOS 9o

22. **B**   The NPV method uses the required rate of return (an external market determined rate) and the IRR method uses the internal rate of return (internally determined).

   LOS 6b

23. **B**   Positive excess kurtosis indicates leptokurtosis, where the distribution is more peaked and has fatter tails than a normal distribution. This gives a greater area in each tail than the normal distribution, meaning that there is a higher probability of large positive and negative returns compared to a normal distribution. Equity return series distributions are more likely to be leptokurtic than normal.

   LOS 7l

24. **A**

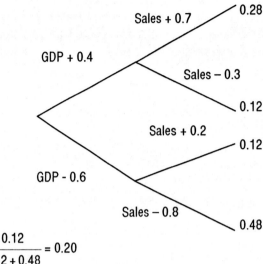

$$\frac{0.12}{0.12 + 0.48} = 0.20$$

We know that industry sales fell, so we are dealing with the subset of GDP increased and sales fell (= 0.12) and GDP decreased and sales fell (= 0.48). We are interested in the probability that GDP increased.

LOS 8j and 8n

25. **B** Expected return of portfolio: $\dfrac{5+7}{2} = 6\%$

Standard deviation of portfolio = $\sqrt{8^2 \times 0.5^2 + 9^2 \times 0.5^2} = 6.02\%$

-6% is two standard deviations away from the expected return. 2.5% of observations lie below this point for a normal distribution.

LOS 9l

26. **B** $\left(1.054 \times 1.081 \times 1.098\right)^{\frac{1}{3}-1} = 0.07751$ or 7.75%

LOS 7e

27. **A** The analyst is using the current list of companies in the Russell 3000 and testing their returns over 20 years. This ignores other companies who were in the Russell 3000 over the period, giving survivorship bias.

LOS 10k

28. **A** The inflation premium compensates the investor for expected inflation and the maturity premium compensates the investor for increased risk to due longer maturities. Both are additional to pure time preference.

LOS 5a

29. B $\chi^2 = \dfrac{(n-1)s^2}{\sigma^2} = \dfrac{23 \times 5.5^2}{5^2} = 27.8$

LOS 11i

30. C In a triangle pattern, the range between the high and low prices narrows. With an ascending triangle, this is because the high prices trend line is horizontal and the low prices trend line is rising.

LOS 12d

31. B There is more money invested in the second year, so the money weighted return will be more heavily weighted towards the second year. In the second year, the stock market performed badly, meaning that the money weighted return will have the lower value.

LOS 6d

32. C A larger sample size will reduce the standard error. This will increase the test statistic, making the p value smaller. The p value is independent of the significance level selected for the test. A higher p value makes it less likely that the null hypothesis will be rejected (since it implies a smaller value for the test statistic), meaning that there is more chance of a type II error being made.

LOS 11e

Economics

33. A Non-satiation or the 'more the better' assumption means that a consumer would never turn down more of a good even if it was free.

   LOS 14a

34. B When supply of a factor is perfectly inelastic, all the income is economic rent and taxing the good will have no effect on efficiency.

   LOS 15a

35. C By charging different prices to different buyers, consumer surplus falls and economic profit increases.

   LOS 16d

36. A The rightwards shift in aggregate demand is anticipated and will be compensated for by a leftward shift in short run aggregate supply, leaving the economy at potential GDP (ie at the same output but at a higher price).

   LOS 17i

37. C The number of women going to work will increase the labor force and the increase in the number of college students will decrease the labor force.

   LOS 18d

38. B Fiscal policy setting is the role of Government.

   LOS 19i

39. C Shut down point is when a firm stops production but still fixed costs in the short term. In the short run a business can operate at a loss providing it covers its variable costs. If however variable costs cannot be covered in the short run the firm will shut down.

   LOS 15e

40. A An open market purchase will increase the supply of bank reserves in order to reduce the federal funds rate. This will reduce interest rates, increase the supply of loanable funds, increase aggregate demand and lead to a higher inflation rate.

   LOS 19k

41. C For example, when the quantity of money increases rapidly, aggregate demand increases rapidly, giving a high inflation rate. The wealth and substitution effects are reasons why the aggregate demand curve is downward sloping. Technological change causes LRAS to shift to the right.

   LOS 17i

42. B Ideally revenue sufficiency is an obvious attribute of a tax policy. Fairness does not override efficiency but should be balanced.

   LOS 19o

43. **B** Since neither firm can trust the other in a collusive agreement, it will break down and the firms will compete with each other.

LOS 16d

44. **B** Unstable equilibrium occurs if both supply and demand curves have negative slopes and the supply curve is less steep (cuts the demand curve from below).

LOS 13e

Financial Reporting and Analysis

45. B

	$
Opening fixed assets	3,290
Net capital expenditure	600
Depreciation expense (missing figure)	(510)
Closing fixed assets	3,380

	$
Net income	560
Change in current assets (1,700 − 1,450)	(250)
Increase in accounts payable (890 − 720)	170
Depreciation expense	510
Cash flow from operating activities	990

Note: the above approach works even if there were disposals of fixed assets, as any cash inflow from the sales and profit/loss on disposal will net off to give the same answer as above.

LOS 27e

46. A The portion of the finance lease payables due within one year will be included in current liabilities, reducing the current ratio. The higher asset value will increase financial leverage (assets ÷ stockholders equity). The interest expense is high in early years and low in later years, giving a higher net income in the later years, increasing net margin.

LOS 32i

47. B All accounting changes for inventory valuation are made retrospectively, except for a change to LIFO, which is done prospectively.

LOS 25e

48. A Going concern is an underlying assumption rather than a qualitative characteristic.

LOS 24d

49. C Under both US GAAP and IFRS, research costs cannot be capitalized. Under IFRS, development costs may be capitalized.

LOS 26g

50. **B** The effective interest rate is the IRR of the cash flows, which is 3.095%

Time	Cash flow	PV at 3.095%
0	(9,500,000)	(9,500,000)
1-4	200,000	742,000
5	10,200,000	8,758,000
		-

The liability after one year will be 9,500,000 + 3.095% × 9,500,000 – 200,000 = $9,594,025.

Note that the issue costs are deducted from the issue proceeds under IFRS. Under US GAAP they are shown as a separate asset.

LOS 32a

51. **B** The net carrying value of the asset will be lower each year for accelerate methods compared to straight line depreciation until the asset is written down to its residual value. Asset turnover (Sales ÷ average total assets) will therefore be higher in each year.

LOS 30c

52. **B** There were 400 units in opening inventory, 130 units were manufactured and 140 units were sold, meaning that closing inventory is 390 units. Under the periodic system, these would be all treated as being part of the opening inventories, giving a value of 390 x $250 = $97,500.

With a perpetual system, we have to do an ongoing calculation.

	Number of units	$ per unit	$
OI	400	250	100,000
Sales	(50)	250	(12,500)
Sub-total	350	250	87,500
Manufactured	80	280	22,400
Sales	(60)	280	(16,800)
Sub-total	410	-	93,100
Manufactured	50	310	15,500
Sales	(30)	310	(9,300)
Total inventories	390	-	99,300

99,300 – 97,500 = $1,800

LOS 29e

53. **A** Annual depreciation expense for accounts = $10,000 over five years and for tax = $12,500 over four years.

	Accounts book value	Tax written down value	Timing difference	Balance sheet liability
31 Dec 2012	40,000	37,500	2,500	40% x 2,500 = 1,000
31 Dec 2013	30,000	25,000	5,000	30% x 5,000 = 1,500

2013 income statement expense = increase in liability = 1,500 – 500 = $500

LOS 31d

54. **C** Although inventory turnover has fallen, the high growth in sales suggests that obsolescent inventories are not a problem. The ratio of receivables to sales has fallen, suggesting that the company is not offering favorable credit terms (lengthening the period of credit would cause the ratio of receivables to sales to increase). The ratio of payables to cost of goods sold (it is not possible to calculate purchases for both years) has fallen, suggesting that the company is paying off its suppliers more quickly, possibly to take advantage of advantageous prompt payment terms.

LOS 28b

55. **B** Goodwill = the excess of the purchase price of the fair value of the assets less liabilities, including any identifiable intangible assets.

	£
Tangible assets	3,500,000
Intangible assets	800,000
Liabilities	(800,000)
Net assets acquired	3,500,000
Purchase price	5,000,000
Goodwill	1,500,000

LOS 26e

56. **A** Full provision is required for deferred tax liabilities. Deferred tax assets are only recognized to the extent that they are expected to be realized in the foreseeable future.

LOS 31b

57. **B** 5,500 + 9,000 + 6,000 = $20,500.

Inventories should be shown at the lower of cost and net realizable value. Where NRV has increased after a previous writedown to NRV, the writedown should be reversed.

LOS 29f

58. **C**

	Accounts book value	Tax written down value	Timing difference
Fixed asset	36,000 asset	34,000 asset	2,000
Interest receivable	5,000 asset	-	5,000
Total	41,000 asset	34,000 asset	7,000

LOS 31d

59. **A** Under US GAAP, if the carrying value is less than the undiscounted future cash flows, no writedown is required.

LOS 30h

60. **C** Present value of lease payments:

$$6,500 + \frac{6,500}{1.07} + \frac{6,500}{1.07^2} + \frac{6,500}{1.07^3} = 23,558$$

Opening receivable = 23,558 − 6,500 = 17,058

Receivable at 31 December 2012 = 17,058 + 7% × 17,058 = $18,252

LO 32h

61. **B** Since the revaluation surplus is taken directly to stockholders equity, so is the related deferred tax.

LOS 31j

62. **C** 2013 purchases = 12,100 + 1,100 − 1,000 = 12,200

$$\text{Payables turnover} = \frac{12,200}{\frac{1}{2}(2,900 + 2,612)} = 4.43$$

LOS 28b

63. **B** Changes in accounting estimate are accounted for prospectively. Changes in accounting policies are usually accounted for retrospectively, except for a change from LIFO inventory valuations under US GAAP, which is accounted for prospectively.

LOS 25e

64. **C** Weighted average of common shares:

$$90,000,000 \times \frac{3}{12} + 100,000 \times \frac{9}{12} = 97,500,000$$

Number of shares after conversion of preferred stock: $5,000,000 \times \frac{2}{10} = 1,000,000$

Net income before common and preferred dividends:

$130,000,000 - 110,000,000 + 5,000,000 + 5\% \times 5,000,000 = \$25,250,000$

Diluted earnings per share: $\dfrac{25,250,000}{98,500,000} = 0.2563$

LOS 25g

65. **B**

	$
Operating cash flow	9,998
Post tax interest (3,200 × 0.7)	2,240
Capital expenditure	(5,090)
Free cash flow to the firm	7,148

LOS 27i

66. **B** Dealing or trading securities are an operating cash flow, rather than investment which would be for longer term investments.

LOS 27a

67. **A** In order to allow for different tax rates and different capital structures, the return should be based on average total assets for the denominator and a pre-interest post tax earnings figure for the numerator.

$$\frac{1,538 + 595\left(1 - 0.7\right)}{\tfrac{1}{2}\left(10,500 + 9,290\right)} = 19.8\%$$

LOS 28b

68. **A** In times of rising prices and constant inventory levels, LIFO will report a higher cost of goods sold as it will charge the latest goods purchased to cost of goods sold. This will reduce its gross profit, reducing its gross margin and will mean that it reports a lower income before tax, reducing tax payable.

LOS 29c

Corporate Finance

69. **A** Cost of overdraft: $\left[1+0.1\times\dfrac{1}{365}\right]^{365}-1=10.5\%$

Cost of CP:

Price: $100-10\times\dfrac{30}{360}=99.167$

Yield: $\left(\dfrac{100}{99.167}\right)^{\frac{365}{30}}-1=10.7\%$

Cost of not taking discount:

$\left(\dfrac{100}{99}\right)^{\frac{365}{30}}-1=13.0\%$

LOS 40g

70. **B** $(5-2)\times\dfrac{25}{15}=5\%$

The sovereign yield spread is 5 - 2 = 3% and this is adjusted by the ratio of the equity index's standard deviation to the standard deviation of the dollar denominated government bonds.

LOS 37j

71. **A** Having legal, financial or other such expertise is desirable. Working previously for senior management suggests lack of independence. Having many other directorships suggests inability to devote adequate time to the post.

LOS 41d

72. **A** The discount rate where the projects have the same positive net present value must be below 14% (it is actually 9.583%), since project Y has the higher NPV at a discount rate of zero but the lower IRR, indicating that its NPV falls at a faster rate than that for project X. At discount rates of above 25%, the investor would reject both projects, so he is not indifferent as to which project he would select.

LOS 36d

73. **B** Shareholder Y will *most likely* be on the shareholders register on the holder of record date, so the dividend will be paid to him.

LOS 39b

74. **B** As the level of sales increases, the impact of fixed costs becomes less and less important.

LOS 38b

75. **C** Payback period has been found to be popular amongst companies, alongside NPV and IRR.

LOS 36f

76. **C** Large companies issue CP, which is not collateralized. It is the money market that sets the rate.

LOS 40g

77. **B** If we exclude the additional $20,000 of fixed costs, the profit at level II would be $280,000. This gives an increase in profits of 64.71% ($\frac{280}{170} - 1$) for an increase in sales of 50% ($\frac{600}{400} - 1$). This gives DOL = $\frac{64.71}{50} = 1.294$.

LOS 38b

78. **B** Present value of the project's future inflows is $\frac{20,000,000}{0.08} = \$250,000,000$. The market value of the company will increase by this amount (since new shares are being issued to finance the new investment – if debt had been issued, the market value of the shares would only increase by the net present value of the project).

10 million shares will be issued to finance the project, meaning that there will be 110 million shares in issue. The share price will move to $\frac{100,000,000 \times 20 + 250,000,000}{110,000,000} = \$20.45$.

The increase in stock price is $0.45.

LOS 36f

Portfolio Management

79. **B**   Systematic risk: $\sqrt{30^2 - 20^2} = 22.36\%$

Beta: $\dfrac{22.36}{20} = 1.118$

Expected return: $2 + 1.118 \times 4 = 6.47\%$

LOS 44e and 44g

80. **A**   Banks need their securities portfolios to have liquidity so that they can be sold quickly to meet short term liquidity demands.

LOS 42b

81. **B**   Unless the risks of the individual managers are perfectly positively correlated with each other, the diversification benefit will mean that the risk for equities in total will be less than the total of the risks for the individual managers.

LOS 45g

82. **B** $\sqrt{11.5^2 0.5^2 + 6.2^2 0.5^2 + 2 \times 0.5 \times 0.5 \times 11.5 \times 6.2 \times 0.6} = 8.0\%$

LOS 43e

83. **A**   The efficient frontier is curved, not a straight line. The market portfolio is only relevant when investors have homogenous expectations. The efficient frontier contains all portfolios that have the maximum return for a given level of risk.

LOS 43g

84. **A**   Securities should only fall in one asset class (i.e. they are mutually exclusive). Asset classes should be different from each other (low correlations) and contain similar securities (homogeneity within the asset class).

LOS 45f

Equity

85.　**B**　The comparables method is based on the fact that similar assets should sell for similar prices (the law of one price) and requires a benchmark multiple for comparison purposes. There is no explicit consideration of future earnings prospects.

LOS 51g

86.　**C**　Since the Russell 1000 includes the largest 1,000 stocks in the Russell 3000, the larger stocks must have underperformed the smaller stocks. An equal weighted index will give a higher weighting to smaller stocks than a market capitalization weighted index, meaning that the equal weighted index will outperform the market capitalization weighted index.

LOS 47d

87.　**C**　The repo rate is the rate charged on a repo transaction. The money borrowed by the investor from the broker is called the margin loan. The interest rate on the loan is the call money rate.

LOS 46d

88.　**C**　The purpose of the portfolio is saving, but the specific trade is based on information that the investor believes that she possesses.

LOS 46a

89.　**A**　The fixed dividend before conversion reduces stock price volatility. The right to convert gives the opportunity to participate in the company's profits. The preferred dividend is generally higher than the ordinary dividend.

LOS 49b

90.　**A**　High barriers to entry reduce the threat of new competition, increasing rates of return. High industry fragmentation tends to increase competition among companies, giving lower rates of return. Higher capacity levels increase supply relative to demand, reducing prices and rates of return.

LOS 50e

91.　**B**　The P/E multiple is calculated as $\dfrac{D_1/E_1}{r-g}$. By increasing the payout ratio, the P/E multiple would appear to increase, but this ignores the fact that a higher payout ratio reduces the net income retained, which will reduce future earnings and dividends growth. This is referred to as dividend displacement of earnings.

LOS 51h

92. **A** Survivorship bias means that the poorly performing hedge funds are not included in hedge fund indices, which consequently are biased towards better performing funds. Many hedge funds report their performance to only one index provider. Hedge funds decide which providers to report performance to, meaning that the constituents determine the index rather than the index provider determining the constituents.

    LOS 47j

93. **A** In an efficient market, the intrinsic value will not be significantly different from the market price. The investor is likely to have underestimated the risk of the dividend flows and discounted the dividends at a discount rate that is too low.

    LOS 48a

94. **A** A small number of companies control the bulk of the global market for branded drugs. The top few companies have a large proportion of global market share for confections and candy. Small players in the oil services market compete effectively in specific areas.

    LOS 50j

95. **B** If net income decreases at a slower rate than stockholders equity, ROE will increase, but this may not be a positive sign for investors. Increasing levels of debt finance (e.g. through a share repurchase) could increase ROE if the cost of debt is sufficiently low, but will increase financial risk.

    LOS 49h

96. **C** Momentum based trading is based on short term share price patterns i.e. market information. The weak form states that market information cannot be used to predict future price changes.

    LOS 48f

Fixed Income

97. **A**   Negative convexity means that the slope (duration) of price/yield line is decreasing as yields fall and increasing as yields rise. Modified duration assumes that the slope is constant. This means that the actual price increase will be lower than that predicted by modified duration for a fall in yields and the price decrease will be higher than that predicted by modified duration for a rise in yields. The duration approach therefore always overestimates the new price.

LOS 55g

98. **B**   For appropriation-backed obligations, the liability for making up shortfalls in the issuing entity's obligation will only be met by appropriation of funds from general tax revenue if this is approved by the state legislature. The pledge to cover liabilities is not legally binding.

LOS 56j

99. **A**   Following the downgrade it is most likely that the credit spread will have widened. The downgrade represents a higher chance of default and/or a lower recovery rate in the event of default.

LOS 55k

100. **C**   Sources of liquidity from strongest to weakest are: cash on the balance sheet; working capital; operating cash flow; bank credit facilities; equity issuance; and finally asset sales.

LOS 56j

101. **C**   US CP is issued at a discount rather than being coupon bearing, and is not generally marketed at retail investors directly. They are, however, negotiable so can be traded freely prior to maturity.

LOS 53e

102. **C**   The call price ensures that the investors receive a yield equal to the bond's yield on its issue. It is also referred to as a yield maintenance provision.

LOS 52f

103. **B**   The normal yield curve is upwardly sloping.

LOS 54g

104. **B** $$\frac{3}{1.013} + \frac{3}{1.017^2} + \frac{3}{1.024^3} + \frac{103}{1.0265^4} = 101.42$$

The relevant spot rates are 2.6% (= 1.3% semi-annually), 3.4% (= 1.7%), 4.8% (= 2.4%) and 5.3% (= 2.65%). They are obtained by adding the zero volatility spread of 0.4% to the Treasury spot rates.

Note that using the yield to maturity for the Treasury security plus the nominal spread does not give the same answer, presumably because the coupon rate for the Treasury security is not 6%.

LOS 54h

105. **B** Volatility risk relates to the volatility of the bond's yield. This is distinct from the bond's duration, which measures the change in price given a change in yield. Option values for bonds are affected by yield volatility, meaning that volatility risk is a greater factor for bonds with embedded options.

LOS 55i

106. **C** On the run Treasury securities have the highest liquidity and are priced around par.

LOS 54g

107. **B** The slope of the price yield function increases at an increasing rate as yields fall and decreases at a decreasing rate as yields rise. This means that the assumption of a constant slope will give rise to a greater error as yields fall.

LOS 55b

108. **C** The original yield of the bond is 6.199%.

Time	Flow	PV at 6.199%
0	(99.47)	(99.47)
1	6	5.650
2	6	5.320
3	106	88.500
		-

With no change in the yield, the price one year later will be:

$$\frac{6}{1.06199} + \frac{106}{1.06199} = 99.64$$

The change in price due to the change in yields is $100.92 - 99.64 = 1.28$

LOS 54b

109. **B** Yield curve risk relates to nonparallel shifts. Interest rate risk relates to parallel shifts. Duration only considers parallel shifts.

LOS 55b

110. **A** Agency bonds are issued by quasi-governmental agencies, such as Freddie Mac. The State of California issues muni's and the European Development Bank is a supranational organization that does not issue agency debt.

LOS 53e

Derivatives

111. **B** The premium paid to buy the put option will reduce profits if the stock price rises. The protective put will only outperform the covered call if the stock price falls by a sufficient amount, since the protective put has already incurred a loss through paying a premium and the covered call has premium income to cover the first layer of losses. A lower strike price gives a lower premium.

LOS 62b

112. **A** Options markets give information about volatility of prices, not about the price itself.

LOS 57d

113. **B** The interest rate that is used to calculate the IMM index is the interest rate on a Eurodollar time deposit, which is LIBOR and is an add on interest figure (contrast T-bills where the interest figure is discount interest). However, it is deducted from 100 to give the IMM quote.

LOS 59f

114. **B** In an equity swap, the fixed payer would pay fixed and receive the return on the equity index (a variable amount). If the equity index falls, the fixed payer has to pay an amount equal to the fall in the equity index in addition to the fixed amount. Consequently, he may have to make a variable payment.

LOS 61b

115. **C** It is possible to calculate arbitrage values for forwards and futures based on price only indexes. Since price volatility is the major issue for hedgers, rather than dividend volatility, it is not important to use a total return index for hedging purposes. An investor with any stock portfolio could use the S & P index forward or future to hedge the systematic risk of the portfolio.

LOS 58d

116. **C** $42 - \dfrac{39}{1.05} = 4.86$

LOS 60k

Alternative Investments

117. **C**   Real estate investments are relatively illiquid.

     LOS 63c

118. **A**   The smoothed pricing of assets for hedge funds leads to understated volatility. Hedge fund indexes do not include all hedge funds of a particular strategy as hedge fund managers decide whether to be included or not. Exclusion of defunct hedge fund results will lead to survivorship bias.

     LOS 63e

119. **A**   Angel investing is usually at the early stages of company financing, for example to transform the idea into a business plan.

     LOS 63d

120. **B**   A university endowment will have a long term horizon and relatively moderate liquidity needs compared to the bank and the pension plan.

     LOS 63c